'Oh, What A Beautiful City'

A Tribute To

THE REVEREND GARY DAVIS
(1896-1972)

GOSPEL, BLUES AND RAGTIME

Compiled by

ROBERT TILLING

BOOK DESIGN BY ADAM BOOKBINDER

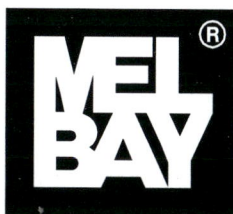

MEL BAY ® · **STEFAN GROSSMAN'S GUITAR WORKSHOP**

1 2 3 4 5 6 7 8 9 0

Buck's Rock Camp, Conn., Bob Carlin, 1969

For Mother Annie B. Davis (1895-1997) for being so patient with my original research.
Also to my wife Thelma for her support and encouragement.
To Roy Book Binder and Woody Mann for their friendship and inspiration.

ACKNOWLEDGEMENTS

I should particularly like to thank all of those people who have given so freely of their material for this book.

Every effort has been made to trace the copyright holders and photographers. The author apologises for any unintentional omissions, and would be pleased, if any such case should arise, to add an appropriate acknowledgement in future editions.

Special thanks to: Paul Oliver, Stefan Grossman, Roy Book Binder, Woody Mann, Peter Mourant, Linda Bailhache, Louise Jackson, Clive Coutanche, Jacqueline Mézec and Adam Bookbinder

The Association of Cultural Equity, Alex Atterson, Stephen Baird, Jack Baker, Alan Balfour, Bob Bater, Bishop T.J. Boston, Blues Magazine, Blues And Rhythm, Blues Unlimited, Blues World, Blueprint, Blues In Britain, British Institute of Jazz Studies, Tony Burke, Cambridge Folk Festival (UK), Cadence Magazine, Dave Clarke, The Library of Congress: Washington D.C., Al Cochrane, David Colebeck, John Cowley, Paul Crawford, Bob Eagle, Ken "Easy Ed" Edwards, Allan Evans, Mayor George D. Evatt, Gray Court S.C., Tim Ferris, Folklore Productions, Folk Roots, Alan Fones, Dave Foster, Seth Goldman, Michael Gray, Manny Greenhill, Mitch Greenhill, Bob Groom, Sheldon Harris, Jeff Hathaway, Glen Hinson, Lee Hoffman, Davis Horn, Indiana University, The Independent Weekly, Gerry Jackson, Mike Jahn, Robert Javors, Stanley M. Jay, Jazz Journal, Jazz Monthly, The Jersey Evening Post, R.W. Jones, Mike Joyce, Juke Blues, John Kruth, Laurens Advertiser S.C., Andy Lawson, Living Blues, Kip Lornell, William Maikin, Kathy McNichol, Melody Maker, David Menconi, Jerry L. Mills, Roger Misiewicz, Udine Moore, Gerry Murphy, Alice Ochs, The New York Times, The New York Post, John Pearce, Nick Perls, Bill Phillips, Tom Pomposello, William Price, Michael Prince, Raleigh News and Observer, Mrs. Tiny Robinson, Rolling Stone Magazine, Ernie Roscouet, Steve Rye, Sounds Magazine, Sing Out!, Smithsonian Folkways Recordings, Talking Blues Magazine, Rev. Eric Thacker, Jeff Titon, John Ullman, University College of Los Angeles, Elijah Wald, Wayne State University, Val Wilmer, Robbie Woliver, Andy Wood, World Arbiter Records and Peter Yarrow.

FRONT COVER: Photograph by Alice Ochs (with Meegan Ochs, 1968) • **BACK COVER:** Courtesy Hans Theessink (USA Festival, circa 1968)

'Oh, What A Beautiful City'

CONTENTS

PREFACE by Paul Oliver 1

INTRODUCTION by Robert Tilling 3

PART ONE: Chronology 4

PART TWO: Musicians, Friends, Students and Admirers 24

PART THREE: Selected Concert Reviews
with Quotations by Rev. Davis 86

PART FOUR: Selected Record, Compact Disc,
Video, Book and DVD Reviews 108

PART FIVE: Selected Obituaries 130

PART SIX: Discography and Appendix 136

PART SEVEN: Selected Bibliography 160

Philadelphia Folk Festival, c. 1969, Bob Patterson

Preface

When I first heard his music in live performance he wasn't even playing it. It was in 1956 I think, at the Roundhouse pub on the corner of Wardour and Brewer Streets in London's Soho where Cyril Davis and Alexis Korner ran the London Blues Club, which met in a smoke and beer-laden upstairs room on Thursday nights. There was a succession of notable visitors who came there to listen and generally, to sit in: Big Bill Broonzy, Brother John Sellers, Derroll Adams and Jack Elliott among them. Not Gary Davis of course, but startlingly, his music. Anyone who felt like singing or playing blues had a chance to sit in too - quite good, aspiring, not so good, but keen. There were two brothers one evening, with Scots accents, tall and good-looking, who played one or two swiftly executed, accomplished duets. Then one of them began to sing a gospel song with a dazzling guitar accompaniment and followed it with a charming song, 'Candy Man' with a ragtime influenced setting.

Afterwards I went over to talk to him. He was an artist, Rory McEwen, but he'd spent a while in New York learning from the man who had taught these songs to him, Reverend Gary Davis. More important to me than the songs themselves was the guitar playing, with its smooth runs, unexpected breaks and swinging rhythm. Rory didn't claim any credit for them himself but regaled me with stories of Blind Gary. As yet a trip to the States was a personal dream, but I knew I just had to get the records of the man whose music was so exhilarating. Shortly afterwards at Dobell's Record Shop ("Every jazz fan is born within the sound of Dobell's") I bought a copy of "American Street Songs" on Riverside RLP 12-611 - Pink Anderson singing Carolina Street Ballads on one side, and Harlem Street Spirituals by Reverend Gary Davis on the other. I marvelled, as I still do, at the bell-like notes that open 'Blow Gabriel', the conversation between guitar and player on 'Twelve Gates to the City', the delicate solo with its poised blue notes on 'Oh Lord Search My Heart' and the complement to the final verse with its falsetto final syllable. In contrast, the impetus of 'Samson and Delilah' and the ragtime figures so effortlessly performed on 'Get Right Church' before a "vocal" cry on the treble string answered by a yelp from the singer. I knew every track by heart and managed to slip one of them into "Blues Fell This Morning" - 'There Was a Time When I Went Blind', an infinitely poignant song it seemed to me.

The following year Brownie McGhee and Sonny Terry came to England and with the pestering zeal of the young enthusiast I played them records for their comments and recollections. One of the first was an old favourite - 'Rag, Mama, Rag' by Blind Boy Fuller. "That's old Gary in there" they both laughed, almost in one voice. I hadn't realised it but quickly made a note which in time made its way, like hundreds of others, into the discographies that other collectors like John Godrich and Bob Dixon were putting together. When I played them the Riverside album and we talked about Blind Gary I had to fit in their jokes about him and his fondness for whiskey with the picture that I had been forming in my mind. It was a picture reinforced by a photo on the cover of a copy of "Record Changer", of an oldish-looking, contemplative head half-hidden in shadow, with the light catching the metal rims of his spectacles, a picture of a religious singer profoundly immersed in his music. Not everything they said quite accorded with my mental image, though some of it did. But I hadn't yet found room for the humorous side, for the human side of the man.

Somehow, he'd taken on some kind of symbolic stature in my mind: I imagined without quite realising it, a man as big as his music, with a powerful voice to match the volume that I used when I played his records (I'd acquired a few, including a precious 'O Lord, Search My Heart' on Conqueror 8561). When I met him, finally, I had to readjust, he was smaller, much smaller, than I had expected and his voice had been overstrained with street singing. He seemed thin and frail, later still he took on a pear-shape which gave him some stability as he leaned over sideways at an impossible angle to talk or exchange a joke. At times he seemed so disconnected that I wondered if he would be able to play at all. Then he'd take up the big Gibson, which hardly ever left his hands and which lay in his lap when he was talking. And suddenly his fingers found the strings with the dexterity that they always had, the calloused thumb picked the bass figures, the thumb of his left hand hooked over the fingerboard to fret the bass E string. His playing seemed so effortless and he was himself animated by it, swaying to his own beat, stomping his feet flat-footed, left and right. Lips peeled back, brow furrowed at the centre with a converging frown, he seemed to sing from the back of his throat, head back one moment, down and talking to the guitar the next. He was, after all, a man totally immersed in his music.

Each time I heard him, each time I managed to snatch a spell of conversation among the back-stage denizens who, like myself, milked every visiting blues and gospel singer dry of information, I got to know him better. Or so I thought and felt, for a while. But I wondered then, and wonder much more now, how much I or indeed anyone outside his immediate circle in New York really knew him. We knew his music, or what could be heard on record, and added to it the brief experience of the live performance. What does it tell us about the man? Or of what his music meant to those that had listened to him or played with him all those decades ago in the Carolinas? What does a blind gospel singer think about when he goes on the streets to play for coins, what does his music mean to him? We believe we know the answers, but I wonder if we really do.

For a blind musician whose life is giving out music and its messages to audiences he cannot see, the image of the world must be very, very different from our own. Even the messages themselves are translated into different patterns to fit different conceptual frameworks: for one it is a message of hope and deliverance, for another it is blues with a spiritual content, the so-called "holy blues". For another it is an analysis of the music on guitar, with a breakdown of the keys that the tunes are played in, the chord structures and progressions. For some it is folk music, for others it is the playing of a poor man on the sidewalk edge on a cold night.

Standard techniques of biography can probably never get to the heart of a blues or gospel singer from the rural black South who has come to terms with, or adapted to urban liv-

ing, street violence, the changing years of racial segregation and subsequent white adulation. So a man, a musician like Blind Gary Davis, lives in the minds and memories of innumerable listeners, relatives and friends in countless ways. An "official biography" places the events of an individual's life in its social and cultural context, seeks to "get inside" the subject, and narrates the conclusions of research in a logical, and generally, chronological order. But even such an ordered biography is at best, a skilful selection of what seems to the biography to be relevant, laid out sequentially like the unfolding of the years.

It's one way, the most familiar way, of writing about somebody of note or influence. But anyone who has known the subject of a biography also knows the sense of dissatisfaction that it leaves: the facts are there, yes, but it's not the person that I know. Reason and history fight with the memory of the personal experience, and people live on in memories - and, in the case of musicians, in moments of time captured on records.

Robert Tilling's book is not a narrative biography of one of the most remarkable and gifted of all black folk musicians of this century, though it is about such a man. It is a collage, a gathering together of facts and ephemera, of memories and memorabilia. It's a collected documentary of pieces of a well-spent life, in association with the impressions, emotions, experience of some of those who have shared for a time in his singing and music and have been enriched by it. It is spiced by the comments and asides, the quips, homilies and compact wisdom of the man

himself which afford glimpses of the personality within.

To make such a compilation requires knowledge, sensitivity and affection; Robert Tilling has just such a combination in relation to his subject. He has known Blind Gary Davis personally, more closely than most of us who have enjoyed his music, both in Gary's home and in his own. Tilling is an artist, a painter who brings the sensibilities of one whose life is largely spent in perceiving and responding to subtleties and nuances of light, shade and colour. He is moreover, a teacher, whose reason for being in education is to relate to others and to coax from them their creative talents and to be acutely aware of them and to nurture them as they appear. And he is a musician, a guitarist with a total involvement in Gary Davis's playing and who has absorbed every facet of his skill and artistry: not to become a "Gary Davis" himself, or to make a career out of the reflected glory, but to understand the man and his music as much as possible from within.

This Tribute to Blind Gary Davis then is not a measured biography carefully told; it is a kaleidoscope of images which illumines through shafts of perception the fragments of fact that lie impersonally abbreviated in a "Who's Who", that are pinned to matrix order and release numbers of a discography or that are grabbed from the past of nearly half a century ago in three minutes of recorded sound.

Paul Oliver

Introduction

"I am here to love you, you understand".

Collecting material for this Tribute has been a delightful and fulfilling adventure. It appears that nearly everyone who has come in close contact with Rev. Davis, or "B. Davis" as he was affectionately called by family and close friends, has in some way been touched by his music and philosophy.

He was a charismatic character with a devoted following both from his church and from the music world. He was indeed a 'Pied Piper'. Of all the contributions that I have received nothing has been critical either of his character or of his music.

Rev. Davis was very much a man of this world, as the Chronology here will testify; he was certainly a devout and committed Christian. He was tolerant of his fellow man and often his only real criticism, and usually always in humour, was of his contemporary musicians. His often caustic comments were usually followed by a chuckle and a grin! But he could be full of praise for those he truly admired and he took particular delight and pride in the success of his guitar students.

He did possess a wonderful sense of humour as those who were fortunate to see him in concert or meet him in person could tell. There are also many stories of private times when he would tell, and often sing, the most bawdy songs and jokes. For most of his life he enjoyed a drink and a smoke, and greatly enjoyed the company of young people. He was no saint but he certainly is an angel.

Many of the 'students', of which a number are included in this collection, who visited him initially just for guitar lessons, would be greatly affected by his personality and in some cases it would change their whole life. A number of them that I have spoken to in recent years speak still with tremendous admiration and devotion.

I am hoping that this Tribute will complement the existing writings already published and perhaps give a deeper insight into this fascinating man. I have tried to illustrate the unique personality of Rev. Davis to show how as well as being a powerful and influential musician, that he was also an interesting man with his influence going far beyond that of his music alone. Perhaps two of his other great gifts were his hard won philosophy and his skill as a storyteller, which his included words I hope will show.

I should like to thank all of those people who have given their material so generously for my original book which was published in 1992 and for this updated and revised edition. There are some people from the original edition that I have not been able to contact again to request permission and I hope that they will be happy to be part of this new publication. It is a great testament to the memory of Rev. Davis that no one refused permission for me to use their material.

It is hard to believe that thirty-eight years have passed since his death; during those years we have seen his reputation and popularity grow from strength to strength. His prowess as a guitar player is undoubted and his admirers increase continually. Meeting him, and Mother Davis, has enriched and enhanced my life. I hope this Tribute will perhaps encourage even more to discover and appreciate his great gifts.

Robert Tilling
March 2010

New York City, 1954, John Cohen

Publicity Photograph, c. 1965, Lenny Schechter

Part One

Chronology

Special thanks to Mother Annie B. Davis, Bruce Bastin and Stefan Grossman.

Although Reverend Davis was not ordained until 1937 I shall refer to him as 'Rev. Davis' throughout the chronology. All of the quotes printed boldly are by Rev. Davis.

BORN APRIL 30, 1896

Born on a farm, on Bethel Church Road, Laurens, South Carolina. It is not known who owned the farm or how it was managed. His father was John Davis and his mother Evelinia Davis, of whom very little is known. Rev. Davis rarely spoke of his parents or his early childhood.

There is some confusion over the year of his birth but 1896 is the most often used. This date was given to the author by Rev. Davis and by Mother Annie Davis. On his application form for admission to the South Carolina Institution for the Education of the Deaf and Blind in 1914, it was given as 1897. On his first marriage certificate in 1919 his age was given as 23 years. On the January 1920 Census for Greenville, South Carolina, his age was also given as 23 years. The year on his 1937 Welfare File is given as 1895.

On a number of occasions a middle initial 'D' is given, possibly Daniel.

The eldest of eight children with six dying in childhood. A younger brother survived but very little is known about him.

"My mother had only two children that lived. All the others died when they were babes."

Blind after three weeks old. This was recorded on his 1914 application form to the South Carolina School for the Deaf and the Blind, Cedar Springs: Cause of Blindness: "Medicine of Doctor who made a mistake." The degree of blindness was given as "Nearly total."

Possible cause of blindness Ebuphophthalmus (Congenital Glaucoma). Rev. Davis was possibly able to distinguish light, dark, colour and shape, which enabled him to get around on his own.

"I could tell the look of a person but to tell who it is. I'm not able to do that."

"You see ever since I'd know'd myself I'd been like this. That's all I remembered but according to the story and the statement of my grandmother I'd taken sore eyes when I was three weeks old. And by me being an only grandchild there wasn't a family, you understand. They done everything they could to bring my sight back. They taking me to a doctor and the doctor put some alum and sweet milk in my eyes and they caused ulcers in my eyes. That is what caused me to go blind."

"The Lord took away my sight and I am His disciple."

CIRCA 1900

Lived as a child in Gray Court, South Carolina, thirty miles south of Greenville, and was primarily brought up by his grandmother Evelina Cheek. It is thought that his father gave him to Evelina as, he or his wife, were not capable of bringing up a blind child. Virtually nothing is known of his parents at this time. His only younger brother Buddy is thought to have died in 1930 and that he also played guitar after being taught by Rev. Davis.

"... red tin-top house with honeysuckle vine climbing up the side of it ..." (Earliest memory)

"I come right out of the woods! Down where the frogs have prayer meetings ... I ain't nothing but a country boy."

"... you couldn't hear nothing but owls after sundown!"

CIRCA 1902/03

Takes interest in music and at first the harmonica. His uncle was a harmonica player and encouraged him to play.

"The first instrument I played was a mouth harp. My uncle would go into town and buy himself one and then he'd buy me one. You could get a good one for twenty five cents."

Rev. Davis played solo harmonica all of his life. There is no evidence (there are no released, or known to the author, recordings of him playing harmonica with other musicians) that he played other than solo. He would often play spontaneously and there are many instances of him playing on aeroplanes and in cars. He would often humorously guess the speed of a car by holding his harmonica out of the window listening to the wind blow through it!

Gray Court, South Carolina, 1980, Robert Tilling

"Davis must have felt the tension (while waiting a long time on an airplane waiting to take off), and took out his harmonica and played the most moving, most appropriate, most feeling music I'd ever heard from him. And the airline hostess came over and made him stop playing - saying that it was annoying the other passengers. Then she turned on the 'musac'." JOHN COHEN (*Musician, folk music historian, photographer, film maker and member of 'The New Lost City Ramblers'*).

He would play harmonica (usually in the key of G) at many of his concerts; a number of harmonica titles have been recorded.

"I taught myself. That's something you can't teach nobody no how. You can teach somebody to dance but you can't teach nobody how to blow the harmonica."

CIRCA 1903

First interest in stringed instruments. He often stated that he first played a banjo when he was four years old.

"First thing I learned to play was an old banjo, you understand, I say old banjo because I learned how to play that. I just was going up and down ... plunk a plunk ... I thought I was doing something with that banjo... "

Around the age of seven he wanted a guitar and started to make homemade instruments from his grandmother's cooking pans. He often told with great humour and joy of how he was in trouble for doing this!

"I got more whoppin' tearing up my grandmother's pie pans. They found I was music inclined, you understand, that I had music in me. So every time my grandmother go buy a pan she buy me one because she know'd I'd tear it up first! So my mother bought me a guitar when I was seven. "

"I started making guitars out of pie pans. Drill holes through a piece of timber, you know, and got me some copper wire and made some strings. That's how I got started. First thing my mother bought me was a banjo. I was only four or five years old. Then she bought me a guitar and I have been playing one ever since."

He often mentioned that it was his mother who bought him his first Washburn guitar for eighteen dollars. His mother was seldom at home but obviously was taking some interest in his welfare at this time. There is no mention of his father being around during this period.

"The first time I heard guitar I thought it was a brass band coming through. I was a small kid and I asked my mother what it was and she said it was a guitar!"

CIRCA 1904-1910

Living in Gray Court, South Carolina. He was able to help

around the farm and, in particular, looked after the chickens and pigs. He could call them with his harmonica and could imitate their sounds.

"My grandmother mostly raised me. You see, my father gave me to my grandmother when I was a child because he knowed that there was no confidence to be put into my mother. She was always from one place to another, going from different towns and dances. Things like that. So my father gave me to my grandmother. I had one brother. He was a good guitar player. I taught him. He used to keep me up all night long to teach him how to play the guitar."

"You see, in those days white and colored didn't associate like the people in the northern states. I had too much experience about white folk then 'cause my grandmother always raised me up from white people. They always told me that it wasn't so good to dwell around white people's children. They loved to play with me but my grandmother didn't like me to take up too much time playing with white children."

Rev. Davis stated that his father was always in trouble with the police and died circa 1906.

"He was killed in Birmingham, Alabama. We heard the High Sheriff shot him."

"My mother married again when we stayed there at the Calhoun Wallaces."
It is possible that the Calhoun Wallaces were the land owners where his mother worked. (A Randolph Calhoun Wallace (1850 – 1924) was born in Laurens County, South Carolina, and may have been the landowner).
It is possible that he stayed with his mother and stepfather for a while then went back to live with his grandmother permanently circa 1906).

Becoming more interested and proficient at guitar playing, he was also singing in the Center Raven Baptist Church, Gray Court, South Carolina. He would play spirituals on the guitar for his grandmother.

"I showed myself and kept messin' with that thing. It laid around about a week. I got hold that thing and I kept knocking that thing."

Although he was mostly self-taught he did initially have help from an uncle.

The first song that he learned was "Little Darlin' You Don't Know My Mind."

"When I started to play guitar, you understand, I started to go around the picnics playing for white people. That's the way I made money, always have made money playing guitar. I couldn't keep none, I

QUESTIONS TO BE ANSWERED BY THE PETITIONER FOR STATISTICAL INFORMATION.

＊—＊

1. Name of the child or children?

Ans. *Gary Davis*

2. When and where born?

Ans. *[Laurens?] County   April 1897*

3. Cause of deafness or blindness.

Ans. *medicine of Doctor who made a mistake*

4. Total or partial?

Ans. *nearly total*

5. Any attempt to restore hearing or sight, and if so, by whom was such attempt made and with what success?

Ans. *no attempt to restore sight*

6. Has he had scarlet fever, measles, mumps, small-pox, or whooping cough?

Ans. *no measles*

7. Has he had any cutaneous disease, such as itch, tetter, scald head, &c.?

Ans. *no*

8. Has he any chronic disease, or is he liable to any sudden attack of sickness, fits, &c.?

Ans. *no*

9. Any like affliction, say deafness or blindness, in the connection previous?

Ans. *Cant hear perfectly at times & is nearly totally blind*

10. Were the parents related before marriage, and if so, how?

Ans. *no*

11. Give names of parents, brothers, sisters, post-office address, and such other information as may be profitable either to the pupil or the Institution.   *Evoline Chesh Gray Court # 4 R.D*

Ans. *Clay Martin Laurens SC*

12. White or colored?

Ans. *Colored*

Laurens SC aug 26 1914

The Parties herein concerned have no Property returned for Taxation in Laurens Co.   J N Thompson, co. Auditor

---

Page from the 1914 application form to enter the South Carolina School for the Deaf and the Blind, Cedar Springs

South Carolina School for the Deaf and for the Blind, Cedar Springs

make it anyway. When I wasn't doing nothing I used to have a good hand raising chickens!"

"... the Lord put something in my hands so I could take care of myself."

Listening to local musicians including Will Bonds, from whom he learned "Candyman". Thought to have heard "Eagle Rocking Blues" and "Delia" for the first time.

"Well I remember a lot of musicians, men that I set down and listened to when I was a boy and one was a remarkable guitar player. He taught me to play the first chord on a guitar. His name was Craig Fowler. He was the first man I took notice of."
(Nothing is known of Craig Fowler).

"That (the blues) broke out in 1910. I couldn't tell you where it came from. I first heard them from a fellow coming down the road picking a guitar and playing what you call "the blues". When I started playing the guitar there was no such thing as a piece coming out called "the blues". They played other songs. The blues, they just began to originate themselves."

"I'm going to tell what the blues is. It's like when you fall in love with a woman and it be so long between dates before you see her. You know you have the blues."

CIRCA 1911-1914

This is perhaps one of the most interesting periods of his early life when he was the member of a small string band which played for both white and black audiences in the Greenville, South Carolina area. Although only sixteen years of age when joining the band he was obviously by then an outstanding player. He was already popular and in demand for parties and dances.

"I played everything when I started out, everything."

The string band played mostly in Greenville, South Carolina. It is thought they did not travel much outside of that area.

"They always send for me when they had a dance!"

"I used to play for dances for white folks alright. When I was in the country I used to play for white folk's picnics. Every time they'd have a picnic they'd come and get me."

The band had six to eight players and included Will Bonds (of whom nothing is known) and the outstanding guitar player Blind Willie Walker (1896-1933) who recorded in 1930.

"Well, it had two guitars, two lead violins, a bass violin and a mandolin."

Although the band was popular and gained lots of work, Rev. Davis did not feel they were ambitious enough with their music and he wanted to travel and make more money.

"Well, after I got started with them I thought maybe I could get them somewhere you know. I found they didn't want to go nowhere. You get out playing guitar places, next thing you stop at some old woman's house, you understand, spending the night. All that kind of stuff and I'd be looking for money and they'd be looking for women! I won't be bothered with no kind of women when I ain't got no money in my pocket!"

It is not certain if the band ended in 1914 or when Rev. Davis decided to leave. It appears that he did not like playing with other musicians, who he could not trust or rely on.

"I'm always gonna play by myself because whenever I run across anything and I don't like it there won't be nobody to get mad."

1914. AUGUST 26

Applies for, and is given, a place at the 'South Carolina Institution for the Education of the Deaf and Blind', Cedar Springs, Spartanburg, South Carolina. No reason is given why a place is applied for at that time, but it may be that the grandmother was no longer able to look after and keep control of an eighteen-year-old young man. The application form is signed, with her mark, by his grandmother Evelina Cheek.

The degree of blindness was given as "Nearly Total". It also mentions that, "Cannot hear perfectly at times."

He was admitted to the school as a "Beneficiary Pupil" on the 28th August 1914.

He only stayed for six months, where he learned to read Braille and may have taught some music. He may also have learned to play piano. Rev. Davis said he left the school because he did not like the food. There is no record at the School of why he left but it is likely that he also did not like the restricted way of life. (There has been some suggestion that up until his late teens he could see to a certain degree, but his sight failed by 1914).

CIRCA 1914-1919

There is very little known of this period but it would appear that he was living in the Greenville/Spartanburg, South Carolina area. He was playing music for both white and black audiences and his probable only income was from music but he may also have had some help from family and friends. He was playing on the streets and at social gatherings.

"I was born and raised in the country. I ain't nothing but a country boy! After I got twenty years old I started standing around different towns you know."

"Street playing, you understand, you ain't sure about a thing and it keeps you on your pins."

Rev. Davis spoke very little about this period.

1919. JUNE 17

Married in Greenville, South Carolina, to Mary Hendrix, also from Greenville. Her age is given as twenty-eight and his age as twenty-three. They were married by Judge W. Scott.

Detail of Marriage Certificate, 1919

"After I married, me and my first wife started travelling. I was playing from town to town. Anywhere! Playing on the streets, then I would get run off by the police more times than I can remember."

A Jack Jordon (of whom nothing is known) remembered Rev. Davis playing on the streets of Greenville, South Carolina, at this time and often with female singers.

1920. JANUARY 7

Fourteenth Census of the United States - Greenville City, South Carolina, states:
Gary Davis aged 23 years given as head of the family and working as a musician on the street. His wife Mary aged 28 years working as "wash and clean at home". Both given as born in South Carolina.

Living in Greenville and making some income from playing guitar. The marriage lasted about five years and there were no children. A later Welfare File states that he left his wife in Winston-Salem, North Carolina, during 1924.

"The truth of it is that I found out she wasn't my wife but everybody else's wife. I let her go. We weren't getting along too well and after I found out her husband was living, that settled it for me."

"...she quit one blind man for another." (Thought to be a man named Joe Walker)

Bluesman and songster Pink Anderson (1900-1974) remembered Davis in 1923 primarily playing religious material. He would play blues if requested and if he was paid.

CIRCA 1924-1930

Living in Asheville, North Carolina, working as a street musician. He was remembered by fellow street musician Aaron Washington, who remembers Rev. Davis living in Asheville in 1922/23 and was still living there when he left in 1926. For a time Rev. Davis lived on the same street as Aaron Washington who took some interest in his welfare. Rev. Davis also taught Aaron Washington to play spirituals.

"Along then his voice was really strong and he could sing good ... he would sit in the square and play the guitar, mostly he would hold his guitar right up close to his head. It got to the point where everybody seemed to like him. Wouldn't hardly anybody pass without throwing some money to him."
AARON WASHINGTON

Playing music all around the Asheville, North Carolina area and living in an impoverished condition.

Walter Phelps (c.1896-1972), who grew up with Rev. Davis, remembers him living in Asheville, North Carolina, at this time.

His only brother Buddy died in 1930.

"He got killed in 1930. The woman he was going with killed him".

CIRCA 1930

Probable move to Durham, North Carolina, and at first living with his mother, and then at various rented rooms. (It has been suggested that he moved to Durham in 1926 or 1927 but there is no actual evidence for this). There is no evidence of actually when or why he moved to Durham but it may have been because Durham was a busy tobacco producing town with lots of opportunities to earn money from street singing. Perhaps also he wished to be with his mother who could help look after his welfare. Lived with his mother, also known as Belle, at 410A Poplar, Hayti. It is thought he lived with his mother for eight years until she died. This would suggest that he did first move to Durham in 1926, but there is no evidence of this. She worked in the tobacco factories and is known to have lived in Durham until 1938. He had since circa 1924 been travelling a great deal and never really settled in one place for long so a move to a new town was not out of character. An uncle, William Sexton, was thought to live nearby but had very little to do with Rev. Davis.

By the time he moved to Durham he had a wide repertoire of musical styles including the blues.

His first official welfare file opens in Durham during April 1931; later in July he is given permission to sing for money on the street.

CIRCA 1931-1932

Meets the guitarist and singer Blind Boy Fuller (Fulton Allen 1907-1941), probably while performing on the street. There is no evidence of when they actually met but Blind Boy Fuller had been playing guitar seriously since 1928 and when Rev. Davis first met him he was already playing on the streets.

A local musician, Willie Trice (1910-1976), remembered that when Rev. Davis first met Blind Boy Fuller he taught him new ideas on the guitar including how to play in the key of A.

Willie Trice, himself a good guitar player, also around this time remembers Rev. Davis:
"... he never let a string be still ... he could make a piano out of a guitar ... he could make five hundred chords when I was trying to play two."

"I met Gary in 1931 at the White House; that's the place they have the tobacco sales. One night me and a friend picked him up and carried him out to the country. Gary was the fastest man I ever heard. I never heard a man pick a string like Gary. You might find somebody make some of his chords, but you don't find anybody pick a string like Gary. Fuller used to say, "All of us boys can play, Willie, but Gary is our Daddy!" He called him the Daddy because he was Daddy of the guitar players, not because he was older than us." WILLIE TRICE

The Trice brothers often took Gary around to house parties and dances.

New York City c.1935

"Oh, yeah, I was a 'blues cat' then. What I mean by 'blues cat' is that I played blues and blues again and again. I would go to parties, dances, and things like that. Chittlin' struts and all that kind of stuff."

Rev. Davis always spoke well of Blind Boy Fuller.

"Well as a man he was a good natured fellow to meet, very kind. Well thought of and everybody liked him, wouldn't do nobody no harm at all. He do like most blind men do when they have a family or wife, do all they can to take care of them. "

It is almost certain that Rev. Davis taught some guitar to Blind Boy Fuller and a lot of his influence can be heard on some of Blind Boy Fuller's recordings. It has been suggested that Blind Boy Fuller only played with a slide when he first met Rev. Davis.

"He done pretty good but he would have done better if I could keep him under me, you understand. After he learned a few things he figured that he could make it. That was just it."

CIRCA 1932-1935

Living in Durham, working as a street musician and often working with Blind Boy Fuller. It has been suggested that Rev. Davis was ordained in 1933 but this is not true and he was certainly not ordained in 1935 when he made his first recordings.

"I was not a preacher then."

After his mother died in June 1934, (leaving him a small insurance, which he soon spent), he lived in various rented rooms in Durham and often in an impoverished condition. He was very independent and rarely had anyone to lead him around. He was more of a devout Christian but still played the blues and enjoyed drinking. It was stated in his welfare file during December 1934 that he was renting rooms with a John King and, "Man sleeps in the kitchen of a two room duplex house. Home very poorly kept. House is in a dilapidated condition."

Not long after his mother died he moved into 410B Poplar, the apartment next to the one his mother had lived in, which was the home of Ella Whitaker, and her daughter Mary Hinton. Ella had known Rev. Davis's mother, and took Rev. Davis in because he was so helpless. They were particularly worried about his smoking and concerned that he would start a fire! A welfare file of the time described the apartment as a comfortable home. It is not known how long he lived there.

1935. JULY 23-26

Makes first recordings for the American Record Company (ARC) in New York City. He was brought to New York City to record by Mr. J.B. Long who was a talent scout for ARC. He was a store manager (owned by United Dollar Stores), in Durham, North Carolina. He sold blues records and was also very interested in recording local musicians. He scouted for new artistes often by holding talent competitions.

He wanted to record Blind Boy Fuller and Rev. Davis was asked along both as a friend of Fuller's and for his outstanding guitar playing. Another friend who often played and led Fuller, George Washington (known as Oh Red or Bull City Red), the washboard player and vocalist, also went along.

They travelled to New York by car with Long's wife and young daughter. They stayed on corner of 133rd Street and 7th Ave. Rev. Davis recorded fourteen solo tracks and played guitar on tracks for Blind Boy Fuller and with Bull City Red. *(See Discography for full details).*

"Yes I made that. ("*I Saw The Light*") Bull City Red sang and I played it on a National guitar. Blind Boy Fuller played one too, J.B. Long bought him one after we came up and made records for the first time. He bought it in Richmond, Virginia. It went for fifty dollars."

Although J.B. Long did not get along with Rev. Davis he still had a great deal of admiration for him as a guitar player:

"Oh, he could play the guitar up and down, any way in the world..." J.B. LONG

Rev. Davis was not happy about the money arrangements and for some reason felt that he was not being paid enough.

"I thought fifty dollars was some money. When I found out that he was getting the royalties and I wasn't getting but the fifty dollars. He had me covered on that, you understand, but I waked up, you understand. He never got me no more."

Rev. Davis also found the timing of the recordings difficult and had to be touched on the arm when the time was up.

"What you stopping me for? It weren't long enough! "

"I didn't enjoy (the recording session) too well and I enjoyed it alright too. I could hardly catch on to it until later on. They'd give you a beer to drink but I didn't want any liquor. I played a steel-bodied guitar then."

1936

Receives first official regular Blind Pension of twenty-four dollars a month. This was reduced in 1941 to twenty dollars.

"What I want to know is how you expect me to live on that much money!"

CIRCA 1937

Meets the harmonica virtuoso Sonny Terry (Saunders Terrell 1911-1983) in Durham, North Carolina, who probably moved to Durham in 1937 and lived with Blind Boy Fuller for a while. Sonny Terry played with Blind Boy Fuller and this is no doubt how they met. All three frequently played together on streets and at social gatherings and as Bruce Bastin describes, "... surely an unforgettable sight let alone sound, as these three musicians played on the sidewalks".

"He was a tough man with a guitar ...The song I heard him sing on blues was "Ice Pick Blues". Man that was a killer. The guitar talked ...I loved him singing that song about Samson and Delilah. Boy he could kill that." SONNY TERRY

Rev. Davis is also remembered at this time often playing piano but the only released recording of him playing piano is on Adelphi Records (1973).

"Ain't that a piano?" I said, "Yes" and led him over to it. And he played the piano ...played that same song he played on the guitar ...sounded just like it. He liked an instrument he could carry with him." WILLIE TRICE

The white musician Sam Pridgen remembered seeing Rev. Davis play on the streets and said he "...followed him like a puppy dog...I never knew anyone who could make chords like Gary could."

Another musician, Jamie Alston, from Orange County, about fifteen miles from Durham, also remembered him playing on the streets in Durham, and also said how Rev. Davis would often go to the record store to listen to his own and other recordings.

Given an eye examination in July to determine eligibility for acceptance by the North Carolina State Commission for the Blind. The prognosis was given as "hopelessly blind".

CIRCA MAY 1937

Ordained a Minister in Washington, North Carolina. His welfare file dated July 21 1937 stated "that he was ordained two months ago in Washington, North Carolina".
No official ordination document has been found. It was thought for many years that Rev. Davis was first ordained in 1933. The misunderstanding has been since the release of the Riverside LP in 1957 when it stated in the sleeve notes that he was ordained in 1933.

"Everything I get I get from God and I just love you to know that."

Wholeheartedly involved in the church and attending services and Revival Meetings in the Durham and Raleigh, North Carolina area. Singing less blues and popular music, concentrating on gospel music.

"Well, how did I come to be a preacher? Now you see that was for me to come to. I was chosen."

Rev. Davis's welfare file dated July 1937 tells that he was concerned about saving souls and that, 'Much ability is shown in his steel guitar which would be a source of income, but it appears M (representing 'Male'), has scruples against this type of endeavour'. There is a great deal of interesting information about his time in Durham in Bruce Bastin's book "Red River Blues".

1938-1941

During 1939, J.B. Long was interested in recording Rev. Davis again but Rev. Davis was not willing and remembered his "falling out' with Long. It is probable that Long wanted Rev. Davis to sing blues but he was no longer interested and only wanted to record gospel songs. He also felt that Long did not pay him enough for the sessions. He believed that Blind Boy Fuller was paid more than he was getting, and felt he should be paid the same amount as Fuller. Rev. Davis records did not sell well which make the original discs very hard to find today.

During 1939 Rev. Davis applies for a `Talking Bible', which was a set of records especially made for the blind.

Spending more time away from home preaching and visiting churches. He was still playing for money from time to time as was suspected by his social worker, "…I asked him about his guitar; I'd seen him come in with it and wondered if he had been playing somewhere. He admitted he had been out playing but wouldn't say where. He said he would play for me if I wished and I urged him to play me a number. His ability as a guitarist is unbelievable.

I have never heard better playing."

During the summer of 1940 his Welfare Caseworker suggested that, "he stopped playing on the streets for money and claims to be a Minister of the Gospel."

During the late thirties Rev. Davis told a Welfare worker that he was far more interested in saving souls than in remuneration for his services, and that he had no church to mention but attends all church services. Also that he takes a very active part in the church work, preaching whenever he can get an engagement and playing the guitar whenever desired.

Although more devout, it is probable that he continued to play around the city of Durham and particularly in the Pettigrew Street area. This was a tough part of town including cheap eating houses, poolrooms, a movie theatre, grocery stores and barbershops. A welfare worker commented that "while he plays around the barbershops, this has been considered as entertaining rather than begging since the barbershops permit him to do this in order to help draw their customers".

1941

Attending Revival Meetings and is transported to them by fellow worshippers who also provided his food. Still living in an impoverished condition.

Blind Boy Fuller dies, February 1941.

CIRCA 1942

Meets his second wife, Annie Belle Wright, from Wake County, North Carolina, while at a Revival Meeting in Raleigh, North Carolina.

1941-1943

During April 1942 his social worker says that he was still playing on the streets and in barber shops probably on Pettigrew Street, also where Blind Boy Fuller had played. He tells his worker that he did not get a permanent preaching position due to his lack of hearing. It stated on his 1914 Blind School application form that he had a hearing problem.

He is advised by the Welfare Caseworker only to sing in the barber shops and not on the streets as it is illegal.

December 1943 marries Annie, (no official documents have been discovered to date. It has been suggested that they were married in 1937 but Mother Davis told the author it was during 1943). Mother Davis told the author that they did not live in Raleigh but in Durham, North Carolina after they were married. (It has been suggested that they lived in Raleigh).

1944

Moves permanently to New York City living at East 169th Street, in the Bronx, where they lived for the next twenty years. His wife moved first and worked as a family cook and Rev. Davis followed shortly after.

"I had never heard nothin' good about New York before I came up here."

From January 1944 he was a resident of New York City.

"... Gary Davis's career now belongs to New York."
BRUCE BASTIN.

Starts to play on the streets, particularly in Harlem, and continues preaching and working with various churches in the city.

"Yes I played in the streets there and I got run off the street by police and got put in jail. All kinds of stuff like that. Still kept on playing, you understand."

"Not so much that I liked it, but that's the best I could do. I was glad to get away from it. 'Cause there's too many different kinds of people you meet up with in the street, and it's not recognised. They call it beggin', pan handlin'".

Street performing was banned in New York City from 1936 until 1970.

Rev. Davis was arrested in New York City on three occasions during 1948, 1957 and 1964 for "Public Loitering".

"...any street that I could make a few dollars."
(Asked what was his favourite street to play on in New York City)

CIRCA 1945

Records in New York City, a guitar instrumental, "Civil War March", which was played on a wooden guitar and was released later on a Folkways Record album (1967). Regularly playing on street, and working actively for the Baptist Church with his wife Annie.

1946

The Watkins School of Music, 152 West 131st St., New York City, publish sheet music, "Message from Heaven", ("There is Destruction in This Land"), for 35 cents.

1946 -1950

Visits Durham, North Carolina, during February 1948 to preach and play at a Revival Meeting and to visit his relatives. During stay falls on the ice and brakes his wrist. (It is possible that he also broke his wrist on his left hand as a boy which may account for his ease to play very difficult chord positions, due to a badly set wrist).

"I had just come up from South Carolina (1971) visiting Pink

New York City, 1954, John Cohen

Anderson in Spartanburg and was telling B. Davis about my trip. He was very interested in all that I saw down there. He said he never met Pink but remembered Simmie Dooley (Pink's partner) as a great guitar picker and had heard about Pink. He said that the last time he was down in the Carolinas was in the late 1940's. His uncle, a last living relative, was sick and he wanted to visit him before he died, and to attend the funeral. So he took the train down there and it was a very cold winter. While there he slipped and broke his wrist! His uncle lived on, I believe he said, for another three or four months and he stayed there until he died so that he could finish up the purpose of his trip. He was so glad to get back to New York!"
ROY BOOK BINDER

Teaches guitar at Brownie McGhee's, "Home of the Blues", which he opened in 1942 on 125th Street, and closed in 1950. It is uncertain when Rev. Davis started to teach there or for how long.

One of the first students of the school was the blues guitarist Alex Seward (1901-1972). The school opened to encourage musicians to develop in all aspects of their music. Rev. Davis was a popular teacher.

"I had Blind Gary Davis teaching guitar ... he was an extraordinary teacher". BROWNIE McGHEE

13

At Home, New York City, 1954, John Cohen

Mrs Tiny Robinson becomes a close friend of Rev. and Mrs Davis during this period. Mrs Robinson was great support to them both throughout their lives. She was the niece of Martha Ledbetter, the wife of Huddie "Leadbelly" Ledbetter. Rev. and Mrs Davis would often visit Martha Ledbetter's and Tiny Robinson's apartments, meeting many musicians including, Woody Guthrie, Sonny Terry and Brownie McGhee.

Records two songs for a 78rpm for the Lennox Label, during January 1949. It is probable that the session was arranged by Brownie McGhee.

Performs at the Leadbelly Memorial Concert at the Town Hall, New York City during January 1950.

"I first saw him in 1950 at a midnight show at the NYC Town Hall - it was a memorial concert for Leadbelly who had died a few months earlier, and a lot of jazz and folk singers were there. However, a single spotlight was there for Davis who emerged from behind the curtain. We sensed his blindness and were stunned by his guitar playing. There was no explanation of who he was or how he got there!" JOHN COHEN

1951

Interviewed in Rev. Davis's home by the scholar and philanthropist Elizabeth Lyttleton Harold, the wife of Alan Lomax. The recorded interviews resulted in a three hundred plus page document. He was living, with his wife Annie, in dire poverty. He spoke freely and candidly about many aspects of his life and times.

"There is absolutely no controlling him or guiding him. He says what he pleases, when he pleases to say it, all very pontifically. I think the resemblance to the authoritative African wise man or witch doctor is striking…I am pleased that the fruit of our slowly ripening trust and friendship is ready to be plucked at last. Rev. Davis is a wonderful, poetic, old gentleman. He is also as bitter and grieved a ghost of human decency and dignity as ever haunted this weary strumpeted old earth." ELIZABETH LYTTLETON HAROLD (April 11 1951)

Also during 1951 interviewed at home by Dr. Ellen Steckert:

"The interviews were conducted in a crowded living room with a table that took up so much space in the centre that the children who emerged from the kitchen and who wished to leave by the front door had to crawl under the table in order to gain their exit. At the time Reverend Davis claimed to have had his most recent guitar stolen and I believe Ken Sidon and Richard Hatch did something to procure a new instrument for him. Gary Davis also claimed to know no songs except those which were religious." DR.ELLEN STECKERT

1951-1954

Regularly playing on the streets of Harlem:

"**Oh! I used to,** (play on the streets of Harlem), **that's where I got most of my robbing done. I have had five guitars like this stolen. Every time I sat down someone took something.**"

"It was in the early 1950's Davis would play on the streets and would often be found at Eddie Bell's guitar store in Midtown Manhattan (near Tin Pan Alley). Sometimes he'd be sleeping in one corner. The Bells were very nice to him. I recall that one time Davis fell asleep in the street and someone stole his "Miss" Gibson." JOHN COHEN

"Gary, while singing on the streets would on occasions fall asleep and someone would make off with his guitar - usually a Gibson J-200. He would save up for another. The musical instrument dealer (the late) Eddie Bell was always sympathetic towards Gary and would let him pick out a new J-200 and hold it for him until paid for. Gary would stop by Eddie Bell's store frequently and play his "lay away guitar". Customers would donate change, dropping it into Gary's tin cup. Such donations would go towards buying Gary a new guitar." HARRY WEST

Rev. Davis recorded titles with Rev. McKinley Peebles by John Cohen during 1953 at Davis's home.

"Rev. McKinley "Kinny" Peebles (also known as 'Sweet Papa Stovepipe', 1897- 1985) had been a very good friend and close associate of Rev. Davis and remembers playing with him a lot on the streets and in churches. Apparently sacred-gospel performers could be just as competitive as blues performers. According to 'Kinny' Peebles they teamed up to win popularity contests in churches! Their association lasted about five or six years in the late 1950's (possibly 1950 -1955) but 'Stovepipe' failed to be discovered when Davis was by the white music audience". ANTON MIKOFSKY.

Studio Photograph, New York City, c. 1958

Courtesy Folklore Productions

1954-1960

April 1954 records an album with the harmonica player Sonny Terry for the Stinson Label. Produced by Kenneth Goldstein.

"I don't see how anyone could live that long inhaling all that rust!" *(of Sonny Terry)*

Many young and aspiring musicians are being inspired by his playing and singing including Dave Van Ronk, Happy Traum, Tom Paley, Gino Foreman, Ian Buchannan, Winnie Winston, Dick Weissman, Erik Darling, Barry Kornfeld and John Gibbon.

Enjoys the company of young guitar players helping with advice and teaching.

"I keep telling you, you want to come to my house and learn how to play guitar. Don't be scared of money, come on honey! I ain't going to kill you. It ain't but five dollars a head and I guarantee when you leave, you'll leave knowing more than before you came there. If it ain't no more than I took your money!"

"You come to me and I'll teach you how to play guitar, not fool around with that guitar".

"I only charge five dollars a lesson – a cow can't give more milk than it's worth!"

January 1956 recorded by Kenneth Goldstein for the Riverside Label.

"As soon as the recording started everyone in the room came to the immediate realisation that this was going to be a great session. Gary was at his best, without a doubt. Of the nine songs recorded in a little over two hours, only two had to be re-recorded. I have often followed the principle that good artists, folk or otherwise, are their own best critics. They know what they want to say and therefore are the best ones to decide whether or not they ended up saying it the way they intended. As soon as we played back the first recording Gary broke into a huge grin. There was no doubt about it. He was listening to himself the way he wanted it to sound." KENNETH GOLDSTEIN *(The Record Changer, Vol. 14 No. 8)*

Probably the first two British guitarists, brothers Alex and Rory McEwen, visit Rev. Davis for lessons, during the early part of 1956.

During 1959 Larry Johnson first meets Rev. Davis and takes "lessons" and they became close friends. Larry Johnson plays harmonica with him on the Adelphi Label (1973) and has made many recordings in his own right.

"I met him sometime in 1959 during the winter and it was a thing for me playing harmonica with him, you know. Well, there he was, an old blind man, and at that time it was before like what we call 'discovered'. And Mrs. Davis was going out every day doing domestic work. And there he was sitting around the house all day by himself. Well, now, there I was in Harlem getting drunk all day. And I always did like music; well, I was just having a good time. Life didn't mean much, whether I died or not. I really didn't care and then I met Gary. And in there he sat, such a good musician. He inspired me and I always respected him as a Minister, and I used to go and see him every day and I'd sit around and play harmonica and he'd play the guitar." LARRY JOHNSON

Playing less regularly on the streets.

"I've often heard people say it's a shame for such a fine artist to have to sing on street corners, but Gary rather enjoys it. Once when singing in midtown Manhattan, a passer-by remarked that he played very much like Reverend Gary Davis, to which Gary replied that he knew Reverend Davis quite well." BARRY KORNFELD (Sing Out! *March 1960)*

1958. FEBRUARY 22ND

Appears in a "Hootenany Concert" at Carnegie Hall, New York City; others appearing include Pete Seeger and Jerry Silverman.

FROM 1959

Making regular club, coffeehouse and festival appearances

including Newport Folk Festival, Philadelphia Folk Festival and the Mariposa Folk Festival.

1960

Stefan Grossman first meets Rev. Davis and becomes a student and close associate. Makes many recordings of all aspects of his music and, in particular, encourages Rev. Davis to release more recordings of his blues and ragtime tunes. A great debt of gratitude is owed to Stefan Grossman for bringing so much of Rev. Davis's music to our attention.

Becoming in demand to make records.

"You know, searching amongst leaves sometimes you find a piece of gold every once in a while."

New York City, 1964, Photographer unknown

On August 24th makes his first record for Prestige/Bluesville label.

"With his battered - weather beaten Gibson guitar which had served him so well on the streets of Harlem, Davis immediately became the focus of attention in the magnificent cathedral ceilinged studio. As the first notes of his fabulous guitar playing came through the speaker in the control room, it was evident that this was to be Davis at his very best. The recorded results are certainly proof of this." LARRY COHN

1961-1963

"By the early 1960's Davis was something of a 'star', playing all over. Manny Greenhill got him jobs at festivals... I think that his first real break into the college circuit happened at Antioch College when some of his students had Davis fly out. Apparently he was very tired when he got on stage and fell asleep in front of the audience. The kids just sat there for an hour, digging the whole scene. I believe he also fell asleep during a concert at Yale but other performers carried on the show. I cherish the memory of the Antioch show, for both Davis and for the kids' good taste. It is his agility on the guitar and his resilience as a person that have stayed most with me." JOHN COHEN

Mother Annie Davis would often accompany Rev. Davis to concerts and festivals.

"At the 'Club 47' there is the added pleasure of hearing his wife, at her seat singing and humming throughout, as involved in the performance as Reverend Davis himself." LINDA KALVER

Appears at many clubs and universities including, Village Corner, Toronto; Ash Grove, Los Angeles; Second Fret, Philadelphia; First Step, Tucson; University of Wisconsin and Columbia University, New York City.

Being represented by Manny Greenhill of Folklore Productions Inc.

"The very first concert I arranged for Rev. Davis was in 1957 when I brought him up to Boston (Mass.) to perform at the Y.M.C.A. He was accompanied by the banjo player, Barry Kornfeld. Perhaps a year later when he was up in Boston again

New York City, circa 1957, Photo Associates/ Courtesy Elijah Wald

London 1964, Val Wilmer

and I remember it was a very grey winter's day, I had a call from a local guitar store owner, a Mr. Wurlitzer, who said that Rev. Gary Davis was in his store choosing a guitar. He had tried all the guitars and had picked out the very best guitar in the store, a Gibson J-200, but he had no money to pay for it! Mr. Wurlitzer said he was prepared to give a twenty per cent discount on the $500 guitar but how could it be financed? So I went down to the store which was near by and as soon as I arrived Rev. Davis came close to me and whispered in my ear, "You know I'm worth it", and of course he was and over the next few months he paid off his guitar which was one of his very best "Miss Gibsons". It was later in 1963 that we signed a formal contract and I have represented him ever since. He was indeed a wonderful man and his life touched and influenced mine in many ways."
MANNY GREENHILL

Rev. Davis continued to give informal guitar lessons at his home and many, now well known, musicians, visited him for advice, or were indirectly influenced by his music, including John Townley, David Bromberg, Taj Mahal and Bob Weir. Everyone who visited their home was warmly received particularly by Mother Davis and there are many stories of her generosity and hospitality.

During 1962 the folk trio, 'Peter, Paul and Mary', recorded a version of "If I Had My Way" ("Samson and Delilah"), and from the royalties Rev. and Mother Davis purchased a home on Long Island, where Rev. Davis lived until his death.

"I got two homes by pickin' guitar. I want you to know that. "

Bob Dylan sings a number of his songs, and his first album includes, "Baby Let Me Follow You Down" (version of "Baby, Let Me Lay It On You"). It is also thought that during 1961 Dylan wanted Rev. Davis to marry him to Suze Rotolo.

1964

First concert tour of the U.K. with 'The American, Blues and Gospel Caravan', appearing at major concert halls including London, Birmingham, Brighton, Bristol and Liverpool. Other musicians on the tour included Sonny Terry and Brownie McGhee, Sister Rosetta Tharpe and Muddy Waters. The tour received wide press and Muddy often praised Rev. Davis on stage affectionately calling him, "My Pastor".

Appears in a short black and white film made in New York City, "Blind Gary Davis in New York".

Appears on British television programme filmed by Granada Television, U.K.

1965

Second tour of the U.K. with concerts including the cities of Birmingham, Manchester, Liverpool, Bristol and London.

"'Ramblin' Jack Elliot topped the bill with a repertoire of hill-billy songs, but the man who took most applause was blind guitar player and singer, the Rev. Gary Davis."

LIVERPOOL ECHO, June 1965

Appeared in a concert on Friday, September 24th held at the Carnegie Hall, New York City. The event entitled "Sing In For Peace" an anti Vietnam War concert. Other performers included Joan Baez, Phil Ochs, The Freedom Singers and Pete Seeger.

1966

Third concert tour of the U.K. with concerts including the cities of Aberdeen, Wolverhampton, Keele and London.

1967

Appears on television on "Rainbow Quest", WNDT-TV New York City, with Pete Seeger.

1968-1970

Continues as a popular and much in demand performer at major clubs and festivals, including the Newport Folk Festival (1968), Philadelphia Folk Festival (1969) and at Harvard University (1968).

Author first corresponds with Roy Book Binder who was travelling and learning from Rev. Davis and has since become a close friend. Through Roy, the author has made many contacts that have helped with the compiling of this book.

1970

Appears in the film, "Black Roots", which was produced and directed by Lionel Rogosin, and also included Larry Johnson. The film received excellent reviews.

"Burning sincerity! Warm, earthy, peppery and humorous."
NEW YORK TIMES

The film was shown on British television during December .

"The choicest programme of the week is undoubtedly Lionel Rogosin's film of a group of black people talking, arguing, reminiscing, and singing." THE SUNDAY TIMES (U.K.), 5th December, 1970
Rev. Davis becomes ill during the late summer.

"Rev. Davis is doing O.K., but he doesn't sound as strong as when I first met him. Today I was going to go to church with him, but instead I am meeting two friends, also students of his. Meeting people through Rev. Davis has been one of the gifts that he has given. Besides his friendship, we have all met others and grown in many directions. We have so much to thank him for. I hope that Rev. Davis knows that we feel he is a great man, not just a great player."
ROY BOOK BINDER (letter to the author)

Appears on television show "Like It Is" (ABC-TV).

1971

Last concert tour of England, during July and August, with

an appearance at the Cambridge Folk Festival, and includes a visit to the author's home in Jersey, Channel Islands.

Other cities visited included Norwich, Sheffield, Manchester, Hull and Bristol. The successful tour had wide press coverage.

"B. Davis came back so tired, but he is now back to his usual self with students coming in for lessons daily."
MOTHER ANNIE DAVIS (letter to the author)

Last formal recording studio session for Biograph during March.

The Davis's home, 109-42 174th Street, Jamaica, New York City, 1972, Robert Tilling

"One of the most interesting parts about the session is that after setting up and getting the proper sounds we decided on some of the gospel material with Gary and he made it very clear to us that he only records one take of any song. He says that if there is a mistake, it's not his fault but the engineer's. We then proceeded to record some 25 sides of Gary Davis. Amazingly enough, there were no mistakes in any of them. Gary also insisted on recording without a break. This is an amazing fact in itself since the session ran for about 5 hours, and although we were getting tired, it seemed that Gary was a bundle of energy who would have continued for ever."
ARNOLD S. CAPLIN, *President of Biograph Records Inc.*

Rev Davis always liked to try and record in one take when in the studio.

"... once is as good as a hundred, twice is as good as a thousand..."

Rev. Davis was taken ill during October and spent some time in hospital.

1972

During January Rev. Davis spent some time in hospital. On February 26th had a heart attack, and after a short spell in hospital he was discharged back to his home.

During March/April the author visited Rev. and Mother Davis. Rev. Davis had not been well but was still receiving students and guests.

(It is possible that a French film about Rev. Davis was released, but the author has no evidence to support its existence).

April 24 gave his last concert at the Youth Development Association Center, Northport, Long Island, New York.

May 5 he was taken ill while travelling to Nuetonville, New Jersey, and suffered a cardiac attack at the William Kessler Memorial Hospital, New York, from which he died.

May 11 his funeral service was held at the Union Grove Baptist Church, 1488 Hoe Avenue, Bronx, New York.

May 12 his interment took place at Rockville Cemetery, New York.

Poem from funeral sheet:

"With eyes that were always closed and now body still,
He always did the Master's will...
Sleep on Gary, and take your rest...
We all loved you but God loved you best.
Sleep on Brother."

"The loss of my husband was Heaven's gain."
MOTHER ANNIE DAVIS (letter to the author)

1974

"A Tribute to Rev. Gary Davis" concert was held on November 10th at the Studio Museum in Harlem, Fifth Avenue, New York City. Performers included Rev. Dan Smith, Sweet Papa Stovepipe (also known as Rev. McKinley Peebles) and Rev. F.D. Kirkpatrick.

1997. DECEMBER 29

Mother Annie B. Davis dies aged 102 years.

"Mother Davis was a God fearing Daughter who loved the Lord. A devoted Mother, Grandmother and a true Friend to all she knew."
From Funeral Sheet, January 3rd 1997

2001. AUGUST 25

A North Carolina State Historic Marker was dedicated at 1201 Fayetteville Street, Durham, North Carolina. The text of the marker reads: "***Bull City Blues*** *– During the 1920's – 1940's, Durham was home to African American musicians whose work defined a distinctive regional style. Blues artists often played in the surrounding Hayti community and downtown tobacco warehouse district. Prominent among these were Blind Boy Fuller (Fulton Allen) (1907-1941) and Blind Gary Davis (1896-1972), whose recordings influenced generations of players.*"

2003. FEBRUARY 6

The Folk Alliance honoured Rev. Gary Davis with a Lifetime

Achievement Award. The award was given at the organization's 15th annual conference held in Nashville.

2004. JANUARY 20

Concert entitled "A Tribute to Rev. Gary Davis" held at the Kaufman Center, Lincoln Center, New York City with Jorma Kaukonen, Roy Book Binder and Ernie Hawkins.

References

I am particularly indebted to Bruce Bastin for allowing me to quote so freely from his two books, 'Crying for the Carolines', Studio Vista (1971), and 'Red River Blues', Macmillan Press (1986). Also to quote from his interview with Willie Trice (Talking Blues Magazine, 1979).

Thanks to Steve Rye, Richard Noblett and John Offord for the use of their interview with Rev. Davis (Blues Unlimited, November and December, 1966). To Gerard J. Homan for the use of his interview with Rev. Davis (Blues World, 1972). I am particularly grateful to Richard Lieberson and Udine Moore from whose taped interviews many of the quotes by Rev. Davis are used (1970).

A number of quotes also come from an essay by Alex Shoumatoff, an edited version of which appeared in 'Rolling Stone' (March, 1971).

Special thanks also to the following who sent information or who gave permission to use their writings: Dr. Ellen Steckert, Sam Charters, John Cohen, Bill Phillips, Kip Lornell, Larry Cohn, Allan Evans, Woody Mann, The Association For Cultural Equity, and Stefan Grossman. Lastly to Mother Annie Davis who answered all my letters and requests.

Robert Tilling

Related Information of the time living in Durham, North Carolina.

Some years ago the Durham County, North Carolina welfare department case file on Gary Davis came to light. He became case 282 there in December, 1934. While much of the material is routine bureaucracy, there are often interesting and perceptive insights from the various social workers concerned. There is no wish to enter into every personal detail but some comments throw light upon his musical activities and the motivation for his work and his final move north to New York.

The file on his social history states: "In appearance he is always neat and clean. He has a very aggressive manner except when discussing his personal situation. At this time he talks very little and leaves the conversation to whoever happens to be with him ... He has a religious obsession which influences his activities in an almost impractical manner. He stated that he was more interested in 'saving souls' than remuneration for his services. He has no church to mention but attends services at all churches. He takes a very active part in the church work, preaching wherever he can get an engagement and playing the guitar whenever desired".

The file goes on to talk of his playing guitar, which caused both them and Gary much soul searching, for any income made

New York City, 1956, Lawrence Shustak, (Reproduced from Record Changer magazine)

from "soliciting alms" would have made his grant invalid. Many of the case-workers sensed or turned a blind eye to his activities and frequently there are such comments as "There have been some questions as to whether or not he may have been soliciting during his frequent absences from Durham". At one point in the social history there is the delightful understatement that "He seems to possess some musical aptitude and his playing has been very well received". It also refers to him having taught music at Cedar Springs Blind School in Spartanburg, South Carolina, which he attended in 1914.

Gary certainly continued to pick up "a little change" around Durham and nearby towns and he probably took off partly because he felt restricted by the welfare department in Durham, which in fact reduced his cheque in 1941. Gary felt that it was because he earned a little on the side, which he never liked admitting and could not bring himself to lie about although a case-worker explained to him that it was because, "the County was averaging too much per grant and that a number of grants had been cut to make up for it".

Gary felt that the department, "had stopped him from preaching and singing on the streets and that since God had called him he just had to preach and that he had to keep himself a little presentable so that he could do just that. He said that people did not give him money for preaching like they used to because they knew he got a grant and that they felt like he had as much as they did". There can be little doubt that about this time Gary considered moving, and before long had left Durham for nearby Raleigh, taking with him his new wife Annie. Gary's welfare file offers an interesting slant on this. "He continued to live about from place to place with unrelated people until he was married to a Lake County woman in December, 1943. Little is known about the wife except through an account from Mary Hinnant, with whom she had previously boarded. This woman seemed to think that the marriage was a good thing since the man would have 'someone to look after him'. It was learned from correspondence that he had gone to New York to be with some of his wife's relatives". This was in January 1944.

In February 1948 the welfare department received a call from one Mary Hinton (the correct name of the Mary Hinnant mentioned above) to say that Gary had fallen during the severe cold weather and strained his wrist. It appears he had been worried about the welfare department's attempts to locate him in New York; simply, in fact to transfer his case. Gary was obviously worried that his small income might be cut and had come back down.

Whatever one's assessment of the difficult situation of the welfare department's attitude towards income, there is no doubt that Gary was well respected. His social worker, Mrs. Laura Miller, wrote him as "Dear Reverend" and her first meeting with him brought this comment in her report: "I asked Gary about his guitar ... He admitted that he had been out playing but wouldn't say where. He said that he would play for me if I wished and I urged him to play me a number. His ability as a guitarist is unbelievable. I have never heard better playing."

I doubt any of us would disagree with that 1941 evaluation of his music.

BRUCE BASTIN, August 1977

●

First time I saw Gary was in Durham. The next time was when he just left a little party and he was playing that song, "Billy the Rabbit Skin", you know, play it and knock the box on his leg. (Shows he meant knock the body of the guitar on his leg as a rhythm device.)

He had an old wooden guitar. The songs he played was mostly spiritual songs. He could play the others but he didn't do it often. He could play guitar just like Joshua White, yes sir. (White was also from Greenville, South Carolina, and had first recorded in 1932, the year that Willie first met Davis. Within a year, White was a very popular recording artist.) He could play like Fuller only faster. You couldn't make no chords he couldn't make, now. He was educated on them strings. He started playing when he was nine years old, he said. That's all he ever did. Yes sir, he's the best. Mr. Satherley (the Artist and Repertoire Manager for the American Record Company, where J.B. Long took his artists, and whose name Willie always pronounced as "Sadler") said, when Mr. Long carried Fuller up there when he made records, said Gary was the playingest man he ever seed in his life. Never seed no man like that play guitar. Mr. Long didn't take him back on account of, I don't know what it was. Gary wanted to play spirituals, Mr. Long said Gary was kind of bull-headed. (Davis accompanied Fuller on his first recording trip but never returned. He and Long argued, probably over Davis's reluctance to sing blues, although he did record two. Long always stated that Davis's vocal grated, but it is likely that Davis's "bull-headed" attitude annoyed him.

Later, in 1938, Long offered Davis another trip to record,

but he refused, saying that he wasn't being offered enough money.) But Gary didn't know about making records, you know. He said it weren't long enough. They stopped him and he said, "What you stoppin' me for? It weren't long enough. "That messed that'n up and they had to play it over again. When he got through playing, you know, and they'd touch him to quit (Davis was blind and unable to see the red warning light that came on, to forewarn artists to end their songs) and he signed his songs off, he'd grab them and say, "Is that'n all right?" He wanted to know they was all right, and he was too nervous too, you know. He'd never done it before. Didn't sound like it on the strings though, did it? Mr. Satherley just looked at him and he didn't miss a lick nowhere. He wasn't just playing two or three strings; he's playing all of them".

He had a little old wooden guitar. I used to trade every week, you know, till I get a better one. I spoke to him and he spoke to me and said, "What's that in your hand?" (Willie hadn't mentioned that he had his guitar with him and feels it substantiates Davis's amazing ability but if Willie was on Pettigrew Street, he was probably on his way to Fuller's, and would almost certainly have his instrument with him.) I said, "I've got a stick here, Gary." "Let me see it." I handed it to him. He tried a few chords and said, "You're right, Willie. You ain't got nothin' but a stick!"

WILLIE TRICE (Courtesy of Bruce Bastin)

●

Through the Depression both men depended on the Durham County Welfare Department for periodic aid. And our few glimpses of their lives during this period come from the reports of their caseworkers.

In order to be eligible for their 23 dollars a month assistance, Fuller and Davis had to conceal the irregular income from their music, and the welfare records reveal a constant cat-and-mouse game with officials trying to determine their clients' eligibility.

"Yes ma'am", Davis told an official who managed to find him in his rented room. "I know you been here several times, but you know I am inclined to preach the gospel, and I got to be gone a lot since God called me". The worker asked if he made any money on these trips. Davis wryly answered "The only success I have is saving souls, which is pay enough". Before the caseworker could continue, Mary Hinton, Davis's kindly landlord, interrupted, complaining that the heat was about to kill her. That started Davis on a sermon about being prepared to die. Taking his text from "Be ye also ready", Davis launched into a detailed sermon on the necessity of preparation for the inevitable "flight to glory". He concluded by giving the worker a pamphlet he had written on the constancy of death, a theme which runs through many of Davis's songs.

On another occasion, Mary Hinton elaborated on Davis's religious convictions. "His mind runs backwards, you know, and I believe it's because he has just thought about the Bible and religion too much. A person can think too much, and I believe Gary has. He sometimes wakes me up at two or three o'clock in the morning going to bed, falling over a chair. He sits up and reads his Bible that late."

Courtesy BILL PHILLIPS/SAM CHARTERS

Last concert, Northport, New York, April 24th 1972, Doug Menuez

23

Bucks Rock Camp, Conn., c 1965, Photographer Unknown

Part Two

Musicians, Friends, Students & Admirers

Here is a poem I love truly. Could you please, if you can, place this in the book. This poem is just like me!

"I shall pass through this world but once.
Any good, therefore that I can do
Or any kindness that I can show
To any human being
Let me do it now. Let me
Not defer it or neglect it for
I shall not pass this way again."

Mother Annie Davis

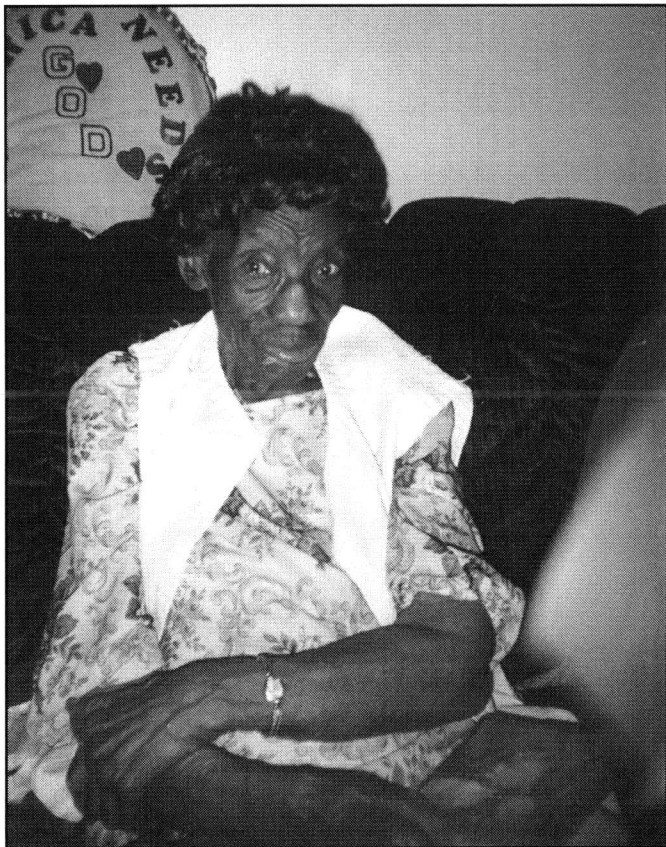

Mother Annie Davis, New York City, 1990, Robert Tilling

I am writing this letter about Rev. Gary Davis, I knew him for many years, in fact 20 years. Rev. Gary Davis was a very dear friend of mine, he was a loveable man.

He preached to my congregation, the Union Grove Baptist Church, and played his guitar many times, the people were inspired by his message. His devoted wife was by his side to see him getting back and forth spreading the good tidings and joy to men's and women's souls.

Rev. Davis preached one time I would not forget. Subject, "If you love me prove it", text St. John 21, 15-17. One of his songs was, "I am going to sit down by the river and won't be back no more". I preach from the text Cor. 2, 5-1. I used for a subject, 'The Christian Moving Day'. His funeral was well attended.

Rev. F.C. Crawford D.D.,
Union Grove Baptist Church, Bronx, New York, May 23rd 1973

●

God's Earthly Moses

There once lived a man I knew
To seek fame and fortune wasn't his game.
The man I'm talking about
B. Davis was his name.

He would go around to and fro
Preaching and singing where he'd go
Telling everybody to be at ease.
If God feed the little birds,
He can surely take care of you and me.

Now lots of people did B. Davis wrong
They even sometimes cut the guitar from his arm
But in spite of that it didn't take B. long
To get another guitar and go on singing his songs.

He made so many people glad as can be
That was just like B. Davis can't you see.
One day B. Davis finished all of his songs
For you see God called "B. Davis come on home,
You already did what I told you to,
There is nothing else on Earth for you to do."

Listen B. Davis might have finished his songs on Earth
But now he have had a new birth.
I saw him in a judgement seat
I imagine somewhere at Jesus feet.

My little daughter saw him let you know
That B. Davis is somewhere resting in peace
Waiting for that great day
Then once again we might hear B. say,
"I'm going to sing a brand new song,
I'm so glad
I'm so glad we all made it home."

Sister Evangelist R.B. Artis 1974
Your Friend In Jesus Christ
(A good friend and neighbour of the Davis's)

I would like for everyone who knew the man to know that he turned to God fully before he died. He testified to the Glory of God and his Wondrous Works. I think his widow Sister Annie B. Davis, (my very good friend), might have told you about this ... that he wanted to put up a church for God and he said, "God have been so very, very good to me, I feel like I should put up a church in remembrance for all the good he did for me, and I don't have all that much time left to do it." He told me this one morning after I had driven he and Sister Davis to attend several business's they needed to attend to.

One day I was at their house and this day the house had quite a crowd, mostly young people. I remember like it was yesterday. I began to sing a Spiritual song. After I finished B. Davis said, "Was that you just finished singing Sister Artis?" We told him yes and he said, "Woman do you know who you are? Do you know that God has chosen you as a special person to work for him, and he has given you a seeing eye to see that others can't. You have a seeing eye to look right through a person and can tell right away just what he is."

I noticed that he became very, very alert even to the things

New York City, 1960, Photographer unknown

around him. Sis. Davis wanted him to rest this day but he raised his voice with authority and said, "Woman don't tell me to rest. I have to say what I am saying for God and I don't have all that much time to say it." So you can see what I have mentioned here that Rev. Gary Davis knew that his time was fast running out and he knew his dying day was near.

Although he was very ill he pressed on forward going to several churches in freezing cold weather. I have no doubt in my mind he make it up with Jesus so he could be caught in the rapture of the Last Judgement when Jesus takes back all the faithful to meet the King.

I am now working in the evangelical field with the encouragement I received from B. Davis and his word to me have proven time, he said, "God wants you to work for him". He told me the same day as he told me God had given me the

seeing eye. To make me sure God wanted me to know he was speaking through Rev. Davis that day he sent two signs and wonders to me. First, he let my little girl, Lorrie Ann, who was only nine years old at the time, make sign. She is small in stature yet she put a picture up as high as an eight foot man could reach and there was not a thing in the room for even me to stand on to reach as high as she put up that picture. (I am 5ft 6in tall!) When I looked up I said, "Lorrie go to bed it's very late", she said, "Mama, look what God did for B. Davis. Took him and put him to rest."

The next sign I saw in a Vision. I saw B. Davis in a very huge chair with a very tall back and very wide arms. His arms were on each arm of the chair and he looked like the pictures you sent to Sis. Davis only he was not smiling and he had a very serious look on his face and looking straight ahead. He said to me, "You know you cannot get anything you want." I was in awe because it was so real. Something said it was a judgement seat.

So you see there is no doubt in my mind he make it up with God so he could receive his Soul at his death.

A letter to the author from Sister R. B. Artis *1974*

•

As you may or may not know that the late Rev. Davis was my adopted father as well as my uncle. Some things I could tell you about my uncle you may already know, however when he was a young man in the South he would get his guitar on his back and never stop playing also he would walk down the road playing his guitar and the men would put their wives in the house! As you know anything that my uncle could say he could play and that was the reason the men didn't want their wives around when he would play like that, in other words my uncle would let his guitar do his talking. For example he would ask me for a glass of water with his guitar many times.

Joseph McLean

•

Meeting Gary Davis

I was 19 (1953) in the spring of my first year at Antioch College when I met Gary Davis. Antioch was an experimental school that had a work study programme in which students had the option of working for part of their year and studying on campus for the remainder. I took a job in New York, initially at the reception desk of the ABC Studios on 66th and Broadway. I did not like it much and chose as my second job the New York Library down on Tompkins Square on the Lower East Side. I loved this job. In fact I went back to it during my second year at Antioch. It was while I was on this job and living in an apartment on East 80th Street - what was then Yorkville, now "Yuppieville" - that I first met Gary Davis.

The job was essentially that of a library clerk who logged in and out the books, but it evolved into a storyteller position. The library had storytellers in those days that made the rounds of the library system and told stories on Saturday mornings in New York to groups of children of different ages. To qualify you had to memorise the story. I remembered I used the Thumber's Thirteen Clocks. Later what I did was sing and tell stories with my guitar, but that is another story.

Here is how I met Gary Davis:

I had become addicted so to speak to the blues during my first year at college. I had always played guitar and sung, but mostly folk songs with maybe a little blues something or other thrown in, it was not until college that I truly became addicted. I stayed up long hours to the detriment of my school work, learning everything I could from my first Antioch girlfriend who played better than I did – at least for the first month or two I knew her. Niela and I later parted, but I'll always be grateful to her for giving me that early taste of what it's like to play the blues. I started out trying to copy blues riffs verbatim. I am slightly embarrassed to say now, but Josh White was one of my early heroes, and I learned to play most of his licks from records.

In New York during my work-study period I met my first true love – a girl named Yaffa. She introduced me to many joys, among them some fancy folk dancing and singing, including beginning lessons in the Hambo, a dance that, much later, endeared my second wife to me. Yaffa had a lovely voice and sang plaintiff hill tunes with a thin pure, silvery quality. She also loved the real blues and we travelled to hear it whenever we could. In those days a centre for the blues was a place in Harlem called 'Felton's Lounge' just below 125th Street on Lenox Avenue. There was an easy feeling in Harlem in those days, unlike now, where "white boys" with some talent and a love of the music were more than welcome to the musical scene and I spent all the time I could up there listening to Brownie McGhee and others, sometimes accompanied by Sonny Terry who lived a block and a half away and would drop in on an occasional Saturday night.

The music was intoxicating. I would go home and try to reproduce what I had heard. While Yaffa would stay up encouraging me or fall asleep exhausted I would continue to play into the morning.

One evening Brownie McGee told me that if I loved the old music I should hear the "Rev". The "Rev" was Gary Davis, Reverend Gary Davis. I said I would very much like to hear him, where could I find him? Well, often the Rev might be found on 135th Street, near the White Tower playing on the street or sometimes taking a nap in the back of the White Tower. He would stand out in all weathers with his tin cup playing for quarters, nickels and dimes.

So, one evening Yaffa and I set out to find him. We went first to Felton's and were told that he had been seen up on the 135th Street that evening, and so we went there. Now, while Harlem was in those days generous in its hospitality to white blues lovers in a blues bar, people walking the street posed a somewhat different problem. One had to negotiate the curious, somewhat hostile stares. In the White Tower on 135th Street and Lenox we asked after a blind black reverend with a guitar. We were told that the Rev. was not here, and that was all – not hostile, just blunt, and a clear end of conversation. So, we went back to Felton's and spent the evening listening to Brownie and commiserating with ourselves for not having found him.

The following day I started calling around to the folk music institutions in the city. There was a folk music bookstore on McDougall Street with a knowledgeable proprietor (I can't quite remember his name) who said that he thought that Gary

Chicago Folk Festival, 1962, Tom Paley

had once or twice had some of his songs published in Sing Out!, a lefty, socialist folk magazine. So, I called. Sing Out!, they told me that, yes indeed they did publish some of Gary Davis's songs but they certainly would not release his number to some young person who was not even an acquaintance. They only dealt with people in the music business with legitimate needs to know.

So, Yaffa and I decided that we might as well try the telephone books. We tried Manhattan in which there were several Gary Davis's but no Reverend Gary Davis and we did not try any of those numbers. We then tried the Bronx, sure enough there was a Reverend and Annie Davis in the Bronx. We called and the telephone was answered by a young woman who said that Reverend and Mrs. Davis did not have a phone in their home, but she would leave them a message. We got the address and said that we would try to call back later, or Mrs. Davis could call us. We did not think that very likely as she did not know us, and it did not happen in the next several days.

The next time we were at Felton's we talked it over with Brownie McGee. He said we should try him again at the White Tower stand on 135th Street and if he was not there Brownie assured us Gary would not mind us trying to find him at his home. Well, he was not at the White Tower, and it was quite a trip trying to find him at his home. We first went to a totally wrong area of the Bronx ... something that would be dangerous now but wasn't then. We went back to the Bronx elevated and travelled to, I believe, East Tremont Street in the dead of night. By the time we got there it was nearly 2.00 a.m. We finally found the walk-up brownstone with the right number. At this early hour of the morning, we decided that we would go up to his apartment and knock very softly. If they were sound asleep they would not hear us and we would just go away. But if they were awake then it would not be so bad barging in on them at this time of night. So we walked up two flights to the Reverend Davis's apartment and knocked softly on the door. Immediately Annie, his wife, called "Who is it?" We identified ourselves as the two young people who had called trying to met with Reverend Davis and that we were sorry to disturb her at this late hour. She said "Come on in children, come on in!" She opened the door and said that the Reverend had just got back - back from where we did not know, and we should just come in and make ourselves comfortable.

She said "You got to excuse me, because I got a leader in my leg!" So, we sat down in the kitchen while she went into the back and massaged her leader, or did whatever needed to be done to it. When she came back in she made us some tea and told us that Reverend Davis would be with us shortly, he had just come back from preaching. Preaching at 2.00 in the morning? Well perhaps God worked on a different schedule than the Reverend.

Gary Davis came into the kitchen in a moment and he shook our hands and then touched our faces. He particularly liked touching Yaffa's face, he said he wanted to "touch everything he could on her, anything she would let him!" He was in fine spirits. He said that he could not play his "Miss" Gibson, his usual guitar, because it had recently been stolen and he was waiting to get enough money to get another one. Apparently his guitars had been stolen on a regular basis, $300

Gibson guitars which in those days was worth quite a lot of work on a street corner.

He brought out an old battered guitar. I do not think it was a Stella but it was of that ilk, a cheap guitar. He began to play. I was mesmerised. He made that cheap old thing really sing. He had music in his fingers that was unique. A style all his own with some special kind of magic. Even on that battered old instrument it sounded wonderful to us. He made the guitar ask Yaffa for a kiss, and of course he got one. He sang and played through the night for us.

Annie insisted on making breakfast as the light was just beginning to grow in the eastern sky. We left around 6.00 in the morning and found our way back to the big city in a sort of a dream.

So, that was the beginning of a long love affair with Gary Davis. On leaving we told him how wonderful his music was and we arranged to try to get together so that I could take "lessons". We later made an arrangement to meet in Manhattan at the house of Hudie Leadbetter's (Leadbelly's) niece Tiny Robinson. She lived in an apartment house on the Lower East Side where Leadbelly used to live and where his wife Martha still did, one floor above. I had met Tiny through several folk singing contacts as she was the girlfriend then of a twelve string guitar player, Fred Gerlach who played nearly all of Leadbelly's songs, nearly as well. We were part of a folk singing group that used to hang out in Washington Square and play music on a Sunday and that's how I first met Tiny. She

Buck's Rock camp, Conn, c.1965, Clifford Strachman

graciously invited us to meet at her apartment and a tradition began, in which I would have my "lesson" every Tuesday evening. The lesson was essentially Gary playing a song and saying to me afterwards "Well, you got that John?"

I was his first student. If he treated the others like that I wonder any of us learned anything, but we certainly were diligent. I tried to get him to play slowly, which curiously, was very difficult for him. I did learn a lot of songs. I also acquired a sense of how he lived. It was a poor, tough existence, but he had a joy of life that was unusual for a blues singer in those times. John Lee Hooker, Muddy Waters, even Hudie Leadbetter, they all had some success, but also some tough, mean times. I felt Gary's love of life transcended all the hardships in some fundamental way.

He loved to tell stories, loved to get a little drunk. He required a cigar every time I met him. That soon escalated to two, one for now and one for later. But, it was not manipulation, it was a love of good things. He loved to brag to us about all the young women that he had, and how he could tell by touching their faces how beautiful they were. In the 1960's he began to have some commercial success, beginning with a record that he made for Folkways which I was instrumental in engineering. Later he played a long series of concerts with Brownie McGee and Sonny Terry.

He touched my life deeply, and I regret losing contact after I returned to graduate school to pursue my own career. I did not see Gary for the next 8 years. The last time I saw him was when he came to my (second) wedding in 1970, for which I was deeply grateful. He sang me there a ragtime blues I had never heard before. It was always hard to get him to sing the blues unless he was a little drunk. He said that the Church did not like it and he was supposed to only sing scripture and gospel. What he sang was "She's Just Funny That Way". I have a videotape made during the wedding. It brings tears to my eyes every time I see it. A sweet man, for all his hard times. I miss him still.

John Gibbon

•

At the memorial concert for Leadbelly, Woody Guthrie and I were to play together and, though we were to be on near the end we had to sit on stage all the way through the program. We spent most of the time surreptitiously attempting to get our instruments back in tune; the stage was many degrees warmer than the back room where we had done original tuning.

At any rate, at one point, somebody (I think it was Pete Seeger) announced that the next performer was Rev. Gary Davis and led a blind man onto the stage. I had never heard of Rev. Gary Davis, but I had a few old 78 RPM records by "Blind Gary", which I thought were the most incredible playing I had ever heard. All the songs on the records were religious ones so when I realised that the next performer was a preacher named Gary, who was blind and played the guitar, I was very excited. I had wondered whether he was still alive.

Of course, Blind Gary and Rev. Gary Davis were the same man. His playing wasn't so clean as the old records (I never heard him play that clearly afterwards, either) but it may have been more exciting in some ways, despite the buzzes

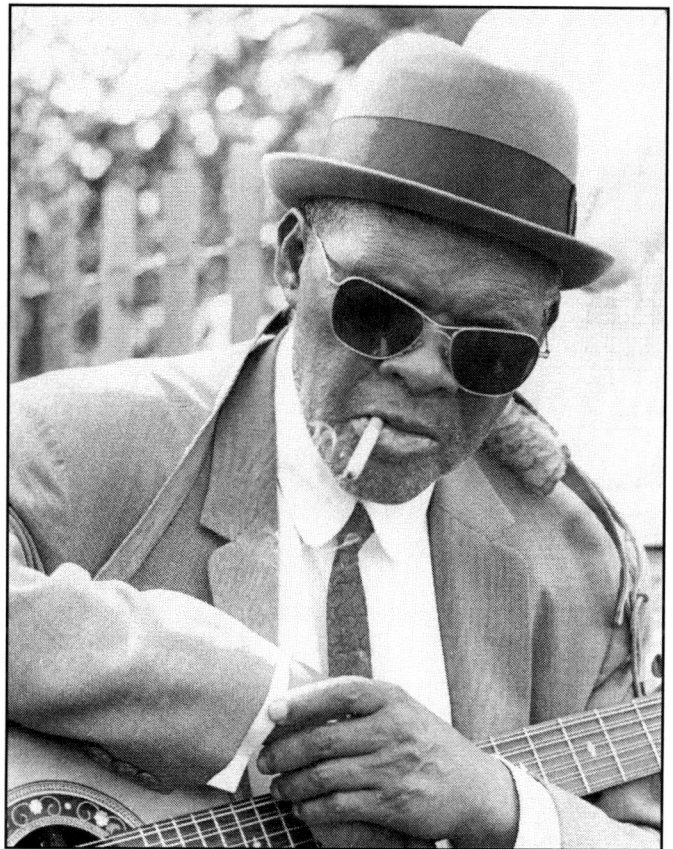

Philadelphia Folk Festival, c.1969, Bob Patterson

and clicks and the fact that the guitar was imperfectly tuned. A hell of a fine guitarist, Gary was... at his best, he and Blind Blake must have been the best of the folk/blues orientated guitarists.

Tom Paley

•

Every two months or so there used to be a "Hootnanny!" at the Pythian Temple (a large hall) on 72nd Street in New York. The entertainment was quite varied. Pete Seeger was always there. Well – I guess it was November of 1956. I went to one of these and about half way through the second act Pete brought in Gary Davis. I couldn't understand what he was talking about. The audience sat politely as Davis rambled on and on. Then he started playing. Need I say what that was like? He started tapping rhythms on the mike with his picks as he kept the guitar runs going with his left hand. I was stunned.

I asked my guitar teacher to show me that. He said he didn't know how to do it – so I stopped lessons and began on my own.

It was little less than a year later that I saw Davis again. He knocked me out a second time. Well – then I got into banjo – and just stopped fooling with the guitar. All my friends (Kalb, Van Ronk, Grossman) were going to Davis for help and I was heading to North Carolina for the Banjo masters.

Two things stood out about Davis:

At Indian Neck Festival in about 1962 (held in Connecticut) he sat up all night and played. He slept in little 3 minute intervals between songs. When I went to sleep that night (2a.m.) he was sitting in a big stuffed chair. When I came to breakfast at 10 – he was still there.

Some people wanted to start a "hip" coffee house right

London, U.K., 1964, Val Wilmer

outside of Philadelphia. They knew nothing about music. They asked about and were told that the Rev. Gary Davis is a big draw. So they booked him in to their neat little coffee house. They were very surprised when he showed up. It seemed they didn't know he was (a) Black (b) Old (c) Blind.

Davis dropped into the Folklore Center in N.Y.C. Mark Silber gave him a guitar to try. It was a J-200 but had a rosewood body instead of maple. Davis played a few notes and stopped. He held the guitar up to his nose and sniffed in the sound hole. "Hey", he said, "why didn't you tell me it was rosewood?"

Winnie Winston

•

The first time I saw him was probably around 1955 or `56. Eddie Bell used to have a very popular guitar shop on 46th Street and 6th Avenue, and I used to go up there to hang out and look at guitars and meet musicians who came by. One day I was leaving the store and there, standing on the sidewalk in front of the shop was a shabby, stooped figure holding an old Gibson and looking very pathetic. A tin cup was attached somehow to a buttonhole in his overcoat, so I dropped in a coin and asked him to play a song. He just stood there for a minute or so without moving. Finally he fished out some picks and started to move around the guitar, feeling his way as if it was all new to him. Suddenly he launched into "You Got To Move" and my mouth dropped open - I couldn't believe what I was hearing. You see, at that time I had only heard pretty smooth blues singers like Brownie McGhee and Josh White. Leadbelly was about the harshest sound I'd ever heard in a singer. But here was something else, and I was dumbfounded! I kept throwing coins into his cup and he kept playing songs and picking the guitar in that cold wind and with people rushing by scarcely giving him a glance. I must have stood there for a full hour, listening to him pick that guitar.

Afterwards, I rushed back upstairs and asked Eddie Bell who he was, and Eddie told me his name and said he was a regular on that corner when it wasn't too nasty out, and he's occasionally come up to the store to rest between "sets" in the street. I remembered seeing his name on a record jacket at a friend's house - a small 10" LP with Sonny Terry blowing harp - so I went over and borrowed the record, then went back to 46th Street a couple of times before seeing him again and asking him to play the songs from the record.

About a year later I saw him in concert with Brownie McGhee and Sonny Terry at the 'Circle in the Square' as a part of a series of midnight folk concerts. From that time on he started playing more in small concert halls and less on the street, although I saw him in another village concert the day

after someone stole his guitar from him - "cut it off my back" as he put it - while he sang in the street. (This happened to him at least twice that I know of. Another time someone invited him into an apartment to warm up and have a drink, and then threw him out without his guitar. Of course, being blind, he couldn't find his way back to retrieve it.) The concert he did that night - at the `Actors Playhouse' on 7th Avenue - was so inspired that I nearly cried several times, and was very tempted to offer him my guitar as a replacement, though I never had the nerve.

During the late fifties I heard him play dozens of times, and we appeared together in the first major concert I was ever involved in, a "New York City Folk Festival" at the Town Hall with Pete Seeger, Gary Davis, and several representative ethnic folk groups from around N.Y.

My friend Barry Kornfeld, with whom I was singing at the time, was a student of Gary's and was leading him around, so we went up to his apartment in the Bronx to pick him up and drive him to the Town Hall. During the trip downtown he was in a very good mood, wisecracking in that falsetto of his, insisting that he was perfectly capable of driving himself, and pretending to sulk when we would not let him take the wheel. At one point we mentioned Sonny Terry in the conversation and he said, "I don't see how anyone could live that long inhaling all that rust".

Happy Traum

•

Whether we godless folkies cared or not, Gary was a preacher, and old time preacher. He could and did wheedle, needle, con, cajole, sass and bully. He could charm the sow out of her ham and the biscuits out of the pan.

Although poor and struggling himself, he could be exceedingly kind, generous, gracious, courtly and funny as hell. He was also a master of intimidation. He'd rant about the Virgin and the Lamb with that stinking butt wagging in his jaw, preaching about sinners with a gin-soaked tongue. He not only looked like he'd been to Golgotha and back, he sounded like it too. He had that fine, foggy tone that could rasp – God's own head cold. His voice was raw and scratchy from years of hallelujah street corners, all those punctuating whoops, shouts, perfectly pitched and rhythmically timed, so true, right up there with the Master Whooper of all time - Sonny Terry. Yet sometimes there appeared a tender vulnerability that softened the edges. A little crying, pleading tone that on songs like "Motherless Children" reached out and tore at your heart.

His true genius revealed itself in the counterpoint of his preacher's growl and the incredible ebb and flow of his rollicking barrelhouse guitar style. Played entirely with his thumb and forefinger, Gary picked ragtime rhythms, blues riffs, chords and melody all twined together like looping calligraphy from some southern Baptist Book of Kells. On stage the Rev.

Gary Davis, I carried him over there, he's blind. He's a good guitar player.

- Jesse Fuller

usually looked like somebody's sweet ol' granddaddy, homely as a mud fence with tadpoles stuck on it. But suddenly a note or the rhythm, or a lyric could take him deep inside himself, and he'd transform into a tormented gargoyle. His shouts became fierce cries issuing from a mouth twisted wide like a spout carved from raw stone. At those moments he had that man/animal look, like a grotesque stone rider found in medieval churches.

Eric von Schmidt (Courtesy John Kruth and Sing Out! Magazine, Winter 2008)

●

I met Gary around 1954 or 1955 in New York. He was introduced to me, indirectly by Bob Harris, who ran `Stinson Records'. Every Tuesday night at that time, Gary would come down from the East Bronx to the house of Tiny Leadbetter, Leadbelly's niece, at 414 E.10th Street, which is on the Lower East Side. She lived about three or four storeys up.

At that time I was 19 or 20 years old, and had been playing the five string banjo for about a year and a half. Playing with Gary was really a trip, because I could never tell what he was doing by watching his fingers, since he used his thumb in such a weird way, so I tried to get into the sound and feel of his music. I remember playing stuff with him that was way over my head at the time. I went down there about half a dozen times, and I recall seeing Martha Leadbetter (Leadbelly's wife, who lived upstairs) one time at a party given by Tiny. There was a sort of comical event when John Lee Hooker mistook Gary for Leadbelly and started complimenting him as such. This was a bit embarrassing for all.

Dick Weissman

●

I have been trying to remember some stories about Gary. I was quite friendly with him for a long time. Originally I met him through Tiny Robinson (Leadbelly's niece) but had seen him regularly in the early 1950's in Greenwich Village, often with Sonny Terry and Brownie McGhee.

I also remember going to a party one night and Gary was there, also Brownie, Sonny, John Lee Hooker and others. It was at the house of a wild folk artist, Dick Weissman. Gary was having a great time, pinching girls and generally carrying on. I remember John Lee grabbing Gary's guitar out of his hands and saying, "Give me that old man and I'll show you how to play". I am fairly certain that it was the first meeting of Gary and John Lee.

One evening I went up to Gary's place in the Bronx. I had bought a new Gibson J-200 and proudly showed it to Gary. He played it, ran his fingers over it and said that it was a fine guitar, much darker in colour than his J-200 ... and he was right!

That was a funny night for every time Mrs. Davis would leave the room Gary would play some blues and every time he hit a 7th note, she would run back into the room and say, "Now Rev. Davis you know you're not supposed to do that!" Another time Tiny Robinson told me a story of how when the Davis's finally got some money they moved to Queen's, New York, and had the new house painted white. A few days later Gary came to the house and ran his hand over the wall. He was not satisfied with the tone of the colour and described it perfectly!

Larry Cohn

With Larry Johnson, Courtesy Marty Van Stan, c.1965

●

I guess you miss Gary?
I guess because up 'till his death I really didn't bother with getting in touch with other musicians. Now I'm beginning to kind of want to be around.

How and when did you come to meet Gary?
About '58 I believe it was, and I was living on 119th Street and 7th Avenue. I came here with three or four harmonicas, I figure, well if I run into anybody that can play a guitar I can join in on `em. And I did. I met Sticks McGhee, Brownie's brother, and I met Alec Seward, a lesser known blues singer, and he knew Gary. He used to always talk about the blind man who played so well. We started drinking one day - I was drinking a lot myself then - that night he decided to take me to meet Gary. Gary liked my harmonica playing and that started a thing with me and him, and by me coming out of the country like I did I was able to talk about records that Gary knew, such as Blind Boy Fuller. I said, "Yeah Gary, I remember hearing that `Step It Up and Go', "Well," he said, "I taught that to him". I said "You're kidding me," (laughter). He went on playing it, and a whole new thing happened. For about a year it just shocked me, you know and then I finally started taking lessons from him.

How were his lessons conducted? Did you just sit and watch Gary play?
Sit and watch and listen.

Would he listen to you?
Yeah.

What kind of comments would he make?
Well, whatever I was trying to play naturally, he could play it better, and he would tell me, "Well, you could do it this way and it would have more effect." I know how to make G one way and he showed me other ways, that kind of thing. With every key, with every chord. It took a long time to remember. He used chords all over the place. All over, it took a long time to get that together. I remember the night I met Gary, I was just drunk as could be, but I told him, I said, "Gary, it's not what you're playing that's knocking me out, it's the harmony you've got with it". That always attracted my attention in music. I never could play lead and still don't, but I said, "Well, I'll chord 'em." So I went at the chords in a harmony way and Gary had all that together. That's usually what I teach. When he played the chords, his hand kept moving, and that's what knocked me out. To play harmonica with him, you had to do

that. Now there's an album out with me and him both - he's playing guitar and I'm playing harmonica - on Adelphi. You can hear where I tried to keep the harmony going against his guitar work. When I met him, we'd sit up days and nights, and play to each other. All that was good ear training, you know. Gary got me into guitar. I didn't even own a guitar. Gary showed me the difference between a good guitar and a bad guitar. If it wasn't for Gary ... everything going on in my life now is because of him. Up till then I really hadn't got serious.

Did he influence your lifestyle too?
His being a preacher. Definitely, man, cause I was standing on the corner drinking every day, I'd probably been dead by now - friends of mine are.

Part of an interview between Larry Johnson and Ralph Rush
Sing Out! Vol 23. No. 3. 1974

●

Brownie McGhee was his usual informative self and was particularly fascinating on the subject of Blind Gary Davis. After innumerable stories about Davis, Blind Boy Fuller and all the historic jazz generals, we became contemporary with an incident from that morning.

Apparently nobody in the Caravan except Brownie knew Davis very well, and they were all a little bewildered by his oft-exhibited flick knife and his general unpredictability and air of authority. At breakfast that morning the waiter

London, UK, 1971, Steve Rye

had seated Gary and Sonny Terry at a table for two. And the conversation opened with a remarkably sinister gambit from Davis. "Terry, I know you're not blind". Sonny, a little taken aback, and respectful of his senior, fumbled for his stick and said, "Pardon?"

"Man, I know you ain't blind. I saw you looking at me last night!"

Steve Voce
Jazz Journal, June 1964

●

When you spoke to him was it clear that music and not religion was his calling?
Yes, music was his calling, that was his vocation.

And the Gospel flowed from his music then?
I think music probably came first. As a matter of fact, I'd bet on it. Both from things that he told me and by inferring about things I know about his life. But he did not want to sing secular songs except for friends in a social context. It really made him nervous when he recorded for I guess it was in the thirties. They put the arm on him to record some blues because blues sold. He never forgave them for that. It bothered him. I don't know if it was the secular music or the devil's music or he just resented having an arm put on him. Either one would be sufficiently good reason but they did put the arm on him and he did resent it.

Was he aware of his influence on younger musicians?
Oh, was he ever! (laughter). Oh God, yes! Look he was the best and he knew it. He hardly ever had a good word to say for another guitar player. He was a merciless critic and he was almost invariably right. I remember one time he did a parody of Lightnin' Hopkins and it was just dripping in acid. And the thing is he knew what Lightnin' was doing and the parody was correct. I remember one time I asked him about Blind Lemon Jefferson. Well Lemon was a little older than Gary but they were sort of contemporaries. And Gary went nowhere without his guitar. He used to call it the "Piano around my neck". He used to take his guitar around his neck even into the john! I mentioned Blind Lemon Jefferson, I thought and still do think that Lemon was a very good guitarist. Gary disagreed (laughter). Gary started to play a very accurate pastiche of Lemon's, Black Snake Moan, and Gary just opened his mouth and let out with his incredible blood curdling scream, and then he stops and says, "Man, he couldn't have sung no louder if someone was cutting his throat." He was merciless. He liked Blind Blake. He used to say Blake was good. He was good. He played right `spodee' guitar. That's the highest accolade I ever heard him pay another guitarist. He rather liked Lonnie Johnson too it seemed. One time I was working in Detroit and I was on stage singing away and I must of done two or three of Gary's things maybe more. I came off and the owner comes and says there's a friend of yours here. Of course I couldn't see into the house because of the lights, so the owner of the club leads me over and there is Rev. and Annie Davis. "Oh my God", I said, "Why didn't I sing some Leadbelly songs". I sat down and Rev. Davis turns to me and says that was "right spodee' guitar". Ah! That was the highest compliment I've ever been paid in my life. I've never been more pleased. I suspect he was being kind. He is the King. He is to Eastern Seaboard guitar what Art

Tatum is to stride piano. Blake had a right 'spodee' right hand. He's got that very nice stride sound but it's very mechanical. The same is true of McTell, although I think McTell had a nicer sense of harmonies and voicing but then again he was playing a twelve, so it's rather hard to say. I've never heard McTell play a six. Rev. Davis if you study what he was doing with his right hand you'll start to see that he doesn't keep any pattern. He'll start to go from a lower to a higher note and then switch right in the middle of a measure to back picking, from a higher to a lower note and never drop the time.

Just nobody like him.

Just nobody like him.

Dave Van Ronk interviewed by Mike Joyce
Washington D.C. 1977

•

The Reverend and I had many times shared billing at coffee houses and concerts during the '50s and he was always an ideal working companion. His authority regarding his own work made him totally uncompetitive and open, and he always just went on stage, set himself up and began to play with the controlled freedom, complexity simply expressed, joy and tragedy blended, that was his great gift. A perfect dialectic: the seemingly guileless, unlettered man of the streets who achieved a sophistication of his own making that ran as deep as human emotion can; knowing and feeling joined and expressed in the presence, the singing, but by far most clearly through the fingers on the guitar which summed up the man.

He despaired of ever getting me to learn any more than my rudimentary knowledge of the guitar. Clearly, I just didn't have his dedication, so he quickly gave up on that. By talking about life, that was something else. We shared that passion, communicating in spare prose our concerns with the oppressed state of working people in our country, especially the most targeted for brutal repression as well, those descended from African slaves. That was why I didn't hesitate when the opportunity arose to ask him to actively participate in an act of solidarity with them.

We were on the bill together at the Ash Grove, Los Angeles's best and oldest theatre for folk arts, now driven to closing by acts of harassment from the police and right-wing terrorists because it also lent a home on occasions to organising efforts on behalf of farmworkers, the Black Panther Party, the anti-war movement, etc. Someone contacted me about playing at a rally to be held in a large public park in a distant corner of L.A., lived in mostly by Blacks and other oppressed minorities. The rally was in support of men working as day-labourers, ditch-diggers, unskilled construction workers and the like who were attempting to form a union. The organisers were relatively inexperienced and had no idea how the rally would go, or if there would be violent disruption of it because of the bitterness of the organising struggle. They thought that some music would be an important element, especially in the case of trouble, as a way of calming and reassuring the workers and their families.

Of course I agreed to sing, but inwardly I felt a wave of trepidation about my ability to reach this audience which had no reason at all to identify with a young white woman with a guitar. I thought of asking Gary to come with me, knowing that his years of experience singing on the streets had taught him to deal with almost any situation. But there was another aspect to this one.

The conventional wisdom in relation to the "ethnic" performer around the so-called folk field was that one didn't confuse these living bits of history (the musicians) with the making of present history. Maybe becoming part of the present would make them seem less picturesque as icons of the past. The relationship between the sum total of their life experiences and its embodiment in the present musician was either missed or denied; missed because they were seen as static possessions, or denied because becoming part of the present they might lose their patina, maybe reveal - perish the thought! - minds of their own, and thus be less conveniently fitted into academic or commercial slots. They would change, have to be re-studied. They would possibly even start making demands. In short, they would no longer be the "property" of one or another folklorist or manager.

Perfect! As a certified maverick myself, I was always on the lookout for others willing to defy the rules of the ballgame. Up to now, I had seen Gary only in the most co-operative of modes, making no trouble and doing his job. Clearly he sensed the best way of getting along with these discoverers and sponsors, who had after all enabled him to get off the streets and onto record albums, concert stages and festivals. But just as clearly, he was his own man from top to bottom, front to rear. I decided to put the question to Sister Annie, his wife, so that it would be easier to turn me down in case. But when I described the situation, it was she who shouted "Of course we'll come!" and the deal was on.

We arrived at the half-wild, unkempt park on the edge of town. A few stragglers lounged here and there, trying to look ambiguous. If the rally was a success, they were there. If it failed, they were just passing through. The organisers didn't have a sense of how to pull things together, being a bit intimidated by the rough look of these men who had led the roughest of lives. This was when Sister Annie took over with the authority of a street corner practitioner. She jumped onto the table nearby and began to preach, not about pie-in-the-sky but about beans tomorrow. Without a need to consult the meeting organisers, she was telling the men just what they needed to hear; someone cares; you are important people; you will be strong if you are united.

Then Gary got up to sing. "Let's get together, right down here!" was his text. "We have a kingdom right down here!" was his promise. The stragglers drew together, sang together, and cheered together. This was a day that would live in memory as their own, whether or not the organising effort was successful. This was the gift of Gary Davis, the man, and this was his art: to give people back their own, polished and perfect, to lift before them a vision of what they can be, of what they inherently are. To give it back in love and anger, with identification and in struggle. A true servant of his people. Because he showed us how, there will be more of him.

Barbara Dane

•

My brother Alex and I set out for America in February 1956, with guitars in hand, determined to learn to play the blues. The journey across the Atlantic took 4 days, and we arrived in New York in the middle of a snowstorm.

Through Alan Lomax, we had an introduction to Leadbelly's widow, Martha Leadbetter, who lived with her niece Tiny

New York State, June 1971, Emma Kopenen

London, 1964, Peter Dyer

Robinson on East 14th Street. That first Thursday evening after we arrived, she gave a party and we went to it. I will never forget the moment she pulled Lead's big custom-built Stella 12-string out from under her bed! The other thing I recall very vividly was the main guest - Reverend Gary Davis. His playing was a revelation; the swift runs, the steel sprung rhythms, the hoarse but beautiful voice, and his humour, irony and lack of self-pity. We had a ball till the early hours, then we went home with him, in an empty bus, and he played the blues for us all the way into that frozen dawn. I tell you, that made a blues man of me for life!

Rory McEwen

•

He taught me for about a year, on and off, in 1957-1958, once a week on Tuesdays. He had previously taught only one other 'white boy', and that was John Gibbon.

This was arranged by Martha Leadbetter and Tiny Singh (Leadbelly's widow and niece) and used to take place in Tiny's apartment on East Tenth Street, N.Y. He was a great teacher. He would give you a basic lick to master and then build on that until you had the system needed to play the backing for many of his songs.

He could always tell if you were faking a particular run and stop to make you play all the notes. Usually, after the lessons, other guitarists came in to play and listen to Gary,

36

including Fred Gerlach, John Gibbon and Frank Hamilton.

I usually rode back Uptown with him on the bus in the early hours. I got off at 81st Street and he at 125th Street. He always played on the bus and once the driver could not bear to miss it, and we stopped for about thirty minutes while we listened to him.

Alexander McEwen

•

Reverend Gary Davis came into the store (led by George Dawson, who was taking him to a friend's rent party) to buy a banjo, but I had already sold it. The Reverend sat down and played George's Mastertone to everyone's surprise... two finger-picking and mountain frailing "Lost John", "Bile Them Cabbage Down", and many unidentifiable (to us) pieces. Stupid on-lookers walked in, didn't understand what they were observing, and walked out. But a lot of people stayed around to hear him... syncopated and then boogie-woogie added to his mountain banjo playing.

Israel G. Young Sing Out! May 1960

•

The only occasion I had to perform with him was at a Folk Festival held at Syracuse (New York) University in 1963. Of course, I had heard him play many times before and after the festival. As you no doubt know, he restricted his public performances to religious and gospel music but once off the stage he observed no such restrictions. He regaled the other performers at the festival with what may be euphemistically described as "bawdy ballads" of the most vivid sort.

He also claimed that he always carried a pistol for protection (although I never saw it) and that we would do well to knock loudly on his door and identify ourselves before entering the room.

All in all, he carried on in a rather high-spirited manner and seemed to be enjoying himself immensely.

Jerry Silverman

•

John often spoke of Rev. Gary Davis and how he loved to hear him play and sing. I met him and his wife at the Folk Festival of Newport, Rhode Island, in 1964. We had a wonderful time together while sitting on the lawn around the hotel.

Mrs. John Hurt

•

"Lo, I'll be with you"

I first met the Reverend Gary Davis in the early 1960's when folk music in the States was enjoying a burst of popular interest. The Reverend was very astute at sizing up people and had his own unique system of checks and cross-checks. I recall an instance in a tobacconist's when he was buying some of his favourite cigars. As he was about to pay for his purchase, he suddenly turned away from the proprietor at the cash register, and, out of sight of the man, bares his quite sizeable roll to me. He pointed to an exposed ten spot and asked in hushed tones, "What is this?" "Ten dollars," I responded. Then with triumph, "I knew I had that there," he turned and handed over the bill for payment. Later, outside, he said to me, "It's a funny thing about money. People want it. You don't find nobody that don't want it."

One afternoon shortly thereafter it was my pleasure to transport Gary and Booker T. White from the San Francisco Valley where they were staying during a gig at the Ashgrove to Sioux and Harry Taussig's for dinner.

The side window was open to let in cool air as we whizzed down the San Diego Freeway heading for the Orange County beach town where the Taussigs lived. Bukka had been discoursing lively and at some length about his life and friends in Oakland and Berkeley. Gary, in front, beside me interjected occasional comments. But Bukka became unusually silent and preoccupied with some private thought. After a while, Gary broke the quiet with an astonishing observation.

> # "One of the greatest guitar players that ever lived and he was a great fellow."
>
> ## – Muddy Waters

"My goodness the State sure has these freeways along here planted with greenery, hasn't she!" Then he took out his Marine Band harmonica from some deep pocket in his coat and began blowing a tune. After a while he cleared his throat, "That's 'Lost John', you know."

What a master of entertainment! He had stunned and surprised everyone by his pronouncement on the freeway landscaping project (he must have heard the rustling of Eucalyptus and Myoporum as we passed), and then held us rapt with his swinging harmonica playing. Afterwards, the conversation returned to its original energetic pace; the blues

Recording for Granada Television, Manchester, UK, 1964

precipitated by a long freeway trip were vanquished.

Harry was in possession of two vintage Martin guitars both in cherry condition. His budget would not let him have both, and so he was puzzling over which one to keep. Both had prize finishes (probably the original finish), quick and clean action and true tones. He consulted Gary:

Taussig:

"What do you think of this guitar, Reverend?"

Harry handed him one of the guitars.

Davis:

"This here is a Martin."

Evidently he discerned the manufacturer by the characteristic cross-sectional shape of the neck. He felt the tuners and tuning head where "C.F. Martin & Co." was stamped in the wood.

Davis:

"Got a nice strip around the neck. This here's got a black ebony fingerboard, huh. That's what it is."

He began to tune, loosening and then tightening the strings. Harry had strung the guitar with compound (silk and steel) strings. Gary noticed this immediately and commented.

Davis:

"This guitar wasn't made for no heavy strings, was it? It ain't good to put real heavy strings on no kind of guitar provided you want to save the neck."

He plays a bit. 'Coco Blues'. Then a few chords up the neck. A run up near the body.

Davis:

"If the neck would just grow longer - boy! Two more frets and you'd be out of a guitar. I need to stretch out too much up there. If this were fourteen and not twelve, I'd just keep it. I'd jump at it in a minute!"

He felt the body.

Davis:

"I like that bridge. It's a neat little bridge. This here's a woman size guitar but it sounds big enough. If you ain't got no case, you can put it under your overcoat."

Next he began to tap vigorously on the face and then the back of the guitar with his fingernail.

Davis:

"Rosewood - made out of the best kind of rosewood."

He tapped even more forcefully. The guitar rang. I do not know for sure whether Harry feared for the finish on the back, but at this point he began to play, on the other guitar, a rather mutilated, but recognisable 'Candyman'. Tit for tat. One mutilated 'Candyman' in exchange for some famous fingernail marks in the thirty or forty year old lacquer job. The distraction, whether intentional or not, worked for Gary abruptly stopped tapping.

Davis:

"You getting that wrong."

He started in with a brisk, solid 'Candyman'.

So began one of the most memorable evenings of spontaneous guitar playing I have ever heard. Gary played for hours tunes such as 'Saint Louis Tickle', 'Slow Drag', 'Buck Dance', 'Bill Bailey,' 'Nobody Knows When You're Down and Out', 'Bout a Spoonful', 'Dark Town Strutters Ball' and many others. I can hear him still…

Don Garwood, *15th May 1973*

●

When I first met the Davis's back on a freezing winter night in sixty-three, they were living in a three-room shack in the Bronx behind a row of condemned buildings in the 3200 block of Park Avenue. I had called the number of a blind old guitar teacher who really needed the money they gave me at the folklore centre on Bleecker Street, Annie had answered and kept on calling me "child" as she told me how to get there, and after an exhilarating trip on the A train and the B train and the C train, a bus ride that began in front of a "flower florist" and a brisk walk through Spanish Bronx, I stood at their door several hours later. Annie let me in, clapping her huge white palms together in delight at the sight of such youth, and I was almost knocked over by the temperature of the room which was easily a hundred degrees hotter than it was outside and as hot as any cotton field back home. The heat was coming from an oil stove in the middle of the room around which two very large elderly ladies in dazzling Sunday hats were sitting, and it was so intense that it had warped the leaves of an old testament calendar that was tacked up on a wall covered with framed prayers, house blessings, and scriptural homilies. Annie told me Brother Davis was at the barber but she had just baked some sweet potato pudding that was still warm inside so I sat down and underwent the scrutiny of the two ladies as I ate as delicately as possible until the Reverend returned and blew the place wide open. He was telling a joke that was making the shy thirty-ish church-going man who had taken him to the barbershop turn red behind his ears. The two ladies suddenly changed into young giggling flirts. One of them went up to the Reverend, took off his stubby-brimmed hat, felt his new haircut and said "My, my don't he look nice."

Alex Shoumatoff

●

Most of all I learned an awful lot about music and the different traditions of the guitar from the Rev. Gary Davis. I met and played music with the Reverend on several occasions. The first time we played together, we traded guitars because he liked the sound of mine - his guitar was perfectly in tune in my hands and mine was perfectly in tune in his. As far as consciously knowing that I existed, after we became acquainted, he always recognised my playing.

I did not spend a lot of time around the Reverend, but I was always fascinated with what he did and where he learned his music. It was a great challenge to play his music. I learned from him several blues in the keys of A, C and G and several of his different tunes, such as Maple Leaf Rag and Piano Blues, both in the key of A; Twelve Gates To the City; and Sweet Papa Low Down. The benefits of playing his music and being involved with him was a profound emotional experience for me.

I admire the Reverend because he persevered for so many years and that he gave a lot of other musicians their start in New York City. His passing was a great personal loss for me as well as for all who knew him, I'm sure. You get so involved with these older people whom you consider masters in music, and when they pass on to another form of energy, they are deeply missed although not forgotten because of their contribution to the world of music. We are fortunate to be able to carry on and continue to play, and I am truly grateful that

I had the opportunity to know such a person in my lifetime. I hope that everyone who heard his music could enjoy what he had to say as much as I did.

Of Sister Annie Davis, I would like to say that she was always a most gracious hostess, invited everyone to hear the Reverend. She made sure that he was always well taken care of and saw to it that he was able to get around even at 75 years of age. I admire her as she brought in an element of the old tradition that you don't see too much any more.

My advice to any person who is studying music is to listen to the music of Rev. Gary Davis - a much admired, respected and loved man.

Taj Mahal

•

"Here's your new student, Brother Davis," Annie said, coming out of the kitchen.

"Where, where, I can't see him," the Reverend said, and boohooed like a train whistle until he felt my hand in his, grabbed it, started back like W.C. Fields, and said, "Great God Almighty, what's this?" Then he felt the fingertips of my left hand for callouses and found there weren't any and said, "So you come to me to play the guitar?" We went over to a corner of the room where there was an armchair, a stool, and a row of banjos and guitars in cases, Mrs. Davis drew a curtain dividing us from the stove and the ladies, the Reverend inspected my new Epiphone, tuned it up for me, took out Miss Gibson, the beautiful flower-embroidered Gibson J-200 he bought in forty-three, immediately placed his fingers in the A minor position on the fifth fret and told me to look at his fingers and play what I saw.

Alex Shoumatoff

•

I ran and owned the main music store in New York City from 1963-1967, and it was a great gathering place for the musicians in the 1960's "folk music scene". Countless musicians hung out there, and needless to say many were excellent guitarists. Rev. Davis would often come there, or use the shop as a meeting place.

The episodes that I think of often concern his ability to figure out things correctly without using sight. One of those

London, UK, 1964, Peter Dyer

39

Romford, UK, 1966, Steve Rye

days the Rev. Davis asked me to call his "driver" to come in front of my shop, on the Avenue of the Americas, and it was six lanes of traffic in one direction. He also asked me if I could wait downstairs with him until the car arrived, (my shop was one flight up). So at the agreed time we descended to the sidewalk and waited amongst that great New York City "din". After waiting for a while, the Rev. in all his blindness shouted, "Here they come!" As I looked downstream on this one-way avenue I noticed an older, say 1955, Buick Special in the flow about one and a half blocks away.

I watched and waited in suspense to see the results of his announcement and see his car arrive. Soon the old Buick was curbside, and the Rev. was efficiently picked up by his driver and away to his next adventure. (Obviously he had heard the particular tone of that small Buick, with 'Dynaflow'... but it was six lanes of traffic!)

One other memory I recall was Rev. Davis's determination to "get along" on his own, and to lessen his handicap caused by the lack of sight.

In 1961, at the University of Chicago Folk Festival, a veritable "glacier" of ice was on the ground up to six inches deep. In the streets were two deep tracks where cars could pass in one direction at a time. This made walking on, or across, these gullies extremely dangerous and even more so when carrying a breakable item like a guitar!

Rev. Davis was so determined to walk without help and I am amazed to this day that he made this awfully slippery and rather unpredictable city trek by himself, that included slips and falls.

Marc Silber

•

It was a hot Friday morning in early July, 1960. The Caffe Lena was only a few weeks old. I didn't know of too many folk performers but had been fortunate to have had one of the earliest, Dave Van Ronk, who recommended several good young artists.

He told me of a young blues singer and guitarist, Ian Buchanan, so I booked him for the weekend. On that hot Friday morning I was walking down Phila St. towards the Caffe. From a block and a half away I saw, sitting on the steps in front of the door, a gaunt young man and a big black man, two guitars leaning against the building, a cane jutting out across the sidewalk. I greeted them and the young man jumped up. "I'm Ian Buchanan; I'm supposed to sing here this weekend. This is Reverend Gary Davis. He needs the job more than I do. Hope you don't mind".

That was the first of many memorable weekends over the next dozen years - sometimes accompanied by his wonderful wife Annie - sometimes by young disciples - Stefan Grossman, Gino Forman, and Roy Bookbinder.

The guitarists he taught and influenced are many - some who had the benefit of his private lessons at his place in the Bronx, others learning from his records. All of them musically enriched by the great legacy he left.

How wonderful to have had the opportunity to meet and know him and give him one other place to share his great gift.

Lena Spencer
Caffe Lena, Saratoga Springs NY.

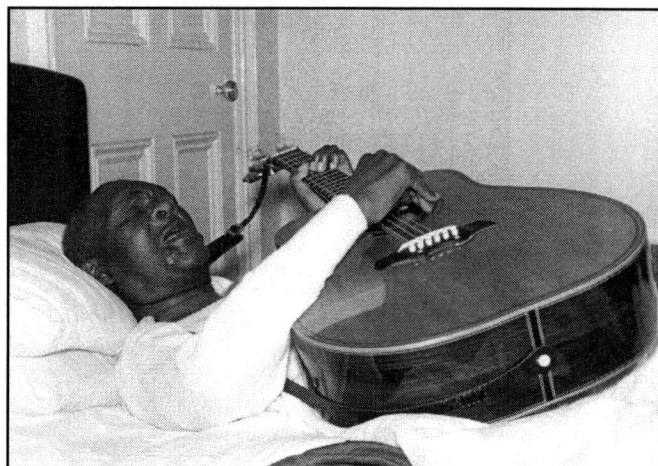

Cambridge, UK, 1971, Steve Rye

•

I first heard of Gary Davis from Danny Hirsh who was my guitar teacher and who was studying with Rev. Davis. This would have been in `63 or `64. He painted a rather awesome picture of Davis. I absorbed that sense of awe, and have never really lost it. I was eleven or twelve years old and was mostly listening to Joan Baez, The Weavers, Odetta, Pete Seeger and other lefty approved kinds of things. I loved Pete Seeger and watched his UHF television show "Rainbow Quest" religiously. It was on that show that I first encountered Rev. Gary Davis and had one of the most profound Art experiences of my life.

It was 1965, I was thirteen and lived in a white middle class suburb on Long Island. Here was this inscrutable black Buddha singing and playing with such incredible power and conviction that it literally sent chills up my spine and instantly expanded my vision of what music could be.

He sang "Oh Glory How Happy I Am" and "Children of Zion". The songs seemed to last forever and gather in intensity as they progressed, drawing me into a new state of mental and spiritual engagement with music. While he wasn't exactly reticent in his exchanges with Pete Seeger, he seemed possessed of a sense of confidence, mystery and superiority that was as impressive as it was uncomfortable to witness.

So in 1969 when Rev. Davis did a week at the Gaslight, I was there every night watching and listening. I finally got up the nerve (I wasn't normally shy in those days and didn't have much in the way of respect for people or anything else, but The Rev. had me hoodooed right from the start) to go backstage and ask if I could have lessons. After some uncomfortable banter which I now know to have been an example of his very dry wit, he agreed.

In December of 1969 I grabbed my tape recorder and my guitar, made connections for the E train to Jamaica then onto a bus and made my way to Gary Davis's ACTUAL HOUSE FOR CHRIST SAKES!! I was petrified. To make things worse, there was a Swedish film crew there shooting the whole lesson which must have appeared like Rev. Davis trying to teach a slug how to use silverware, for all the response he was able to get out of me. I had shut down and become inert matter out of awe, and camera shyness. He was losing patience. I was mortified, and managed to snap out of it long enough to learn a bit of "Candyman". I was 17.

Subsequent lessons went more smoothly. Typically the lessons lasted around two or three hours and on a couple of occasions, when it got late, included dinner, served with much grace and generosity by Mrs. Davis. In spite of the concentration of time spent together, I was never able to become familiar with Gary Davis in the way that Larry Johnson or Roy Book Binder, who I saw at his house fairly often, seemed to be. For one thing, I was very young and it is apparent in listening back to the lesson tapes with the advantage of hindsight that Rev. Davis treated me in an age appropriate fashion. For another, I was and am still so overwhelmed by his music that any pretence on my part of chumminess seemed impossible. I learned a great deal and was enormously pleased when Rev. Davis told me he thought I was a sportin' guitar player!

Studying with Gary Davis was one of the best things I did in my life! Even though I gave up performing a long time ago to devote myself to painting, I did so after having sat at the side of, and learned from someone I believe to have been a true musical genius and an artist of great stature, whose work transcends his time and culture. In a strange way I search for visual equivalents to Gary Davis's music in my painting, the power and intensity, humour, virtuosity and spirituality, are all the ingredients essential to the creation of any enduring work of art in any discipline. The sound of Davis singing "hallelujah" at the beginning of his prestige recordings of "I Belong To The Band" is a sound I search for in my work. I'm also still working on my lessons.

Philip Allen (aka Mr. O' Muck)

•

As the "folk boom" spread in the 1950's, Gary got to play concerts and at many colleges, and on one occasion a student asked, "Reverend Davis, why don't you play a Martin Guitar? Don't you think they sound better than Gibson's?" Gary replied, "Martin's got the tone-ability, but Gibson's got the last-ability!"

I assume the fact that Gary would often get caught in a rain shower while playing out of doors prompted this answer. Apparently he assumed Martins were too delicate to get wet!

Harry West

•

He was probably the most enlightened man I have ever known. He was more content than a hundred Buddhists put together. Once when I was taking a lesson from him and I was having some trouble and getting a little anxious over it, he said, "Danny, it's just as plain as the nose on your face, so don't worry. In time you will get it". He went on to tell me, "Now when I was a boy we had a mule and I was supposed to put him in the shed. I went out there and pulled on that mule, and pushed on that mule and yelled on that mule but he wouldn't do nothin' but go Hee-Haw, Hee-Haw! After a while I gave up. Then a little later it started to thunder and rain, and that mule ran into that shed! So don't worry about that song. When you're ready and it's ready you will get there".

Sometimes when I took lessons the Rev. would slip off into a dream, for ten minutes at a time and neither of us would say anything. He would sit in his armchair and suck on a chip on his Gibson guitar and then all of a sudden he would jerk forward and be really active.

Danny Birch

•

Well, I was friendly with Reverend Gary Davis. I'd met his accompanist and he introduced me to the Reverend and his wife. She fed me chicken and rice. I went to their house and to this record store in Harlem and heard rock-and-roll jamming. It was new to me. I'd never heard Negro soul music. I was in folk. And there were all these folk singers going rock because Dylan was going rock. There were the Beatles and Reverend Davis and all these things. I didn't know what to do with them, so I stopped writing completely to let it all soak in. I met Jake Solman (her first manager) at the Gaslight because I went there with Reverend Davis and his wife. They introduced me to the owner. Mrs. Davis said, I have a girl here; I want you to hear her sing. They had never heard me. It was like Sis and Gordon (Friesen, the editors of Broadside) bringing me on at the Broadside hoot because I'd written a song they'd liked. Well, I did a guest set at the Gaslight, and it was good. Mr. Hood (the owner) liked me.

Janis Ian
Interview with John Cohen, Sing Out! April 1968

•

An old man with guitar
a calloused hand spins silk on steel strings
a bird rises from the throat and floats over dark fields
the fire of life is held in a bead of sweat
our loudest laughter cannot drown the flame.

Ralph Rush

•

In 1962 I lived in the attic of a house run co-operatively by some nice folks who worked in a bookstore ("The Sign of the Sun" - which is gone now) in San Diego, California. They had folk music concerts in the bookstore on weekends, and the performers stayed at "the boarding-house". I remember the Reverend Davis and his wife staying for a while on more than one occasion. I tried to learn something from him, but I was too much the beginner then. On one occasion I sat in his room while he was practicing at night; being a shy kid, I was too tongue-tied to ask if I could turn on the light so that I could see what he was doing, and, of course it didn't matter to him. His wife came in after a while and scolded him for not turning it on, but I never expected him to think of it. I just wished I could play like that, in the dark.

Michael Cooney

•

The Rev. Gary Davis a blind man who's turning 70, was all set to sing his soul out at church Sunday.

He is midway in a two week engagement at the Chess Mate, an espresso coffee shop across from the University of Detroit.

He took his guitar to church Sunday.

His agent understood that he would be "welcomed" and would sing if asked. He wasn't asked. Church members seemed fearful of having an entertainer in the church. So the Rev. Davis, who has been blind since a relative put some kind of medicine in his eyes when he was a baby, was led back to the car of a church member who had invited him to the church.

Playing "Whistling Blues", London, UK, 1971, Steve Rye

"I want to go back in" he said, "I came to worship, not to play. I'm not a blind beggar. I'm a minister."

He was born the son of a poor farmer in Lawrence County, S.C., in 1896. Some say his voice is a little rough and rasps. He sings mostly hymns. Connoisseurs of the guitar say he can do subtle things with it others can't do. "God's been blessing me, I know", he said. "He's kept me living and given me plenty to eat."

Rev. Davis sat facing forward in the car as he reminisced. Somebody who had brought the guitar into the church for him, handed it back to him. If he were to sing, it might have been "Beautiful City" or the blues hymn, "In this Land". When he's at his best, Variety magazine says "there aren't many like him." His performance has been called the "Holy Blues." The guitar breaks into the stanzas and runs into his slurred vocal lines. He's been recording since 1935, shortly after he was ordained a Baptist minister. He likes to sing so much he often can be found strumming away on a street corner in Harlem.

"They struck me deeply in there," he said of the misunderstanding. The pastor was away, the chairman of the board said later and the church members only had been guarding zealously the pre-arranged morning service. "They put me on the ashes side," said Davis. "They stirred me up now, and I can't give you an answer," he apologised for not having much to say.

Asked about his favourite Bible verses, Rev. Davis said: "I like all of the Bible." And hymns? "I sing them all." The gospel singer was led back into the church after church members said he was welcome to worship. The choir sang a stirring anthem, about blessing the Lord with all their souls.

The blind man sat quietly ... in his own soul's world.

H.H. Ward

(Courtesy Detroit Free Press, January 1965)

●

When Reverend and Mrs. Davis moved into their house in Jamaica they got a record player with an automatic changer. Mrs. Davis asked me to check it over and see if it was working properly. The only record they had was an old time preacher serving up hell and damnation. I set up the thing, figured out how it worked and showed Mrs. Davis how it worked. When that was done, she said to me, "Thank you very much, honey. Now would you mind taking it off. It makes the Reverend sick."

I was taking the Reverend to a gig in Manhattan on the subway, when a very pretty woman came and sat with us and started talking to the Reverend. She got off before we did and I told the Reverend that I'd bring him around to see her anytime. He said that he could get there himself and we kidded for a little while as to whether he'd need help finding his way there or not. Finally I told the Reverend that I'd been considering bringing my girlfriend to see him but that I was afraid because he was such a ladies man. He said, "Well, you can bring her. Go on and bring her." I said, "Yeah, but I want to bring her back too." The Reverend said, "Oh you can bring her back, but she won't be satisfied."

David Bromberg

●

Teach In Reverend Gary Davis Style Guitar

"You come to me, and I'll teach you how to play, not fool around with the guitar", he often said. For hour after hour Gary would sit and teach his songs to anyone who wanted to learn them. He would explain a certain song or lick patiently, and stop only when satisfied that he had got his point across.

Both he and Annie loved having people come over to the house, and Gary's students were a great part of their lives. Every now and then Annie would arrange a night for all the students to come and meet each other, play music together, and consume a tremendous dinner that she would spend the day preparing. The atmosphere was always relaxed on these evenings, and oft times proved fruitful for new friendships. Gary would look forward to surprising everyone with a song or two that nobody had heard before, and after dinner there would be more music in the basement until everyone was played out and sleepy. Of course the last person playing would be Gary, singing and playing louder than ever.

One rainy afternoon when the pace had slowed down some, Gary sat calmly smoking his pipe, talking about how well off he was now with a wife that he loved, friends, a home, and time to enjoy them.

Woody Mann

Sing Out! Volume 21, No. 5

The Reverend Davis was a great influence in the development of my playing style, though I favour the use of the middle finger in addition to the index finger that he used. The inclusion of this extra finger smooths the style out somewhat, but the syncopations and thumb/index runs which I can use come straight from Gary.

I feel very fortunate to have been able to get to know him over a number of years. I met him when he was over in England for his first Roy Guest tour and I managed to spend some time with him on most of his subsequent trips. I don't think I ever sat down with him and got him to show me exactly how he played something. It wasn't that I didn't want to - it was just that there always seemed to be so little time and it was much more important just to sit and rap. Just listening to him reminisce brought into focus for me a whole era of American history.

A time of hardship and poverty, of Dance Craze Marathons, of Juke House piano bars, of bootlegging and wire walkers over Manhattan. Listening to Gary talk was a magical experience that rivalled even his singing and playing.

I always figured that there was plenty of time later to get him to show me that double shuffle he used in "Samson and Delilah" or that high C run from "Sally, Where d'You Get Your Liquor" - the next time we met. Well, there wasn't much time. I guess all his friends knew it but to admit it was to somehow dare fate to take him. So we sat with him and listened and laughed and denied the possibility of this wonderful storyteller being taken from us. I'm sadder that I never found out about that double shuffle, but sadder still that I never once thought to switch on the recorder when he was just sittin' and rappin'.

John Pearse
October, 1979

•

The Reverend Gary Davis' Guitar Style

Reverend Davis's guitar playing had an unmistakable sound. Anyone interested in playing his guitar pieces of songs should become acquainted with some of the peculiarities of his technique. His tone was crisp and strident, with a raspy, raw edge characteristic of many 1930's blues players. It was unique, however, in its full resonance, sustain and projection. This undoubtedly came about as a result of his many years as a street singer competing with the noise of the New York traffic. He produced this sound by playing very hard on a very strong guitar. His favourite instrument, the Gibson J-200 (which he called `Miss Gibson') is the largest and heaviest flat-top guitar ever manufactured and he used the heaviest gauge of bronze strings available. It takes a great deal of muscle power to produce a rich sound from this instrument and I have never heard anyone make it sing like Gary Davis could. He wore his thumb pick half-way back, behind the first joint of the thumb. This enabled him to obtain the full power of the palm muscles and kept the pick from slipping out of position. All of his picking was done with thumb and index finger, as with Doc Watson and Merle Travis. When once asked why he only used the two fingers, he replied, "Because that's all you need". Listening to the complexity of

his playing, one must concede the point.

He had extremely unusual left hand technique - his large and stiff looking fingers would slap down hard on the fingerboard with a pressure that seemed to strangle the neck, yet he moved through many awkward fingering positions with great facility. His unusual fingerings derived from the odd angle at which he held his guitar and this, in turn, was caused by a number of chance circumstances: a badly broken arm in his youth, the combination of an enormous guitar and a relatively short man with a large belly and most important, so he could see what he was doing!

His style of playing was in the tradition from which he came - the 'East Coast' style, exemplified by Blind Blake and Blind Boy Fuller. It is a pianistic approach to guitar playing; the thumb keeps a steady 'boom-chuck-boom-chuck' on the bass strings in imitation of the left hand in the stride piano, the melodic lines and fills are full of ragtime syncopation, the chord structures, contrapuntal bass lines and the bouncy, lighthearted character of the music all derive from the ragtime piano. For Gary Davis, this imitation was quite deliberate - he constantly was asking his students to, "make it sound like a piano". Davis used several devices that were flashy tricks of showmanship, quite unusual for a bluesman. He would play a solo with the left hand alone, slapping the strings onto the frets to make the notes, all the while holding his right hand high, snapping his fingers in time. Another device was to stop playing and slap the strings and the box, imitating a little drum break, then come right in with the guitar part without dropping a beat. While not difficult to do, these tricks were inventively timed and uproariously funny. Needless to say, his audiences loved it.

Dean Meridith
Blues Magazine, Vol. 2, No. 2. 1976

•

The Reverend Davis has had guitars stolen from him on the streets of Harlem, where he has also had his brailled timepiece and last few cents taken from him. These occurrences would, to be sure, shake the faith of even the strongest men. But Gary Davis has always had "just a little more faith".

In a conversation on the way to the studio to record this collection, the Reverend Davis mentioned his concern with seeing that his wife was adequately provided for in the event of his death. He discussed the fact that many men were directly responsible for "their women sinning and begging in the streets" because they weren't taken care of. He also discussed other things such as the purchase of a house, a car for his family and other everyday luxuries and necessities.

The purpose of mentioning this, by the way of introduction, is to emphasise the fact that Gary Davis is not a saint; but rather, he is an individual, a performer and a husband who is concerned with the lot of himself and his family in matters of everyday living, much in the manner of any other breadwinner, be he labourer, professor or performer.

Larry Cohn
Notes on "A Little More Faith ", (Prestige Records) 1961

•

But even before his death his father had not been around much, and his uncle, a kind man who played the harmonica,

Keele Folk Festival, UK, 1966, Brian Shuel

Jersey, UK, 1971, Peter Misson

chord formations because of a childhood accident which affected the shape of his hand. Gary may have had an accident, but the theory is hogwash, because jazz and pop guitarists have been playing these and more complex chords since the twenties. Gary did receive some formal music training at a school for the blind in South Carolina, where he learned piano. I would guess that this training accounts at least in part for his more advanced knowledge of chords and harmony. Sis Davis says that Gary didn't stay at the school long because he didn't like the food!

Gary thought of his guitar work as more sophisticated than that of most country blues players. He had a particular disdain for Mississippi artists such as Son House, Skip James and Robert Johnson. He claimed that when you play in open tuning, "you ain't playing the guitar." Of Skip he said, "Nobody would ever hire him for a dance." It surprised me, however, to hear Gary be so critical of the emotional delta vocal style than to the more restrained vocals of Blind Blake, Blind Boy Fuller, and the other East Coast singers. Gary admired Mississippi John Hurt and Libba Cotton, but commented, "they play the country style; I play the city style."

Gary thought of some of his guitar arrangements as imitating a whole band. When teaching me, 'I Belong to the Band', he would distinguish the bass and treble runs as representing different instruments in a marching band. Many of his ragtime pieces he described as "my piano piece."

The variety of Gary's repertoire never failed to amaze me. I would often come and play him a new arrangement I had worked out on some old pop song, and he would counter with his own arrangement, which he hadn't played for years. Once during a discussion of Bob Dylan, he amazed me by playing a stylized, ragtime version of 'Don't Think Twice, It's Alright', and an arrangement of 'Masters of War'.

A number of things tend to indicate, however, that he did have sight as a young man. First of all, there is a song, 'There Was A Time When I Went Blind'. The recitation on 'Whistling Blues' contains much visual imagery. In a discussion of the old National guitars, Gary described all the different models and the colours they came in. (I have had limited experience with blind people, so I was surprised by how colour conscious Gary was). Gary once tried to sell me a pistol; he explained that when he grew up it wasn't uncommon for blind people to learn to use firearms.

Gary told of hopping freight trains, which I would imagine to be pretty difficult for a blind man. He said that when he left home for the first time, he stayed away for a year. Everyone assumed he had died, and when he returned people ran through the streets hollering, "It's Gary's ghost! It's Gary's ghost!"

I hope you are able to find some photos of Gary without his glasses. His facial expressions communicated much, but were appreciated only by those who saw him in his home.

When asked about racial conditions in the South when he was young, Gary said Georgia was the worst. "When a coloured man went into a tobacco store in Georgia, he had to ask for Mister Prince Albert!" (Prince Albert was a popular tobacco).

had taken over his upbringing. "The first instrument I played was a mouth harp. My uncle would go into town and buy him one. Then he'd buy me one. You could get a good one for twenty-five cents." The young boy would sit all day in the barnyard calling to the pigs and the chickens on his harp, and under his uncle's tutelage he became an accomplished country harpist, until he could blow the sounds of the whole coon hunt, the baying, panting, snarling, and whining of the pursuing hounds and the hissing of the tired coon. He always carries a couple of harps in his jacket but hadn't played them since he had got the cold, cause playing with a cold is "too much whiskey for a dime. Make you as drunk as any shot of whiskey."

Discovering that the boy was "music-inclined", his uncle helped him make his first banjo out of a pie plate, and presented him with an eighteen dollar Washburn guitar on his eighth birthday. It was the most important day in his life, the day "the Lord put something in my hands so I could take care of myself". He soon picked up the chords from the radio and from visiting neighbourhood guitarists and by the time he was twelve he was in demand for local fairs, hoedowns, hops, and camp meetings.

Alex Shoumatoff

•

When I was twelve years old (1969) I started to take guitar lessons. After a few lessons Reverend Davis wanted to know what I looked like so he grabbed my head, knocked twice and said, "Is this coconut ripe?"

Gary gave me a Martin guitar.

John Weihs

•

Gary had a knowledge of chords and harmony that surpassed that of almost any other country blues player. He could play in any key, and in church often accompanied the pianist in the flat keys. While a pop or jazz guitarist is expected to have this knowledge, it is virtually unheard of in country blues. It has been suggested that Gary was able to play unusual

Although he would sing bawdy songs, he became indignant when I once asked him to sing or recite `the dozens', (an insult game which often ends in violence). "Don't you go talking on that stuff now; before you know it someone's laying on the floor dead."

Many of Gary's novelty songs with endless verses had a violent streak to them. Are you familiar with, "Come Down and See Me Sometime"? I can't seem to locate the lyrics right now, but I remember sections about knifings, shootings, and a fellow getting a bed-slat in his head.

Gary had strong opinions and conceptions about things. Of Charlie Christian he said that, he was good, but he "couldn't get all the melody" because he played with a (flat) pick. He informed me that there are 36 chords on the guitar and 52 on the piano, no more and no less. (I think I remember his figures correctly). He stated that long playing records are eighteen inches in diameter, and 78's twelve, and that tunes were restricted to under three minutes in order to leave room for the artist's name in the middle of the record.

Gary was a patient teacher, but sometimes, when I pressed for a certain lick or right hand roll, he would beat around the bush. This I think is explained by his comment, "Don't give `em all you know, or they won't come back."

Richard Lieberson

•

I found him, first of all, to be very exciting and secondly incredibly generous. I mean, as a person, his warmth and generosity and sharing of his life's experiences (he was about 66 at the time) - he was willing, anxious and loved to sit down and rap with anybody about himself, about his music or about music in general and to play for hours. If you sat down and had a guitar and were just into learning, he would take his songs apart note for note for you and play them with you over and over again until you got it right. I mean literally stop right in the middle of what he was playing and say: "Did you get that?" and then slow it down if you had to have it slowed down. If you were fast enough to pick it up right off the top, then he'd go on. That's the kind of thing he liked to do. Just willing to be with anyone who came along that wanted to be with him. I visited him on occasions in New York, two or three times, and it was the same kind of experience there. You'd go to his house and his wife would cook lunch or dinner for you and you'd spend your time in the basement with him playing guitar or he'd talk to you about his guitar, asking about his friends in Toronto. He always remembered who I was, always asked about my wife who he really liked. She cooked eggs the way he liked them. Sharing his music, talking about music, reminiscing - just in general being who he was.

I can't recall him ever getting angry. Seeing as how he was blind, he was very afraid of fire. When he was smoking his cigar he would sometimes get very anxious. Occasionally, he dropped it out of his mouth or something and then he'd get very agitated. But I don't recall ever seeing him lose his temper or get angry about anything at all.

Bo Basiuk
Part of an interview, with Al Mattes, Blues Magazine c.1976

•

I first heard the Rev. Davis's music in 1960 through a recording by Jack Elliot of `Cocaine', which absolutely amazed me, and a couple of years later, I heard the original 'Cocaine Blues' on the Pure Religion and Bad Company album.

In 1961 I was living in Bournemouth and playing Blind Boy Fuller and Woody Guthrie music, and again discovered the Rev. Davis playing with Blind Boy Fuller before he became a Reverend.

One day I noticed an album called, `Gary Davis Harlem Street Singer', and persuaded a girlfriend to buy it for her collection. I still have the album, and regard it as one of the finest recordings of the Rev. Davis.

Although I have never been able to play exactly like him, and would not seek to try, as I think over-analysis of any particular style takes the essential swing from the music, his influence on my guitar playing nonetheless is evident to anyone who would listen in particular to his beautiful and compatible bass lines and swing.

I first saw him live in 1964 when he was on tour with Sonny Terry, Brownie McGhee and Muddy Waters, and it was an unforgettable experience. As you know, Sonny Terry had recorded with Blind Boy Fuller and the Rev. Davis many years before, and the high spot of the evening was when Sonny tapped his way out on stage to join the Reverend for a song which brought the house down. They looked in each other's direction and the Reverend said, "Well Sonny, I haven't seen you in a long time". Enough said.

In about 1971, just before he died, he did a final show in London at the Shaw Theatre and was supported by a Gospel Band from Birmingham. I was privileged to be asked to introduce him and compere the show. Backstage in the great man's presence, I found it very difficult to talk to him. He was tired and looked forward to going home and being with his family. He was also trying to sell Miss Bozo - his fantastic old 12-string guitar. He allowed me to play the guitar and I attempted to show my appreciation of him by playing, `Death Don't Have No Mercy' - one of his beautiful songs.

Author's home, Jersey, UK, August, 1972, Robert Tilling

Unfortunately he didn't recognise it and told me "picking won't get it".

I had some photographs taken by another fan of his - a Frenchman called George Chaterlain - who had flown in from Nice especially for the concert. Although the Reverend was tired he played the most amazing concert I have ever seen and must have been on stage for $1^{1/2}$ hours at least. During the concert he kept saying, "I've gotta hug a woman every day the doctor said to live". Eventually and to thunderous applause, the lead singer of the Gospel band came out and obliged and subsequently joined the Reverend in a song. At the end of the concert it's fair to say that he was mobbed by the enthusiastic audience and I think he went back to America tired and happy.

I count myself very lucky to have met him, and very grateful for his music.

Ralph McTell

•

As to myself, I first met Gary through Mark Waller, who drove for Gary for a short time, the summer of 1971. I was pretty much awed by him. Throughout that summer I went to Gary's house about twice a week, and saw him assorted times in the fall while I was in school in Philadelphia.

My favourite story about Gary took place one evening after we'd gone to a church in the East Bronx. He preached, and I'd played some music. Roy Book Binder picked us up to take Gary to a job in a small bar in N.Y.C. The whole way there, Gary preached about how a man should be true to his wife. Accordingly to him, when you were single, you could run around all you wanted to, but once you were married, you had to be faithful. The rest of the time he played his harmonica.

Anyway, we got to the club, and the stage was just really the back part of the bar, with a step up, and a few tables behind the

performer. We all ended up sitting up there. Roy started to play. His back was towards us, as we sat and drank a little something. Probably Gary had his 'special coffee' with a shot of liquor in it. Anyway Gary started to get a little lecherous, as he often times tended to do. He was grabbing for my leg and saying whatever else he felt like to go along with it. So, I changed my seat and was opposite him. On the way down to the club, I'd been singing or humming "Fishing Blues", and now, all of a sudden Gary started singing "I'm a going fishing, I'm a going fishing", and at the same time took his cane, and kept fishing for my leg, under the table, It was quite a scene.

I must say that most of my interesting anecdotes about Gary deal with the lecherous side of his nature. I hope you don't leave out that side of his character in an effort not to offend Gary, because, it was a very strong part of his personality. One time, he was in a hospital, after he'd had a heart attack (this was March before he died). He had intravenous, and oxygen plugged into his nose. He started grabbing at my leg and then proceeded to tell me to close the door, that no one would bother us, and I should get in bed with him. He was always like that when I was dealing with him, and I'm pretty sure he acted that way with other women. Certainly one of his favourite acts on stage was to call for a girl to come up there and he'd grab at her and say, "The doctor says I have to have a woman to live, the doctor says..." And then he'd go into "The Boy Kissing The Girl While Playing Guitar At The Same Time". (And proceeded to embarrass the girl who'd come up from the audience).

One evening that I particularly remember about Gary took place in Penn. where he'd been playing in a college coffee house. John (from England) and Alan Smithline and I were there. We were up playing that night, and Gary was getting a little sentimental or something. Anyway he told me that he'd wanted to teach me everything he knew, and that I should stick with him. That was one of the most meaningful and touching things anyone has ever said to me, and whenever I remember it, it provides me with a special musical push.

Gary was the finest person I've ever known. He was cantankerous, stubborn and set in his ways, but he was also loving, inspirational, and he had a certain wisdom in him, that is rarely encountered. And he certainly inspired love, and he inspired people to create music. He had an incredible ear, and even more wonderful style of playing. One joke I just remember is the one about two bulls, looking down on a field of heifers (one's old and the other young). The young bull says to the old one, "Let's run down and get us a few of those heifers", the old bull says, "Let's walk down and get them all!"

Joan Fenton

•

"You know", he went on, "when I was your age I went to a party one time wearing a white suit and I was sitting there when all of a sudden a whole fight broke out. I went into the kitchen and stole a potato pie off the table and came over to the fireplace

New York, 1957, Kenneth Goldstein

London, 1971, Georges Chatelain

and climbed over the burning logs and hid up the chimney till they quit fighting. When I got out, Good God, my suit was all black."

"Aw come on, B. Davis" Annie interrupted. "You still trying to tell people that story?"

Alex Shoumatoff

•

I was sharing a gig with Gary and I think it was in Chicago. Well we arrived at the gig and as we got out of the car I accidentally locked all the guitars in the trunk!

Gary got very agitated but I told him not to worry for when we get to the club all his fans will be there with their Gibson J-200's and he could borrow one! They were all there and we had a great time!

Ramblin' Jack Elliot

•

Artie Mogul was at the offices of Harms-Witmark Publishing on the day that Rev. Davis was to receive royalties for the tune 'If I Had My Way', which Peter, Mary and I had recorded on our newly successful first album. Just before Rev. Gary was about to sign the publishing agreement, as I understand it, for legal purposes the lawyers felt compelled to ask Rev. Davis if, in fact, he was the author of the song.

When Rev. Davis replied "No" an audible gasp was heard in the room but, before anyone could make a comment, he continued "...it was REVEALED to me..." The laughter that followed was doubtless due more to relief than any sense of humour.

Noel Stookey (*of Peter, Paul and Mary*)

•

The Reverend gave the sermon. Standing at the lectern with "Miss Bozo" (12-string guitar) around his neck, he looked thirty years younger, like an incredibly strong man in his prime. His forehead was creased, sweat poured out, his big nostrils flared open, his upper lip curled up - he looked like Victor Mature straining at the pillars of the temple in "Samson and Delilah". He went wild over the guitar, sometimes playing only with his left hand, sliding up and down the neck while he snapped the fingers of his right hand or slapped them, on the sound box, moaning, shouting, squealing. At times his voice and "Miss Bozo" were indistinguishable. Truly he was "fire-baptised and holy-ghost-filled". Annie was clapping one hand into the other, then turning them over and doing it the other way around, swaying back and forth all the time with her eyes closed. Occasionally she would shake and utter little screams as shivers of religion ran down her spine, and her eyes would pop open, but soon she would get back into the sermon and close them again. Looking at her and at her intently nodding old friends, I flashed that what we were witnessing was unreproducable, not only because it was Gary Davis's unique virtuosity but because it was the traditional trip of the blind religious street singer, an African witch doctor trip evolved through baptism into revivalism, the expression of a transient culture, the old black rural south, which has been broken up and absorbed by American progress, which provides homes for the blind so they don't have to sing on the streets but doesn't provide an alternative for down-home religious catharsis like what the Reverend was putting us through, which is what people like Jeff and Roy and me were doing here. This is what he sang:

"You better know how to treat everybody
For you got to go down. You got to go down.
You better learn how to treat everybody
You got to go down. You got to go down.
Ashes to ashes and dust to dust
The life you're living won't do to trust
You better learn how to treat everybody
For you got to go down."

Alex Shoumatoff

•

He Was a Friend of Mine

Sang his songs on the streets for years
For nickels and for dimes.
Preached the words of Jesus
And drank a little wine.
Travelled around the country
Sang a song for you and me.
He was a friend of mine.

Never wanted nothing
While he served his time.
Taught us all to 'See The Light'
Although he was blind.
Need someone to listen
He always had the time.
He was a friend of mine.

49

With Roy Book Binder, Buck Rock's Camp, Conn., 1969, Bob Carlin

Now `Death Don't Have No Mercy'
Took that friend of mine.
I don't know where I'm going
I feel like I am blind.
Said put your faith in Jesus
The world could be so fine.
He was a friend of mine.

He `Belonged To The Band'
Sang his last song somewhere
Said `Let Us Get Together, Right Down Here'.
He was a `Light In The World'
A voice we all could hear,
He was a friend of mine.

Told me about his boyhood
About hoboing on the trains.
Laughed about Prince Albert
You know his faith hid most the pain.
Can't forget the old man, guitar, hat and cane,
He was a friend of mine.

Roy Book Binder, *1978*

●

I walked in, said hello, shook hands, and really was a little shy at finally meeting the legendary guitarist, musician Reverend Gary Davis.

My main musical influence at the time, Stefan Grossman, had told me that I'd really love to study with Reverend Davis. I was at Stef's house and he went over to the phone and called Reverend Davis right up. I can't remember if Reverend Davis was home but soon after that I walked into his duplex home in St. Albans, N.Y., a part of Jamaica N.Y., a part of the big apple (New York City).

Stef soon left for Europe and stardom and turned me over to Reverend Davis as it were.

O.K. so I am sitting there and Reverend Davis can sense I am a bit shy and he takes over. He finds out I am a black folk singer, different from most of his students of his famous "5 dollar lessons" and right then and there begins to instruct me on the ins and outs of music:

"Man you've got to get out and let the public see what you can do, if you just play around churches, you understand, you will starve to death".

"I play at churches every chance I get", he said, "but when I get ready to make some money I play at colleges and clubs and places like that".

"Let me hear you play something".

"Man I could make you a real guitar picker, I can show you how to put the pepper (seasoning for hot guitar) in it".

He found out I have a family, wife and little girl, Thomasina. This really turned him on.

"Bro. Winslow you can make it in music, you can feed your family, you are good enough now, but I can help you get better".

Between each mini-sermon on the music business, I'd ask him to play another song: "Trying to get home", "Belong to the Band", "Oh, Glory", "I Will Do My Last Singing", all the masterpieces I loved so much seemed to come effortlessly from this great man.

Reverend Davis's music was the best I have ever heard but as good as it was it had to take a back seat to the man himself. He had, along with Mother Davis, the best developed sense of hospitality I ever ran into, and I'm from the home of hospitality, N. C.

This get-acquainted lesson lasted for hours, I think I ate, and I'm not sure if I had my wife and kid with me but I know he met them soon after.

Speaking of the family, we developed a tradition; every time I'd go down for a lesson, and usually they'd go along, we'd stop at a vegetable truck, actually they were black fellows from Georgia, as a rule, who loaded up these tandem trailers with collard greens, turnips, old fashioned hoop cheese, hickory-cured hams, etc. and drove up to St. Albans and parked beside the streets and in effect would sell folks like us who were from the Carolinas (and anyone else of course) a little bit of the south.

My wife started piping this traditional meal when I'd go for a lesson like this; one day I casually mentioned we were vegetarians. This got Reverend Davis's attention and he said to my wife she'd have to show him what a Vegetarian Soul Food Meal was. She cooked one that day and thereafter for the next five or so years until he died. This she did every time she accompanied me to his house.

On one occasion I didn't take the family I went down and spent a whole week with him. Every night (morning really) the sun would catch us still talking about the black experience as he had lived it and how he had used his music "to be somebody". At the drop of a hat he would tell you he was blind but he was a "man". Actually he could see. I was shocked to find this out one day. I had just bought a very loud yellow shirt. He was sitting there in his famous chair and all of a sudden he says, "That's a nice yellow shirt you have on". This caught me completely unawares so I said, "Man I thought you was blind", he chuckled, as only he could, and said, "You can't let folks know everything". That was Reverend Gary Davis!

He didn't like to hear you practice during a lesson, he'd play it for you note for note slowly several times if need be and then once you played it right he'd be ready to move usually to the next phrase. One reason this method worked so well was that he had an uncanny way of knowing which of his tunes you could play. This always amazed me.

I never really learned a lot of his tunes at this time, because after I met him and was learning I had a near fatal auto accident that although it left me unmarked the whip lash I suffered sprained my nerve centre in my neck, and I could concentrate with serious headaches for a only short while. I am fully recovered and after I get this done I am going to review all those Reverend Gary Davis lessons of 1967 to 1972, because as I write this they are so real as to be happening again. I can see the man in my mind patiently going over "Children of Zion" that he taught me I think at our last lesson.

Reverend Gary Davis, Bach, Segovia, Merle Travis, Mose Roger, Stefan Grossman, Richard Picket: these men belong together in their musical influences.

Since Reverend Davis died it is hard for me to visit his house but I do go every so often.

During the time of 1970 my wife was pregnant and we were down there, she shook his hand and he discovered this, he was excited as if it was his grandchild and he said let him name

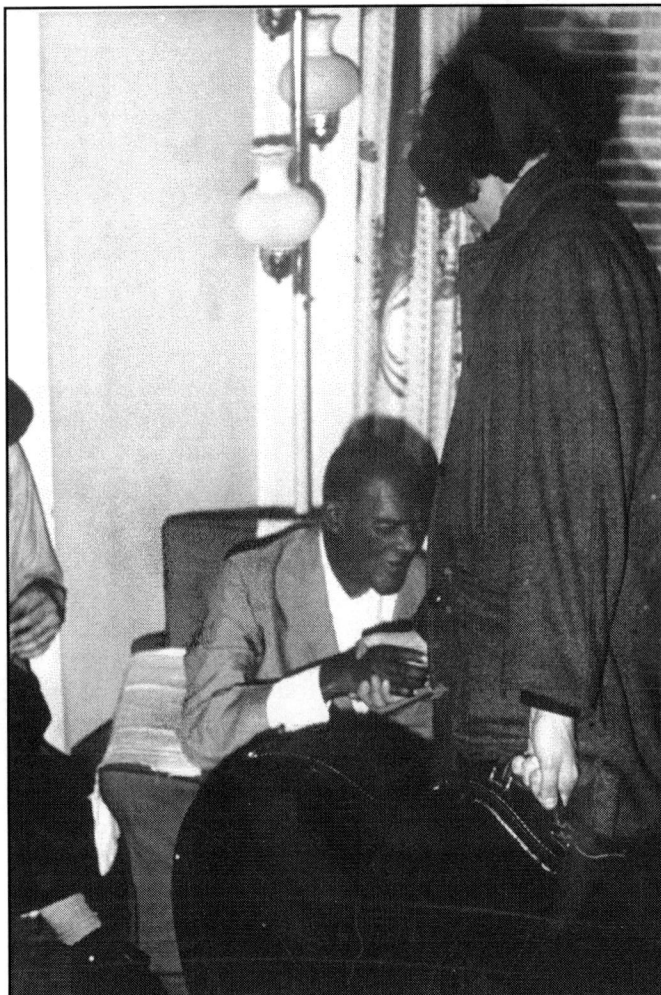

At home with Allan Evans, April 1972, Robert Tilling

the child as it was going to be a boy (it was). I said "What would you name him Reverend Davis?" He said some awful name like John or something of that order, I said, "Reverend Davis if it's a boy I'll name him Gary, how's that?" He agreed, so I have a little boy of 9 years now (a good guitarist even now by the way, studying classical etc.) named Gary T. Winslow. My youngest boy, Carlton, feels as though he knows him too though he's only 5. He knows his music from his records. Some of Reverend Davis's influences are responsible for:-

My having a Bozo guitar –12-string
Knowing about the business of music
Having a little boy named Gary
Knowing how to record and numerous other things.

Another story is in order here, about a year or two years after I met Reverend Davis I recorded an album for Biograph Records.

One day while I was over at Arnie Caplan's house, I mentioned Reverend Davis. Arnie (owner of Biograph) asked me if Reverend Davis was still alive. I said yes and why didn't he do one last recording session with him as he was getting on in years. Arnie said O.K., walked over, picked up the phone (I'd given him the number) and proceeded to get an appointment to go and set it up with Reverend Davis. I went back home and forgot about it. Soon after I went down for another lesson and this was the day they had chosen to do the recording. Reverend Davis asked me to join him and go over to the studio where he

was going to cut an album for the like "final word to all his guitar students".

It was a holiday. There was a parade, so the studio was a block or so away from where we had to stop, so we had to walk; everyone was upset because Reverend Davis didn't walk much or climb stairs. But we walked it. Upon getting there he had to climb a few steps. No one knows it but this is one of the reasons his voice was tired on some of the cuts. He was exhausted but insisted on completing the session for his legacy to us who would follow. He was going to do some of his secular songs so he left Sis Davis home. She would have fussed, she was of her own mind about such things.

To show you what Reverend Davis was made of, he knew he was not up to par, but he wanted those tunes left for a record and exhausted though he was, he cut 2 full records that day of some very difficult music. I won't forget after one particularly struggling cut he said, "People think playing guitar is easy but it's not". His face was wet with sweat.

His followers have developed two schools of thought about these records that resulted from this session viz.:

(1) They should not have been cut.

(2) An appreciation to Caplan and Reverend Davis for being sure the music was left for our consideration and learning; Biograph 12030 and Biograph 12034.

On one cut he says, "This is for you guitarists to get you learnin'". Here he was talking about this legacy he was proudly leaving at this session.

On some of the cuts the guitar may have been a bit out of tune. Some uninformed writer said that the ones there with him should have kept his guitar in tune for him due to his advancing age. First of all, a person like Reverend Davis ascribed to the old blues school of mastering "one cut, no more take it or leave it" and I would never have asked him to let me tune his guitar, if I would've I was caught up in the history of the moment, so I didn't.

Larry Breezer, his live-in driver and student at the time, was amazed when he told him to get his guitar and cut "Candyman" with him. That's the kind of man he was. His music was to share, to make others happy and able to play like him until they could play like themselves.

We felt he'd never leave us, his music is still with us.

Tom Winslow
Folk-Songster/Entertainer

●

It was the Reverend's seventy-third birthday and he was in fine spirits. Someone in England had sent him a box of small cigars which he had been smoking steadily in spite of a bad cold, and by the time we reached the standstill in front of the Midtown Tunnel, he was already on his third cigarillo of the expedition. But suddenly he broke out coughing, choking, wheezing.

"I swear, Brother Davis, you gonna cough yourself to death on them things," Annie said. "You gonna cough yourself right into the coffin. You smoke them things just like a child eats candy."

"Aw hush," the Reverend replied when he had pulled himself together. "I ain't gonna die. I ain't going nowhere. And if I did die, I'd be here just as often as I was when I was alive". He returned the cigar to his mouth.

Alex Shoumatoff

MJ: How did you meet Reverend Gary Davis?

GG: Annie came and she opened the door and I explained to her that I wanted some lessons. So she turned and said, "Reverend, this young man wants to learn some guitar." He was really getting on. It was about two years before he died. So I stood at the door waiting for him. He shuffled up from somewhere and the first thing I noticed was that this guy is very old. I had seen pictures of him on record jackets, and I expected a younger looking man. He came out with a sly smile on his face. Looked real happy. Looked like happiness, that's what he was. We stood in the foyer of the house for fifteen, twenty minutes. He started shaking my hand. I said, "Reverend, I came here and I really would like to take lessons". And he nodded. My hand was staying in one place and his was moving all over. I started talking about this and that he's feeling all my knuckles and then he'd switch hands and on and on it went. For fifteen or twenty minutes he felt my hands, at least. Then we went downstairs to his furnished basement. He had a big, fat easy chair with the right arm torn off the chair so he could sit there and hang the big ass of his Gibson off the end of it. It was real comfortable like that. He sat down and said let me see your guitar. I took it out and he felt it all over for a long time, the bridge, the braces and the back and then told me it was better than his guitar. He had a J-200 a really fine guitar. I said, "Sure, Reverend" (laughter). So he knew something about my hand and my guitar and he asked me to play a tune. So now he was ready to show me something. He started to play and said, "Well, what is it you want to know?" I said, "Why don't you show me something easy." "Easy", he says, "Ain't nothing easy! I don't know anything easy". He said, "You heard about 'Wade In The Water'. You don't wade in the water around here. You've got to swim. You want something

easy, go out the door. That's the only easy thing you'll be able to do around here." "Yes Sir", I said, "Anything you say."

George Gritzbach, in conversation with Mike Joyce
Blues Magazine, Vol. 4, No. 1, 1978

Ballad for Reverend Gary Davis

Have you heard the singin' preacher?
He's been and gone
Set sail for another shore
Ridin' high the dawn.

Shined his light
Some seventy years
On mountains of hate
Boilin' cold with fear.

Gypsy jagged corners found
Your song on the street
Sowin' seeds among the
Tide cast there in concrete.

Singin' hard times
Is how you shoulder them
Livin' is here people
Won't you hold on in.

Though it's been said that your
Sight was gone
One thing I know is true
Few men upon this world askin'
Have seen as clear as you.

You done your last singin'
In this land
Left your sword standin'
In the sand.

Keep your lamp trimmed an burnin'
Under skin and sky
So many words to say
Fare thee well goodbye.

George Gritzbach *1976*

'The Rev'

Who could have guessed his parents were both slaves,
Or that his years were spent on city curbs?
His hands - so young and black and smooth – belied
The years they'd spent in endless work, and yet
Were never still. I wonder why they stayed
So smooth, as if ignoring time and wear;
And always restless, feeling for a new
Seam or a hangnail to explore. His fingers
Dance across the neck of hickory wood,

Cambridge Folk Festival, UK, 1971, Steve Rye

Coaxing rhythms hiding in the strings.
The lifeless steel would breathe beneath his touch,
And fill his world with visions all his own.
From time to time his fingers found his watch,
Which, faceless, let him show how well he saw.
But that last time I saw him seemed so strange:
His hands lay quiet, folded on his chest,
The strings lay quiet, to sing for us no more.

G. Withers

•

Reverend Gary Davis – As I Remember Him

Smithline: I'm having a bit of a problem with "Hesitation Blues".

Davis: You ought to have done had that one by now.

Smithline: Yeah, but I'm sure I have it. I'm not sure I'm playing the right bass notes.

Davis: You got it Smithline. You're playin' it right...

I studied guitar and lived with Reverend Gary Davis during the last year and a half of his life, and during this time I was employed as Reverend Davis's chauffeur. A day doesn't pass where I don't think about Reverend Davis or listen to his music via his records or the tapes I made of him while living at his home. I'm fortunate to own Reverend Davis's 12-string Bozo guitar and play his music on that instrument

Jersey, UK, August 1971, Robert Tilling

ever cognisant of the magnitude of its previous owner.

Gary Davis was one of those human beings who was larger than life. To watch him play guitar and sing caused your mouth to hang from your face. He was great and solid great through and through. He was not a piece of technological gimmickry. He was the genuine article and his voice and his guitar were complete unto themselves. He used no phase shifters, no echoplexes, and was recorded with no overdubbings.

Gary loved to play the guitar and his rhythm, inflections, and deftness of execution were impeccable - as steady as the Rock of Gibraltar. He played with such authority and vitality, that acoustically, the bass notes of his jumbo Gibson guitar, outfitted with heavy gauge strings were powerful enough to make your belly reverberate. For me there was no precedence for this style or expertise in playing and his appeal was the kind of thing where it didn't matter who his audience was. Everyone who was fortunate to hear him knew that the experience was something special.

Gary was a musician's musician, and not just a solo guitar player. He played excellent five string banjo, harmonica and piano - which I saw him play only once in church. He could also play lead style guitar. Best known for his guitar arrangements of string bands, marching bands and Big Bands, they are nothing short of genius - they were so perfectly put together. He had ears like computers and played all different kinds of tunes - things you might not have expected like Bob Dylan's "Masters of War" the "Tennessee Waltz" and countless others. One thing he liked to demonstrate was his ability to play "Amazing Grace" in a few different keys up and down the neck. He was pretty adamant about not playing in open tunings, a technique he considered cheating, although there was one tune which he played bottleneck style in open D-6th tuning.

I had no problem at all relating to Gary Davis and we shared some wild times. He loved to play music, loved to flirt with women, and loved to philosophise about life, and since there were three of my favourite pursuits, I had much to learn from a man who was more than three times my age (and who had been there and back). On more than one occasion, Gary's pep talk spared me the sufferings of unrequited love, and his wisdom helped me to see my situation in a proper perspective.

It was quite a thrill to be with such a star. Gary Davis had legions of loyal fans, and people from all over the world made pilgrimages to his home. Gary would address his visitors by pointing proudly to his guitar and saying, "This guitar over here caused me to be sitting in this house". How true it was. He had waited a long time for the recognition that was due to him. An artist of his stature had belonged on the concert stages many years before.

A favourite topic of discussion among everybody except Gary Davis was the subject of his blindness. He certainly did not like to talk about it. This is the story he told me. When he was a little boy it became apparent that there was trouble with his eyesight - that there was some kind of condition, or some kind of problem. A doctor in town said that he could perform an operation to correct the problem but Gary said that there was no money to pay this doctor. Another doctor said he would perform the operation for no fee, but unfortunately the doctor died. Left untreated, the condition steadily worsened until he totally lost his sight.

Manchester, UK, 1964, Brian Smith

Brighton, UK, 1971, Steve Rye

creative force. Put yourself into your music, put your soul into the music, make your own original stamp on the music.

In 1968 when Issy Young had the Folklore Center, on Sixth Avenue in New York City, he would hold concerts every Monday evening and I used to go practically every week and one evening Stefan Grossman gave a concert there. Rev. Davis came to hear Stefan and Stefan was so excited. All the people at the concert were so impressed that Gary Davis would come to hear Stefan play. Now that showed me something of his humility and gratitude of the teacher, that his student not only listened to him but reached a different place to himself.

Rev. Davis was very interested in people who had their own way about playing the guitar. He wanted them to be thoroughly grounded in technique and be a master of the technique so that they could use their technique in their own song, for your own creativity and so I see him as a person who expressed his own song, and who would expose his weaknesses. He was not an actor in that sense. He would expose who he was and I honour him for that.

Ron Rebhuhn

●

Annie Davis, Gary's wife, is the person who held everything together, and I believe has been grossly overlooked ... she is a very religious person, and a very generous and caring person and without her Gary would probably have succumbed sooner to his excesses. She would keep an eye on him, sometimes perhaps, a bit too much, but she was the one who knew him best. She was aware of Gary's declining state of health and knew that the end was coming and tried to make him conserve his energy so that the "world would still have a Reverend Davis". She had a very hard life, and even in later years when Gary was "making it" and things were easier financially, she still had an immense amount of work to do.

Since leaving Reverend Davis's tutelage and subsequently being exposed to all types of music and stars, I can safely say that his talent has stood the test of time, and in my perception has not diminished by one iota. I live in the Rocky Mountains and when I view these majestic peaks I can draw an analogy to the stature of Reverend Gary Davis, and that is the perfection of his music and the grandeur of the person himself.

I miss Gary Davis, and like I say, a day doesn't go by where I don't think about him. What I remember most about him is the power and honesty of his playing and singing. He could make you cry and he could make you laugh.

Alan Smithline
1979

●

He had lots of time for people which is true of every good teacher. I remember he would charge five dollars but you could stay all day because he was not just teaching guitar, he was teaching you God, and he was teaching you his way of life. He was teaching you who he was and then from who he was you could learn who you might become. I hear him now, saying, "be creative, be your own person, do not be so worried what other people think and do not be a slavish imitator of others".

His idea was that you should become like him, this

One incident that took place in 1971, I believe, stands out. Rev. Davis, myself, and some other students of his had gone to see Stefan Grossman play at the Washington Square Church. Gary was really enjoying the music, grinning, and shouting out encouragement when Stefan's guitar work impressed him. Gary was aware that he was going to die soon, and it gave him satisfaction to know that people would be playing his music, carrying on his tradition, when he had gone.

After the concert, we asked Rev. Davis if he wanted to go home or over to The Gaslight, where David Bromberg was performing. Gary was hot to trot and wanted to go where the music or party was at, so we headed over. Bromberg, incidentally, had once studied with Bro. Davis.

When we reached The Gaslight, the management let the entire Davis party in for free. Gary didn't care for the opening act, and began to make noises imitating guitar strings breaking. "Spoing-doing! There goes the A string! Spoing-doing! There goes the D string! "

Bromberg began his set with an up-tempo bluegrassy number featuring some hot flatpicking, and Gary was excited, cheering him on. David dedicated the set to Gary, and played `Just A Closer Walk With Thee' leaving the stage and coming over to our table, which was way in the back, for his fingerpicked guitar chorus. Next, Bromberg sang Davis's `Trying to Get Home'. David had also written an original tune called `Trying to Get Home', which he introduced by saying that he wasn't a religious person, and that the idea of going home had a different meaning to him. When he completed the number, Gary stood up in the back of the room and began to speak. "I know this ain't usually done in this place but I am moved, and I got something to say".

Bromberg left the stage and took a seat. Gary gave a mini-sermon lasting about ten minutes to an audience of people most of whom had no idea who he was. The sermon was divided into two parts. Gary spoke about how he understood Bromberg, that `Tryin' to Get Home' could mean something different to a non-religious person. I wish I could remember his words, for he was quite articulate and did not speak often about things like this.

The second part of the speech was about "playing the guitar". Gary demanded that the audience respond, like a church congregation, and refused to continue until the audience had answered him.

"You're gonna have a lot of trouble in this world ... playing the guitar".

"That's right".

"People gonna turn you from their door ... playing the guitar".

"Uh-huh".

This went on and on. Finally:

"Play that guitar, boy!" and he sat down!

Richard Lieberson

•

I remember seeing him play in Detroit in 1964 or 1965. He played "Candyman" and I was amazed at how different and better it sounded than all the imitators. The rhythm was remarkably beautiful, somehow beautifully syncopated and regular in a unique way.

One time I was at a party for the Philadelphia Folk Festival, in 1969. The Rev. dominated the whole room, just talking and playing, with everyone gathered around. He had a knack of picking the prettiest girl out of the crowd and giving her special attention.

As a guitarist, I have always had the utmost respect and love for the Rev.'s music. Totally aside from technical prowess, his music is exquisite in its melodic and rhythmic beauty and inventiveness. The phrasing of his melodies is beautifully idiosyncratic, expressing a power and depth of emotion that is stunning. I don't believe in trying to imitate the sound - it's impossible; but the pure joy of listening and learning about what's truly important in music from listening to the Rev. is a gift that has changed and influenced me musically in a very major way.

Eric Schoenberg

•

John Jackson told me how he saw Gary preach for over an hour at one concert, and he found it one of the most vibrant and moving sights he'd ever seen. John couldn't get over Gary's complete independence, he met him once at an airport. Gary was on his own and had been waiting over two hours for someone to collect him. John asked if he was O.K. Gary said he was and "Somebody be along sometime, else I'll go find them ain't no matter". John sat with him quite a while and they cut a bottle together.

Garry Bready
1972

•

I first encountered the Reverend Gary Davis in 1963 and shortly thereafter I became his pupil. But I soon ran out of

Peterborough, UK, 1971, Peterborough Evening Telegraph

57

Possibly Chicago c.1965, photographer unknown

money to live on, much less to pay for lessons, so the Davis's hired me to drive their car. It seems to be the fantasy of each Davis student that he (or she) is the master's favourite pupil. Rather than indulge in this doubtful form of vanity, I prefer to claim with absolute certainty that I was Reverend Davis's worst driver. Still, despite the fact that I nearly twice wrecked their Ford, the Davis's kept me on for a couple of years, giving me an opportunity to get to know Reverend Davis and his music quite well.

John Townley
Adelphi Album Notes, 1973

•

It was the late Reverend Gary Davis who had the most profound influence on both Roy's attitude to music and to life. (For anyone who has met and talked to Reverend Gary it is difficult not to be!) Roy first met Reverend Gary in 1968 after Jack Baker and Mike Katz suggested he went to Reverend Gary for lessons. Roy phoned him, met him, and within a month he left school and was on the road with him! ... "Reverend Davis wouldn't be there for ever and school would be." Roy, on the sleeve notes of his album relates to this time: "Shortly after I met this most influential of the East Coast blues guitarists, as he was trying to teach me one of his incredible guitar solos, he mentioned that he was leaving for Detroit the next day to begin a tour of concerts and coffee house gigs.

As old Gary sat smoking a Tiparillo, sitting in his favourite armchair in front of his electric heater, I mentioned that I had fifty dollars and that I wouldn't mind going to Detroit with him. Reverend Davis chuckled a little, saying that fifty dollars couldn't get me much further than Pittsburgh, Pennsylvania ... Detroit was great! We froze in a Chicago hotel for a week, almost crashed in a plane ride from Buffalo to Baltimore, and we had more weird things happen to us in more weird places than either of us could remember. Gary and I were both pleased that some of his music is on my record."

Reverend Davis regarded Roy as one of his favourite "students" along with Larry Johnson and Woody Mann; Sister Annie Davis still refers to him as " ...good ole Roy..." One of my fondest memories of Reverend Gary is when I was at his house in April 1972 and Roy was sat close to Gary playing Bo Carter's "Biscuits" with Gary laughing and smiling ... Gary always liked a "humorous" song!

Robert Tilling
Blues Link, January 1974

•

Gary's been around for 73 years and hasn't had the easiest life, yet he always looks forward to the good times. Playing his music and singing in the streets of Harlem, Reverend Davis has had more than his share of hard times. More than once, after having his guitar, overcoat, and cane stolen, he has called home and told his wife, "You better come get me. They got everything I had." Reverend Davis has always managed to get back on his feet and was thankful that he was able to get another guitar and start again. He is always looking up to better things.

Roy Book Binder

•

I did a tour with Gary Davis, Paul Simon and Ramblin'

Jack Elliot. We did this tour by car. We were driving like heck through these winding roads. Gary Davis couldn't see the turns so he'd be flying all over the place. When we finally got out of the car, he kept saying, "Free at last. Free at last."

Buffy Ste. Marie
(Courtesy – Hoot! Robbie Woliver, St. Martin's Press, 1986)

•

Reverend Gary Davis-
Some Reminiscences

It was August 1964; I was sixteen years old and enjoying the hospitality and excellent southern cooking of the Reverend and Mrs. Gary Davis. They lived in Jamaica, Queens, a Long Island suburb of New York. Jamaica then was a middle class black neighbourhood, bungalows with picket fences, back yards and barbecues, not at all one's picture of New York.

For me, those days were spent at Gary's side - listening, watching, soaking up as much as I could of his endless repertoire of gospel songs, blues and ragtime guitar pieces. I wasn't much of a guitar player then - the only piece he actually taught me was "Candyman", one of his easiest. His students would come and go as I played the role of 'lead boy' - lighting his cigars, fetching or re-stringing a different guitar. I was impressed by the accuracy of his ear. He would play a phrase slowly while the student watched his fingering, then the student would play the same phrase for Gary's approval. No - the syncopation isn't quite right - Gary plays it again, over-emphasising the accents, painstakingly slowly. The student tries again, and his efforts are rewarded with an impatient grunt and violent shake of the head, which sends an inch of cigar ash rolling down Gary's amply filled shirt. "EFF SHARP!" he growls, pointing to the proper bass note.

One day after reminiscing about the folk scene of twenty years earlier, Gary decided to visit Woody Guthrie. As we drove to the hospital, he displayed uncanny knowledge of New York - although he had been blind before moving to New York from his native South Carolina, he directed us on a complicated route to Brooklyn without missing a stop light or major intersection. As we neared that infamous district, he started fumbling with his pockets and pulled out a loaded revolver and an eight inch switch blade.

For a full ten minutes he stayed there, sharpening the knife and lecturing us on how decent folks have to get themselves "prepared" for a trip through Brooklyn.

Huntington's Chorea is an incurable disease which leaves a man a mere skeleton stretched with pallid skin. It denies the control of one's muscles and an arm or leg will frequently wave about in a spasm of frantic activity. This was the state in which we found Oklahoma's Hard Traveller, in a dingy institutional green room decorated with only plaster cracks and a barred window soiled with years of grime.

At the sight of his old friend Woody became quite excited, whether in spasm or a desire to get up and greet Gary, I don't know. Whatever, he got hopelessly entangled in the sheets and the crib-like bars around his bed and an orderly had to come and sort things out. Gary played and sang for him, then spoke about having the strength to meet the day of judgement and eternal salvation.

It was a moment that touched me deeply. The ageing blind man having lived through all that this century has dished out to black Americans, standing over the hopelessly diseased man talking of hope and salvation in another, better world.

Leaning against a fence post, I listened as `Miss Gibson's' crisp twang drifted out of the tent and into Sunday, slowly being absorbed by the early morning mist. The Pennsylvania Dutch farm was waking up for a new day, serenaded by Gary Davis's fingers waking up for the Gospel songs concert of the Philadelphia Folk Festival. My reverie was broken as I caught sight of a grey pin stripe suit and bowler hat ambling toward me with a bow-legged saunter, like Chaplin's tramp. Pin-stripes stopped dead in his tracks when he heard Gary's playing, cocked his head to listen and turned to me. "Is that Gary Davis in there?", he asked incredulously. I could only nod, I was so struck by this face of leathery wrinkles, rich chocolate skin, the boyish charm in the twinkling eyes. Mississippi John Hurt replies, "Hot Dawg! I ain't seen him in thirty five years!" I followed him into the tent and as I watched their joyous reunion, I felt a warm glow.

For this was more than just the chance meeting of two old

Gary was one of the greatest - I can say no more.

- Pete Seeger

men. The whole folk scene: the self-appointed musicologists of the blues, the thousands of aficionados and aspiring guitarists like myself, the whole network of coffee houses, festivals, small magazines and mail order record companies; it seemed that all this existed for them, so that they might meet here today. The long overdue recognition of their talents, the acknowledgement of their contribution to our musical heritage had given them the comfort and dignity and, finally, the possibility for such joyous moments as this, that they had paid for with suffering and hardship. It had also given them the opportunity to make their mark, to touch others with their warmth and experience and to leave a lasting impression of their life and times.

It is August 1967. Roebuck and Purvis Staples, of the Staples Singers gospel group are with Gary Davis in a Backstage tent at the Mariposa Folk Festival. They are fending off the chill evening air with a heated conversation. Gary has slowed down noticeably - his speech, his movement and his guitar playing all reflect the toil of his seventy-one years. Purvis is trying to convince Gary to retire, arguing that he has done more than his fair share to serve God; that the Lord would want him to spend his last years enjoying the abundance of good things he

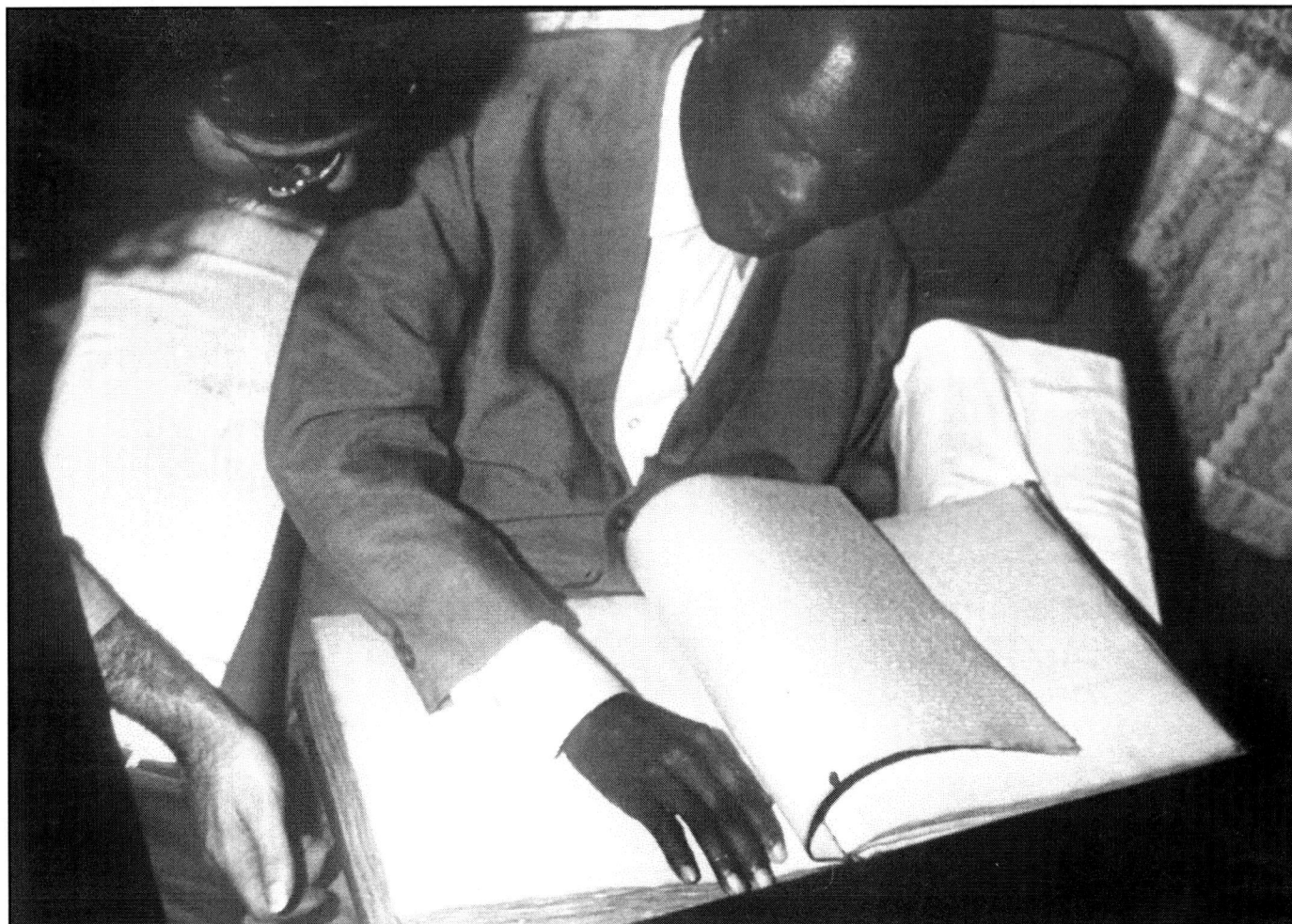

Reading Bible with Roy Book Binder, April 1972, Robert Tilling

created for the uplifting of Man's soul. Gary is adamant and annoyed – "God put me on this earth to spread His Gospel and sing His Truth, and Lo' help me, that's what I'm bound to do until the day He knocks me down dead".

Reverend Gary Davis died May 5th 1972
Death don't have no mercy in this land.
Dean Meridith *1976*
Blues Magazine Vol. 2, No. 2

•

The music and personality of Rev. Davis was a constant inspiration to me and kept me focused at a time I needed it the most. He and Annie made me feel part of the family and the music I learned still is as vivid as my memories of our time together. I feel very lucky to have known him.
Woody Mann

•

I remember the late Rev. Davis very fondly. He came to my shop in Chicago in late 1969 or early 1970. Roy Book Binder, Rev. Davis's travelling companion brought him in.

Rev. Davis played one of my twelve string guitars and he really liked it. Because he was blind, I offered him a discount. He said, "I'd accept a discount if I didn't have the money, but this is your living. Since I have the money, I'd be ashamed to accept a discount. If I didn't like the guitar, I wouldn't take it if you gave it to me. Because I like it, I expect to pay the full price".

The man was not only a great musician, but also a very good and honest person.

He sat and played in my shop for several hours that day. I enjoyed it immensely.
Bozo Podunavac

•

Rev. Davis was playing at a club in Chicago when someone asked him to check out his new Bozo twelve string. Rev. Davis wouldn't let go of it! He wanted to buy it and he did his first set with it. He was crazy about it and would not give it back.

He teased the owner and got the address of Bozo and we took a cab over there the next day. Rev. Davis ordered a guitar and for weeks he waited at home. He was like a kid at Christmas when it arrived!
Roy Book Binder

•

Rev. Gary Davis has been one of my main mentors. Of all the Blues men from the East Coast, from the Piedmont area, Rev. Davis has been the most influential and because of this, many aspiring Piedmont style pickers have used him as their model. I, myself, John Cephas, also used Rev. Gary Davis as a model and I hold him to the highest esteem of guitar players. I learned, in my youth, so much from Rev. Gary. I think there are two great Piedmont blues men that wrote the book, one is Rev. Gary and the other is Blind Boy Fuller. There are none greater.

Without their influence in my life I do not think I would have any position in the blues world.
John Cephas
(Piedmont Blues Man)

Buck's Rock Camp, Conn., 1969, Bob Carlin

•

He was a very fine man and a great guitar player. There was no one else quite like Rev. Davis and I had a lot of respect for him.
John Jackson

•

Thoughts on Techniques and Memories of Reverend Davis

(These notes are greatly edited from a long audio tape sent to the author in 1972).

I spent a lot of time with the Rev. Davis and really he was my moving master in music. When I left school, I went to one semester of college at Tufts University, Cambridge, (circa 1962) and it was actually during that time I met the Rev. Davis for the first time. It was at a small coffee house in Philadelphia called the 'Second Fret' where he was the second act to Jack Elliott. Those were the days when Jack Elliott and that kind of folk music were more popular than Rev. Davis. I had heard his records and loved the way he played, but I had never met the man, but I found out that I could take lessons from him. The result was that I ended up dropping out of college and following him around New York to learn how to play his kind of music. The technique that I learned from him, although not necessarily the musical style, but very definitely the guitar technique, has completely shaped my entire style of musicianship.

I moved to New York, dropped out of college, and I took a few lessons up with him up in the Bronx. He lived in this little tiny place, just below 172nd Street. You went into this dank little tunnel underneath a front range of houses and you went into a small back yard and there was this little house, it was almost like a house you would find in the south. A little one storey building with a front porch and a veranda, it was in the middle of the Bronx enclosed in a block of buildings.

The furniture was all cotton patterned, cotton covered and stuffed, sort of over stuffed furniture, that has been sat on and worn so much that the stuffing is all smashed down.

I remember going there the first time for a 10 o'clock lesson with Rev. Davis and I was just barely awake after a very late night but very thrilled and excited nonetheless. I learned that first time a rag, I forget what he called it, but it was a piece that Jack Elliott had wanted to learn and he couldn't figure it out so I told Jack that I would learn it and teach it to him. And so I went and learnt a tune and it was wonderful. I went back that afternoon and I sat down to play it and I couldn't remember a note and I was in a blind fog, total panic, Oh, my God! you know, because it was wonderful to have learnt from someone who just played it for you. He'd just play for you ... it goes like this, and you'd try and he'd say no, it goes like this, and you'd try it again after a couple of times you got it.

At this point I wasn't totally confident with my psychic powers of learning and so I went to bed that night in a total depression thinking, Oh, God, I'm going to go back next week and I won't be able to play it and he won't want me for a student. Well two days later I woke up in the morning and I remembered it all, note for note, it had sunk in and it was sitting there tolling in the back of my mind somewhere and just hadn't come out. I went back the next time and played it perfectly, and he was very happy and I was very happy and we went on to learn any number of things.

I learnt a lot of his pieces, hardly any of which I play any more because you can hear him playing better on a record. Basically it is a classical style of times gone by, it's not a style that will continue to live on its own except as classical music, it's something to be looked at as a significant part of the past. What lives on to me was several attitudes towards both technique and towards the guitar itself, which I think are probably his greatest and least recognised contributions to music in general, the first of which is the technique itself and I have heard a lot of people, a lot of students of Reverend Davis, Stefan Grossman, Barry Kornfeld, any number of people who have taken Davis's style and they have played it note for note, but it is very difficult to play something note for note of Davis's. If you watch him play the same song many times it is not the same any two times in succession. But they altered the technique not the notes, they adapted a classical technique of bar chords for instance which he never used in his technique, particularly the use of the right hand.

I know virtually of no one who plays Reverend Davis's style, the way he does with just one finger pick and one thumb

Chicago Folk Festival, 1962, Tom Paley

pick, that's all it takes and that's all it should take. When you come down to situations like two finger rolls, many people will do them with three fingers which is very good but it approaches a banjo roll, and when Rev. Davis does them he does it letting the thumb double up for that extra finger, so it comes out, a little bit stronger. The more you use your thumb the stronger it is.

When he played with the right hand he played from his entire body so that a thumb stroke was an extension of the shoulder not of the wrist, or the thumb itself or even of the arm but of the actual shoulder and a body movement. The result is that the thumb and forefinger hardly moved at all when he played. It is one of the things that made it very difficult, unless you were very sharp to learn how to figure out exactly what he was playing, for he was not very delineative visually in his playing in that it was all strictly body motion. It was all strokes of the arm directed from the shoulder, and this was something that was really lost on most of the people that learnt from him. Not too many people could play like that. The only other person that plays like Davis that I know of is Larry Johnson. When he plays Rev. Davis songs they are almost indistinguishable from Davis. I never heard anybody sound that close to Davis and there is hardly anyone that has learned, not just the songs and the music but the technique itself and particularly the right hand.

Another aspect that he did besides using a Gibson guitar, which is a very over bassed guitar with a very slow response, is that unlike other guitarists he did not hold his guitar latterly across the body but at an acute angle. You will note in pictures of

Blind Blake, and a lot of early people like Blind Lemon Jefferson, the guitar didn't face latterly across their body but it went up at a very acute angle. The effect of this is that when you hit the bass string you are hitting it in the middle over the hole where the maximum bass area is, your finger, as a result falls much more to the treble end towards the tail piece. The result is you get a much deeper bass and a sharper treble than you do if you play the guitar latterly across your body. Also when you put the guitar strap straight around your neck rather than over your shoulder as Davis does, it forces the guitar to slant to that acute angle and gives you that over bassed and over trebled effect which is unique to his style of playing.

Another really interesting effect used in Davis's thinking was his tuning, something else that nobody does, mostly because everybody objected to it at the time. I remember in my more innocent days as an early student taking his guitar and tuning it to pitch like a guitar should be, and my goodness it just sounded very nice and in tune to me and Davis would pick it up and say, "Oh dear, Oh dear", and he would adjust the gears until he got it back in tune which was his tuning, and of course had the bass string considerably flat of the treble. Everybody thought it was just out of tune but it wasn't out of tune, every time he tuned it to exactly the same intervals, it was intentionally 'out of tune'. I never really understood until much later and after studying music of other cultures and realising how traditional and ingrained in a primitive music this kind of tuning is.

Another facet of Davis's music that was again lost, was his left hand technique. It was very important because many people had learned classical technique beforehand so therefore it put you in the wrong position to begin with, sticking your elbow out and your fingers across the neck and your thumb behind the neck. It is a disastrous way to try to approach that style of music. You have to do it with your elbow clenched in right into your body and the hand gripped around the neck and the thumb around it on top of the strings, like a baseball bat or golf grip. It gave you a great deal more power because one remembers that Reverend Davis played only heavy gauge strings. You really had to have a strong left hand and good leverage to be able to push those strings down effectively. Hardly anybody plays heavy strings any more, people pick up my guitar and they get immediate pains from playing it because there are very few people that use really extra heavy gauge strings, but Davis always did. Rev. Davis also used his thumb to fret fifth and sixth strings and it is a technique that is not used that much, except among black guitarists who still use a similar technique because it seems to be indigenous to their culture.

His technique of course is a non-visual one, it is basically a tactile technique that comes from not looking at the guitar. It was a style he developed, as did other blind guitarists at the time such as Blind Blake and Blind Lemon Jefferson. He developed a style that really had to be played in the dark because he was in the dark! He developed a technique where the fingers at all times, in all the positions, were always touching each other, therefore he always knew where his fingers were by where they were touching each other rather than where they were touching the neck. The result of this as far as a student was concerned was that it was virtually impossible to tell what notes Davis was hitting because he hardly moved his fingers at all. It was just like a big palm down on the neck and it moved a little bit and all

these intricate notes came out, and neither right nor left hand moved hardly at all. This is the height of efficiency and it is a maximum of output for a minimum of input of energy. Basically it came from the fact of relating to the strings as a tactile entirety rather than as a visual one. It wasted a lot less energy and it ended up making chord positions in a much more efficient manner which has not been copied much by other guitarists unfortunately. It's much easier to play that way and also, although he used intricate counterpoint, he used positioning that always allowed that if you missed the string you were trying to hit, and hit the next one it would always fit in, again because he always stayed within chord positioning. He moved just enough of a finger out of it to get what he wanted. It is the opposite way of looking at left hand technique used in classical guitar and of course, naturally therefore people brought up with that classical kind of fingering would have difficulty relating to his technique. Hardly anyone used it except black guitarists who were brought up non-classically, and if you watch most black guitarists play, it is with a technique that's similar to Rev. Davis. The result is that it would enable you to do counterpoint and syncopated rolls at the same time. In other words there are two lines going on at the same time, a treble, a descending and a bass ascending or vice versa. You could be doing a roll hitting the other things in the chord, which meant that you had virtually three things going on at the same time, in the same guitar lines which is really incredible. Another thing that Davis did with the guitar which has not been much imitated is that he used the guitar as if it were an entire band.

He would use all these different instrument imitations but it was more than just an imitation, he'd play his lines lifted from bass instruments in a band. The treble lines are not guitar treble lines as such but treble lines lifted from the higher instruments, the trumpets, clarinets, and other mostly wind instruments, and brass instruments in the band, and the result of this was a much larger sound of the guitar. It sounds like a whole band, it sounds so large, fantastically large sound on the guitar. It was from using lines that really should have been written for large instruments and this is something that was marvellous in its time.

I think that's what people have most to learn from what Davis himself learnt over a long period, is how large an instrument, how significant an instrument, the guitar can be made into when you have nothing else playing with you and it was the reason he'd never played with many people because he'd had all the parts down himself and if other instruments came in they just interfered.

As for Davis himself, one of the things I noticed when meeting him for the first time, I painfully realised when I chauffeured him was that when he's on the road he never sleeps. He sleeps but he doesn't sleep like normal human beings, he takes cat-naps, five, ten minutes then he's up again, which means if you're taking care of him, driving him around, leading him around you have to be up twenty-four hours a day. This is why I almost wrecked his car a couple of times because of lack of sleep. I once had a rather harrowing experience coming down the turnpike, leading into New York, a very winding road in deep fog and me not having had any sleep for thirty-six hours, the Reverend snoring away next to me. I was thinking, "Will I survive this? Will I be guilty of murdering the Reverend Davis?" but fortunately no such luck!

He smoked a pipe, he smoked Prince Albert tobacco and he would fill his pipe up until it was well overflowing and therefore when it was lit all kinds of burning tobacco spilled on to the rug and started minor brush fires around! This again is non-visible to him so it didn't matter and yet a lot of things were not so non-visible to him. He could pick up a guitar and tell you what colour it was by feeling it. The Russians did the most work on tactile visual colour sense. He could tell you not only what kind of guitar it was, which is easy enough to do, but what colour it was or what colour anything else he touched was. He also had a sort of second sense of what was happening. I remember driving alongside a lake, to our left and he just suddenly said, "Oh, tell me isn't that a beautiful lake over there", again I nearly wrecked the car!

Of course being blind he was very worried about being ripped off, which he had been a number of times. He told me a wonderful story of when he was sleeping somewhere in North Carolina in some kind of flop house. He always carried a knife; he said that once while sleeping, he felt this hand creeping under his pillow where he had put his wallet. He grabbed the hand and said, "What do you want?" and the fellow said, "Well I don't want nothing, I'm sorry, I didn't mean anything". Rev. Davis said, "What you want?" while sticking his knife near the guy's throat. "I was just trying to take your money but I didn't mean nothing", and Davis said that he took his hand out held it down on the floor and said, "Well you're not goin' to steal again", and then he made this simple gesture which was quite visible where the shock value lies in pretending to stab his knife through the cat's hand, which put me in some amount of horror!

I never really experienced how quick he was with a knife until the second day of the recording session when I was supposed to give him his five hundred dollars; he wanted to be paid in cash only. So I got five one hundred dollar bills and he said I don't want to be paid out here, let's go back to the closet. There weren't any closets so we went back into the men's room and when we got in there and I took out the five bills and gave them to him, and I said to him, "You know Gary, I got you all alone here man, giving you all this money all I have to do is rip you off" and he said, "You won't do that" and I looked down and there was a knife at my throat and I said, "You're right Gary I won't!"

Well, a nice story was told by one of the people at his funeral. Two weeks before his death he was shopping around, he wanted to buy a church. Although he had been an associate minister at a church in the Bronx for all the time that he'd been in New York, he had never had his own church. He felt that this was his life's mission so he took this younger cat who was evidently taken under his wing, his ministerial wing rather than his musical one and they went and found this store front type church. He said that Rev. Davis went and paced it off and says, "Well it looks like it's about 200ft by 100ft, I guess, by 50ft", he had paced it off each way and he had made some noises to see how the acoustics were and he'd say, "Well this looks like it". He went and put down the money for it. He bought the church, and he said that he had told the younger cat that he had made it now that he had done what he came here for; he'd finally built a church for God and that he was ready to go, ready to move on. Two weeks later he died.

I used to plumb him for data on early guitar development. The only thing I really got of significance was that I got him to play a lot of other people's material. It is interesting how he'd change it or not change, but the one thing I got from him, that maybe other people did also was the source of "Candyman" because "Candyman" really was the only song he does that's really early guitar style. He told me that he'd learnt it in 1905, which would make him nine years old. A man came strolling through his town in South Carolina and that he'd play this song and he said this is exactly how he played it. Rev. Davis said that was the big hit of the year, everybody was playing "Candyman". That it places in terms of guitar styles really way back, and there's really no record of guitar styles at that time.

I found out very quickly that most of Davis's students cowered before him as "the master", you know, but he was into "bullying" people around a good deal. He liked to be stood up against and socked back in quite physical terms. If he was giving you a hard time you'd say don't give me any of that Reverend and punch him or something in that order and he'd really get into that and he'd punch you back and get into wrestling matches. I never knew any man his age that could squeeze the life out of you, a bear hug from the Reverend could asphyxiate a man.

One of the problems of performance in general with him was that he'd never really get into gear unless there was some real communication, either real communication or super large audience who just adored him because he was a super egotistical cat and he really fed off praise. If it was a roaring audience in praise of him he would do fantastic work but that's the natural performer and otherwise his biggest performances were really at his church where he would do fantastic things where again they were right in tune with him.

John Townley

Rev. Davis taught me, by example, to completely throw out my preconceptions of what can or can't be done on the guitar.

-Bob Weir

The Reverend's music has channelled my life profoundly since I was first introduced to it by Ian Buchanan in 1960. I was 20 years old then and I am now 51. I never had the intense one on one experience that Ian, Stefan, or Book Binder did but thanks to Ian's intervention I was able to immerse myself in the man and his music during the several months I spent in NYC in 1960 working in a hospital at an Antioch College Co-op job.

After I moved to California the next year, I never failed to see the Rev. every time he came to the Coast and for some reason he always remembered me and took a few moments to ask about my well-being and to show me a few more tricks. Even in the twilight of his life when he was no longer as powerful, the strength of his soul was undeniable. To this day, the opening bars of "Death Don't Have No Mercy" off that "Harlem Street Singer" Album still gives me goose bumps and given the right set of circumstances can move me to tears.

That's about it. A brief but not inconsequential relationship. Ian Buchanan was a prime mover in my life, but the sword he wielded was the Reverend. I love and miss them both!

Jorma Kaukonen

•

I thought Rev. Gary Davis was absolutely the best American overall guitarist. He's a total genius. If he had sight he would have been more than a genius. He was crying about the state of things through his material but he never grovelled.

Danny Kalb
(Courtesy - Hoot!, Robbie Woliver, St Martin's Press, 1986)

Back in the early sixties the good Reverend made frequent house calls at the Ash Grove – the now legendary Hollywood folk club. Between gigs he just sat in a rented room with his wife and smoked cigars. He sat there with nothing to do...very bored, like kind of grumpy. And you could pay him five dollars and either talk to him or sit quietly - he would play or you would play. Of course, he had all these songs, and they went about the same way each time. So you could take a close look at some of these tunes and some of these moves on the guitar. And you would sit in front of the guy and play it back to him and he would say, "yes" or "no" or whatever.

I'd go home and I had no idea what happened. Then a month later it began to come back and you could possibly retain some of it. But it turned out it wasn't about the lesson or the guitar music, it was just about sitting with this guy who really was something and not anything like anybody I knew in Santa Monica.

Ry Cooder
(Courtesy Rod Campbell, Folk Roots, February, 1993)

•

Thinking back to when Reverend Davis passed on - I was up in Rhode Island and I called up my room-mate, Woody, to see what was happening and he told me that Reverend Davis was gone. I drove down that day and I remember I got down to the house the day that it was full with all kinds of relatives come down from North Carolina and South Caroline and I came in and sat around with the rest of them. Sister Davis was in her bedroom and I could hear her crying some. After

New York City, circa 1958/59, Courtesy of Stefan Grossman's Guitar Workshop, Inc.

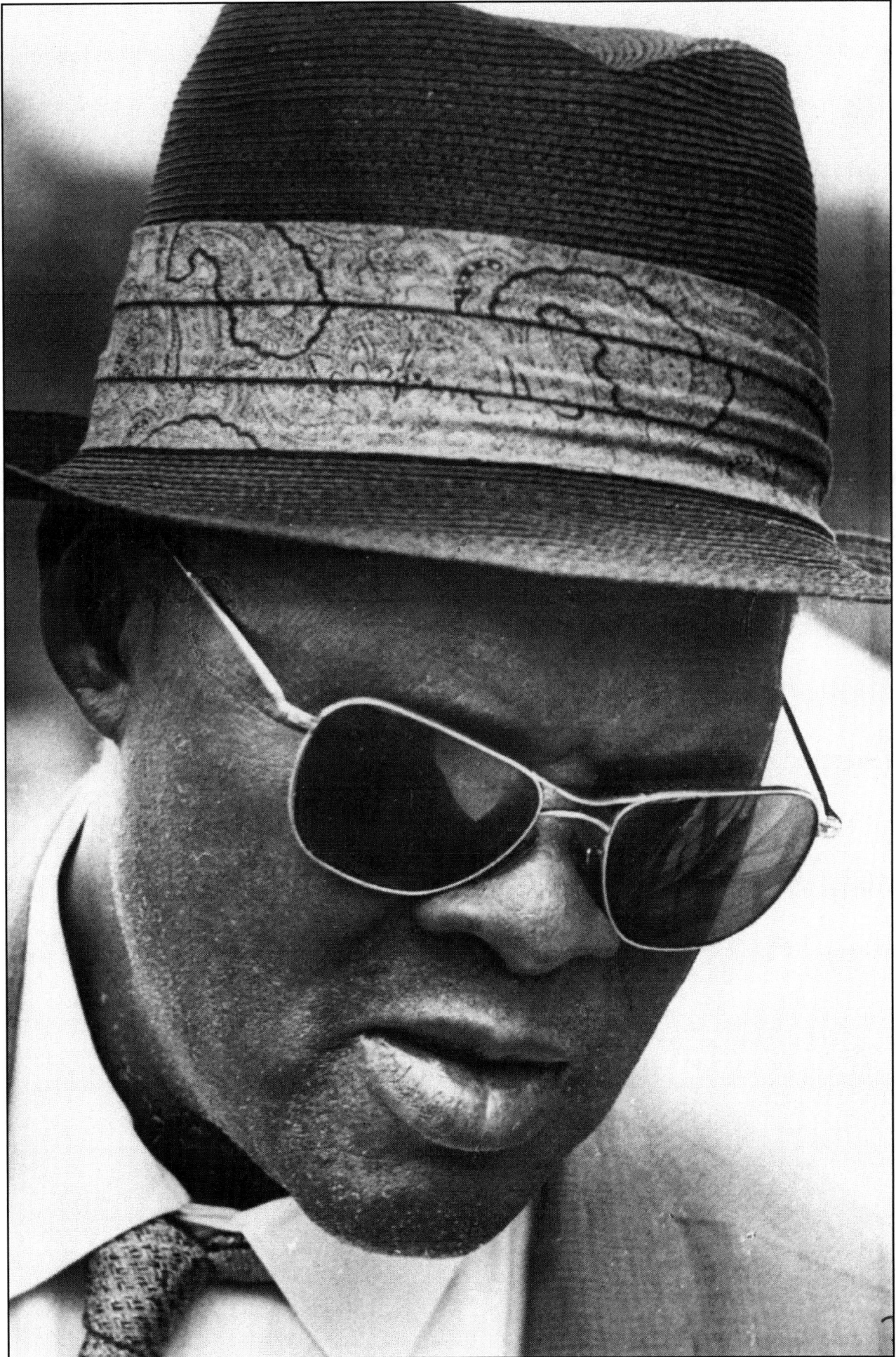

Diana Davies, 1964, Courtesy of the Center For Folklife and Cultural Heritage, Smithsonian Institute, USA

a while Sister Davis came out and I walked over to her and embraced her and we looked at each other and she said to me, "Roy, the best friend that we ever had is gone". And we both broke up and we were bawling like babes. I'll remember that as long as I live - "Roy, the best friend that we ever had is gone".

Reverend Davis was a good friend; he gave me more than anybody. I look back now and I wouldn't be here where I am today if I hadn't known Reverend Davis. He taught me to pick a guitar, and knew about different people on the road - "Watch out for this, watch out for that" - and taught me how to keep on looking up, and things always worked out.

Reverend Davis was a great man. A lot of people remember different things about him. I just remember a friend that I could sit and talk to about anything from politics to religion.

Roy Book Binder

●

Soon my work will all be done
Soon my work will all be done
Soon my work will all be done
I'm going home to live with my Lord

"You know," he said several minutes later, "when you come to that line, 'soon my work will all be done', that song reaches to a streak of gladness".

Alex Shoumatoff

●

During 1969 I went to see Rev. Gary Davis at the Quiet Night club in Chicago - it was a magical concert. He performed wonderfully, and I was in awe of his incredible skill and words would fail me when I saw him walk on to the stage - he was overwhelming, and I felt the world looked much better after hearing him play. There were so many blues players about at that time where their music was about darkness but with Rev. Gary it was all about joy!

I really wanted a lesson from him - just one song so that I could tell everyone for the rest of my life that I learnt it from "The" Rev. Gary Davis! Rev. Davis was staying next door to me with a friend Henry Moore - so I knocked on the door, went in and there was Rev. Davis fully clothed, fast asleep on the bed, and in a chair near by was Roy Book Binder, who was travelling with him.

I said to Roy, himself a player that I greatly admire, that I would like a lesson and he said that he would wake the Reverend up. I replied no let him sleep - I really did not want to be the one to wake him up! So Roy generously taught me "Hesitation Blues" and I was overjoyed to have learnt the song from Roy, who in turn learnt it from the great man himself, and I have been telling the whole world ever since!

Eddie Holstein

●

Years later one can look back at the generosity of B. Davis whose immense patience during lessons helped us absorb much of his music. It was a life's thrill to be honoured in having him as a teacher and witness him imparting such exquisite music. It was overwhelming enough to be able to capture and master the notes. Now, only now when it is too late, does the thought dominate: how did he compose and arrange his works? The absolutely ingenious construction of his religious pieces in C major, when scrutinized, impress as having a guitar part resembling the interlocking gear mechanism of a watch. All the accents, anticipated bass notes and the three part texture (bass, middle voice, high voice - in addition to his voice) were carefully crafted, not a minute detail by chance or out of place. How did he develop this style, a complexity of which no other guitarist or scarcely even any jazz pianist from this time possessed? If only we could have asked him how on earth did his ear lead him to place an A - flat 7 chord before going to the tonic of A minor in Children of Zion! Such an ingenious solution to a musical cadence bespeaks a profound musical sophistication, and this is but a mere detail from the hundreds of songs, each bearing such thought and ingenuity. Davis was as much a composer as an arranger, for even when he adapted a trite ditty such as Cocaine Blues, he transformed it into a profound musical statement. If we could have some hours with him now to ask how he made such poor threads into the finest caftan. His art stands outside of time or being dated, like much of the folk scene, which reflected the impulses of a moment and the need to separate from a society growing further and further into standardization by putting on country clothes.

John Coltrane commented that he was just "dipping into the reservoir". This was Davis's base, a long life of listening and recollection of everything he heard, drawing on it analytically to refer to in his music and to shape it in his own voice. As much as we admired his unique genius in playing the guitar and leonine voice, we ought to try, even from such an impossible distance, to crawl inside his thoughts and place ourselves in his act of making a fine mechanism which guided each piece, thinking it over with such rapidity that all was in place, and in no time, for he is ever the surprise to us, now as great a composer as performer.

Allan Evans

●

Back in 1963, I had just started playing country blues, and was getting guitar lessons from any bluesman that would hold still long enough, including Mississippi John Hurt and Rev. Gary Davis. Usually I managed to corner them backstage at gigs, and was persistent enough to get them to show me a lot of stuff. Of course they were being very kind to me in the bargain!

One night, I went to a coffee house in Philadelphia called "The Second Fret" to hear Rev. Davis perform. "Backstage" that was really upstairs, up a tight spiral staircase, with just enough room for one person at a time to pass. Now, as the Reverend was coming down the stairs, an attractive young woman was trying to go up. As she approached Rev. Davis, she piped, "Scuse me, Reverend!" He at once reached out and accurately seized her by the buttocks, saying, "Did you say, 'Squeeze me, Reverend?, ignoring her as she pushed past him. He then turned and seized the next person coming up the stairs in the same manner, who cried out, "Reverend, I'm a guy!" Rev. Davis did not immediately remove his hand, saying "When you're blind, boy it don't make no difference!"

Rick Blaufeld

•

I was truly struck by Reverend Gary's willingness to allow this young (at that time, the late 1960's) photographer to take his picture, out in back of the Lion's Share. My daughter, Meegan (9 at the time), was enchanted with him, as she posed dancing at his side. He was a very dear man.

Alice Ochs

•

The first time I heard him was a shock I will never forget. I still cannot believe the things that man could do. He was unquestionably a genius, and he became my idol, my guitar guru. It took me a while to assimilate any of his techniques, but he was certainly the strongest single influence on my playing.

Dave Van Ronk
(The Mayor of MacDougal Street,
Elijah Wald, Da Capo Press, 2005)

•

New York, 1964

First, the long subway ride, then, the stares from the locals… what were city folk doing venturing so far out of town? This was rural Bronx, with little wooden houses on scrubby lots, trees and beat-up sidewalks. This was a pilgrimage to a sacred land. Inside there was always the element of soft lighting - a warm glow from a small lamp with a tilted shade - a beautiful, burnished bronze cast to the room…the flavour of an old house from another era, walls adorned with framed plaques reading "God Bless This Home", doilies gracing the arms of threadbare easy chairs, the greyish haze from a cigar, a room filled with too many salvaged and cherished things to fit into one small space, cosier and more wonderful than ever - filled with sweetness and profound meaning to a fourteen year old girl who had already dedicated her life to playing and living inside this absolutely mystical, overwhelmingly meaningful music, blues - one guitar, one voice, one thumping heart and a soul so powerful it could speak straight to God.

Holding court was the magnificent Reverend. With his Jumbo in hand, he danced across the strings with a smile so sly that his mocked irritation was a blessing. On the one hand were the jokes, the flood of wise cracks that always brought a chuckle or a belly laugh, then the reprimands, and your fingers turned to jelly before the master. He growled, he cajoled, he sang with his throaty, raw voice, Gospel tinged with blues, blues coated with Gospel til his wife entered the room, dish towel in hand, to remind him that he was not to digress into the devil's music. This was Reverend Gary Davis's house, this was everything that mattered, this was blues to me in 1964.

Rory Block
2007

•

He would always get angry at me 'cause I would always take off his hat and pat his head and call him "Reverend John" and he hated the name John. He would insist I had the Devil in me! Because only the Devil would call somebody by their wrong name. Which would wind up with him playing the guitar, asleep, only to wake up and say that I don't know how to take care of him! That he wanted to go back to New York

where people knew how to do what he wanted. But I always had Mrs Davis on my side so I could "shut him up!" His main objection was that my hands were too gentle. He said "you don't have real hands". But what are you going to say to somebody like that when you're twenty years old and all they do is complain about what you're doing wrong…which seems to be a trait of that generation always hollerin' at me as if they were my father. Of course, from their heart because they wanted me to get how they played. Of course being a young black kid trying to play that shit they felt as though they had the right to tell me what to do - culturally thinking. And of course I was afraid to complain, because it was culture, and they were "seniors". But of course I'm sixty-six now and I'm not complaining! But that's just the dues that we had to pay. Me, Louisiana Red and Larry Johnson which is probably why we're all crazy today. Unable to play a song without "ghosts" standing around us, pointing their finger.

"Philadelphia" Jerry Ricks
2007

•

Rev. Gary Davis' music was the kind of music I heard as a youth on the streets of Meridian (MS) on Saturday mornings. These blind men had only one source of making a living… before Social Security and other disability programs were enacted…and that was playing for tips on Saturdays.

Rev. Davis, who gave up for a Christian ministry, was a giant of this genre of musicians. His music influenced countless young guitarists in the 1960's and 1970's. Like Ishmon Bracey who would not play any blues in his church going wife's presence, Rev. Davis separated the evils of the blues lifestyle from that of his Christian calling. But he also tutored such protégés as Roy Book Binder and others when possible.

The good reverend would have only been another of a long list of successful blues musicians from the East Coast if he pursued his original career. But his ability to record and compose gospel material gave him a wider following and a broader following in American music.

Gayle Dean Wardlow
2007

•

He would pull out his gun and show it to me, and one time, as diffidently as I could, I said, "You know Gary, you are blind. Don't you think maybe it's not such a good idea…" He said "If I can hear it, I can shoot it."

Dave Van Ronk
(Courtesy - The Mayor of MacDougal Street,
Elijah Wald, Da Capo Press, 2005)

•

It was during one of my lessons with the Rev. at his house in Long Island, (circa 1967), that he fell asleep with a lit cigar in his mouth and burned a piece of binding on the top of his J-200N. Although there was no structural damage to the guitar, he was very upset about it.

Some months later, while he was doing a series of gigs in and around Detroit, Michigan (my hometown) two friends, Rick Meltzer and Lewis Ross, and I took Gary to the Gibson Guitar

Surbiton, London, UK, 1965, Surrey Comet

Factory in Kalamazoo, Michigan to get the binding replaced. The Gibson repair tech informed us that, "We don't repair tops. We replace them". We left and to the best of my knowledge, the burn was never repaired. If not for the music of Rev. Gary Davis, there would be no such thing as the music of Rick Ruskin.

Rick Ruskin
2007

●

I was 14 years old and just discovering girls. And roots music. One day they came into conflict.

I had a "date" (whatever that meant at the time) to meet a girl in Downtown Boston. But Reverend Gary Davis, who was staying at the house, was sitting on the living room couch playing his Gibson J-200. A cigar dangled from his mouth, a cup of "sanctified" coffee close at hand. I kept trying to leave, but somehow could not bring myself to walk out of earshot.

This went on for some time, until the phone rang. It was the girl, waiting for me. I tried to explain, but since I couldn't understand the situation myself, it must have been pretty incoherent. Finally she asked me to turn down the radio so she could hear me better. But it wasn't the radio; it was Davis, weaving his musical web.

The relationship with the girl didn't progress much further. The relationship with Reverend Davis's music has endured through the succeeding 48 years.

Mitch Greenhill
2007

As to Gary Davis…I didn't know the man, but we shared the same manager Manny Greenhill) early on in my career. The thing I remember about Gary was his logical approach to the fingerboard…choosing positions to work out where he didn't have to skip up and down the neck…just across it. This must be common for blind performers. But more uniquely, I would think, was his ability to make an 'out of tune' guitar play in tune. If you handed him a perfectly in tune guitar, he would make little changes which would've normally produced some ugly sounds. But then, when he started to play, it would be miraculously in tune…from his squeezing and cajoling of the strings. And of course you already know about the time on Martha's Vineyard where he pulled out his gun to get paid at George Papadopoulis' club…turning slowly around… threatening to shoot anyone who moved…he got paid.

Geoff Muldaur
2007

Gary and Tom (Hoskins) became the party animals of the tour, ready to hang out with fans, preferably female, long past the time everyone else had gone to bed. With young admirers at his feet, Gary would get out his guitar and Tom would load up the pipe and score a bottle of scotch. The music would continue until the noise drew complaints from next door or until Tom had made sufficient eye contact with one of the girls to bring the proceedings to a close. (UK Tour 1964)

Joe Boyd
(Courtesy - White Bicycles: Making Music in the 1960's, Serpent's Tail, 2006)

I was born and raised in Washington, DC and started playing guitar at age 12 years old, and a few years later, bass guitar, in a wonderful and varied environment in and around Washington. I met Jorma Kaukonen, a few years older, during a record listening session, with my older brother, Charles in 1958.

With Meegan Ochs, 1968, Alice Ochs

We formed a band during Jorma's last year of high school, and in 1959, Jorma then went to Antioch University, Yellow Springs, Ohio, to continue his schooling. During his second year, he worked during the summer in New York City, as part of that school's work furlough programme. That summer of 1960, at age 16, I took the DC-NYC train 225 miles up along the east coast, to New York City to visit him for a couple of weeks, hang out and listen to music in the Big Apple! Of course it was an exciting time for me, away from home and on my own. Upon arriving in NYC, and taking the Subway Transit System for the first time, I remember approaching the subway entrance at Penn Street, abruptly stopping at the sight of a fellow emerge up and onto the sidewalk, with a quite large knife sticking out of this chest, spinning once round and falling over down at my feet. I do remember calling for help, and noticing that people just continued walking on, over, and around this poor fellow. Help did arrive later on, I do believe. Welcome to New York!

After meeting up with Jorma Kaukonen, we started making the rounds of various clubs and music scenes. One of these trips took us to see the great Reverend Gary Davis. He was playing at Gerde's Folk City. I had not had the chance to see him, in the DC area, as he did not travel much. It is one thing to hear the man sing and play guitar on record, but to get to see him was one of the thrills of my lifetime. His performance was so captivating...intricate counterpoint, as well as the melodic and rhythmic approach weaving throughout his singing was like no other. He was able to make the guitar sound so full...huge, as if he were playing in the approach of a piano. Full moving bass lines, jumping from a rhythmic to linear melodies all up and down the neck. Just an amazing amount of musical ideas completed during one passage. Far and above the average blues guitar stylistic approach. And then, that voice. The power and sincerity of his vocal just nailed you to your seat. After that night, I was never the same again! Thank you Rev.

Jack Casady
2007

●

"I was happiest or let's say more fulfilled working with people who really needed attention", he recalled. "And I mean sometimes physical attention. Three of the people I managed were blind, for example. There's no doubt that I had to be there, you know.
...Some of our greatest performers and composers were illiterate people. I'm speaking about Rev. Gary Davis, for example,.... who you have no reason to expect that kind of flowering of music from – even poetry...To me it was the most fascinating part of the business and so I gravitated towards that."

Manny Greenhill
(Courtesy - Folklore Productions, the First Fifty Years, 2007)

●

"Reverend Davis," Leona Greenhill recalls, "would like you to 'sanctify' his coffee, in the morning, which meant to put a little hard liquor in it. He was very proud of his big belly that indicated that he could afford to buy food and eat." And it was a very important day when he was able to purchase his own home, in Queens.

Leona Greenhill
(Courtesy - Folklore Productions, the First Fifty Years, 2007)

●

I first met Rev. Davis in 1963, at the Philadelphia Folk Festival. I was blown away by his guitar playing, and asked him if he would show me some of his tunes. Though I had no money to offer him, he agreed to teach me whenever he was in Philadelphia, which was fairly frequently, as he played often at the Second Fret, a coffee house that featured many of the legendary bluesmen of the day. For the next two years, I often had the privilege of sitting at Rev. Davis' feet, between sets at the Second Fret, while he showed me one amazing guitar lick after another.

He would often let me play Miss Gibson, his J-200, which seemed really easy to play after fighting it out with my warp-necked Silvertone... finally I got a decent guitar, a little Martin O-15. Most of what Rev. Davis showed me was beyond my ability to play at the time, but it remained stored away in my memory, and I was able to remember much of it in later years, as my ability increased. Now 40 some years later, every time I play one of his songs, I'm mentally listening to him playing it. I will always think of him with awe and gratitude!

Rick Blaufeld
2007

●

Rev. Gary Davis, one of the wizards of modern music... like he'd been raised upright and was watching over things, keeping constant vigilance over what was happening.

Bob Dylan
(Courtesy - Chronicles Volume One, Simon & Schuster, 2004)

●

He was a real woman's man. He enjoyed a drink or two with the young ladies. He lived up on some desolate street with his wife, and he loved coming down to the Village to play. For us it was like bringing a master. If he had a few drinks, he really enjoyed himself. He enjoyed being out.

Charlie Rothschild
(Courtesy - Hoot!, Robbie Woliver, St Martin's Press, 1986)

●

He was an incredibly patient teacher when the mood was on him. Being blind, he had difficulty describing what it was he was doing, so his method was to play a thing over and over again, slow it down so you could see just where his fingers were going, and he would correct you by ear. He did not mind if it took two hours to get one lick across. On the other hand he could be very irascible and unpredictable at times, so you would work on his lick or whatever it was, and a few days later you would run into him and play it, and he would growl at you, "Man, you're stealing my stuff."

Dave Van Ronk
(Courtesy - The Mayor of MacDougal Street,
Elijah Wald, Da Capo Press, 2005)

●

...he wanted to be paid in cash, in private, $500, can you believe it? And I had to borrow it from my partner. So we went to the bathroom where I handed him five one hundred dollar bills. As I gave them to him, I jokingly said, "You are out of sight, a poor blind man, I could steal it all," at which moment, I suddenly felt the gentle but firm tip of a stiletto beneath my chin. We both broke down into hilarious laughter...

John Townley
(Courtesy - Adelphi Records, 1996)

•

During the intermission she (Sister Rosetta Tharp) asked for an offstage microphone when Gary sang 'Precious Lord'. 'I don't want to take away anything from him,' she said. I coiled the mic cable and left it beside her in the wings as Gary came out to the start of the second half. When he picked out the opening chords of 'Precious Lord', Rosetta began to moan. She was back in that little country church in Arkansas with her Mother, singing in a primitive style I had never heard from her. Gary lifted his head and murmured, 'Oh Lord, sing it, girl!' Her interjections seemed to transport him to another time and place, re-creating music that few white people had ever been privileged to hear. (UK Tour 1964)

Joe Boyd
(Courtesy - White Bicycles: Making
Music in the 1960's, Serpent's Tail, 2006)

•

I guess the first taste of Rev. Davis would have been from Ramblin' Jack Elliot - certainly on the album, Jack Takes the Floor - "Cocaine Blues", beautiful old style picking. Then, I suppose, the Doug Dobell album - Pure Religion and Bad Company. Wonderful stuff, emulated right down to the photo on the cover.

I can distantly remember actually paying money for a pair

Signing autograph, Jersey, UK, August 1971, Robert Tilling

of little steel rimmed specs in the Paris flea market. The quest for those shoes is ongoing... (The album cover photograph shows Rev. Davis wearing an interesting pair of shoes - RT)

So, when I heard he was playing in London it had to be done. Don't remember the year but word came to The Cousins in Greek Street that evening. He was appearing at the Singers Club - Ewan McColl's, way across town and I was skint. So it meant walking. A young man with a mission. I got there at half time - the interval. People were milling about so I just wandered in and sat down in a conveniently empty seat right at the very front. It caused a bit of a commotion when the dignitaries returned but as the show was about to start nothing too drastic happened.

Then I remember hearing a sort of snuffly sound right behind me - like an old bulldog. I looked round and there he was. As he was called up he dropped his cigar. I got it. It became my treasure, like a saint's relic. Some old chewed thing with a wooden end.

Well, the playing was amazing. There he was, right in front of me. Funny old off-white baggy suit, big Gibson guitar, held high at an odd angle, swaying and rocking gently to the great, great songs: "Death Don't Have No Mercy", "Twelve Gates", "Blow Gabriel" - I could hardly believe it.

I suppose I should mention that on the journey over I'd met a small bunch of brother long-hairs. They were smoking a certain something, and I got some too. It was good stuff and still working in the system. I can remember being fascinated by the old man's eyes - they wandered independently behind the opaque lenses, strange and hypnotic. Maybe I slipped a little lower in my chair, drawn up and transfixed by the weird eyes. Blam! Suddenly it all stopped mid-song and the eyes descended. A croaky old voice said, 'I'm a country boy. I'm a country boy. I'm not a city boy. I don't go round stealing another man's music.'

It was a moment that still haunts me. A ghastly wrench back to reality. The well-known 'swallow me up please, mother Earth.' Well, it didn't end the world and later I got to say hello back at Gina Glazer's place. The great man was nicely relaxed, I remember, drinking hot tea with some whiskey on the side. 'Why hello there, Missy Tea,' he would say, 'I'd like you to meet Missy Whiskey. I know you gonna be friends.' Tip, tip, tip, sip, sip.

It was clear the Reverend enjoyed drinking and it was a pleasure to be there just to witness it. He had a character with him whose job was to drive him home. That guy didn't share any of the enjoyment. He reached the eyes raised to heaven stage early. But with the taste of whiskey in him the Reverend acted very well disposed. We talked and he showed me some of his wonderful two-finger runs and raggy turn-arounds. I had a little go at trying out the harmony on Gina's piano. He loved that and told me he was going to take me along to be his piano player. It must have been good whiskey because I can't play the piano. It seems to me that he was a man with great spirit. I know that he left us some beautiful songs and guitar pieces but there are some sermons out there that I don't think have ever found their way onto record – and that stuff is really on another level.

John Renbourn
2007

At home, 1970, Woody Mann

•

The highest compliment a musician can receive is to be recognized by his or her 'sound' and once you've heard Rev. Davis there will be no mistaking his signature singing or playing 'voice'.

It's entirely fitting and appropriate that Rev. Davis favoured his Gibson J-200 guitar since he played so big.

Mike Dowling
2007

•

I was one day out of high school in Pittsburgh, 1965, when I moved to NYC to call on the Rev. I had his phone number: AX 1-7609. The first thing I did after getting a room up on 98th Street, was call him, introduce myself and get directions. He directed me to Queens where he had a kind of shabby little record store. There were a few gospel 45's on the wall. He was in the back asleep in an overstuffed chair, looking very small. I didn't know what to do so I just sat there for a while, looking at him thinking, wow, I'm sitting here in front of Rev. Gary Davis. I think I finally must have said something and he woke up, really startled, and started yellin' and whoopin', thinking that some one was robbing him. I ran back out on to the street and waited for him to calm down a little. "It's me Ernie, who called you about a lesson." He got quiet, listening, leaned forward and asked, "Did you bring your money?"

That day he straightened me out on "Oh Glory" (he dictated the words, as it had not yet been recorded, and made me sing along), and "Slow Drag". I was clueless about "Fast Fox Trot" and I asked him to play it. He chuckled, and when he played it, it seemed as though he hardly moved his left hand, playing those lines against each other effortlessly. A revelation.

I spent a lot of time with him in New York and Pittsburgh, and driving him places. The last time I saw him before his funeral was in Pittsburgh in 1970. I brought him and Annie in for my wedding. He performed his preacherly duties solemnly and sweetly. He taught me "Will there be Stars in my Crown" as a kind of wedding present. It was raining some that day and I remember Annie saying "When it rains on your wedding day, that's how many tears you will shed".

Ernie Hawkins
2007

•

When I first saw Rev. Gary Davis I had no idea who he was. I had only been playing guitar for about two years. I saw him play in a local church basement - an old man was being led to the stage by two young boys - he was late! The audience was restless. He sat down on the stage with his dark glasses reflecting the few stage lights. He sat alone in silence and tuned his guitar - his hand was shaking and I really wondered if he was going to make it and then a clown yelled out "Play your guitar!" To which he replied, and I shall never forget it, "I'm just waiting for someone to introduce me!"

73

Someone came out hurriedly from behind the curtain and said "Ladies and Gentlemen - Rev. Gary Davis" and he lurched immediately into 'Death Don't Have No Mercy'. I was on the edge of my seat. I will never forget it, there was a lot of energy in that room that night.

Larry Conklin
2007
(Last concert by Rev. Davis, Northport, NY – April 1972)

•

Rev. Davis once told me not to worry about success in the music world, because, as he said (as best as I can recall), "When they want you, they'll come knocking on your door". Another, sadder, anecdote. I used to hang out with him. He would stay, usually, at my brother's house and would have plenty of time on his hands. One day he told me that he needed a shave, so we got in my car and drove to a barbershop in the area near Los Angeles City College. I was quite naïve about racial prejudice in my hometown in those days, the early sixties, and honestly couldn't put two and two together when the barber, seeing who it was needing the shave, told me that he didn't do shaving at his shop. I was honestly surprised and was fairly pleasant in my response, "Really?" He said no, he just did haircuts, with a smile on his face, and we left. I told Gary that I'd never heard of that, and as I remember, he just smiled and we went home.

It took me a while to understand what had transpired.

Bernie Pearl
2007

•

I first heard Rev. Gary Davis from a recording my older brother had bought back in the mid - 1960's. What struck me about him most was how his vocal and guitar were ONE VOICE (which is true of so many of the great players). Although he is not a direct influence on me as far as guitar style, I have ALWAYS been moved by his playing and singing - his syncopation is amazing to hear and makes me smile when I hear it. As one of the great links back to a very different time, we are lucky to have his music.

Roy Rogers
2007

•

What I remember best, of course, were my guitar lessons. There was only one way to learn - and that was to learn the pieces by rote - on the spot! I had just met this man who was so inspiring, charismatic and at the same time a bit frightening to me. I remember that we sat across from each other on a small landing at the bottom of a set of stairs that led to what seemed to be the basement in the house.

London, 1964, Val Wilmer

74

I quickly understood that the way the lessons worked was to learn the pieces by heart. His blindness precluded the possibility of having him write anything out. I was hardly in a position to write things out, either...though I probably should have tried. I didn't want to sit there with a tape recorder, either. So the lessons were about stuffing the "piece of the day" (I recall it was mostly my choice) into my head and then getting back home as quickly as I could to see what was left in my memory and try to assemble the pieces in my room. Reverend Davis was able to play his tunes incredibly slowly...one note at a time: these pieces were exactly as he intended them to be and seemed a lot more "set" that I had expected they'd be. Anyway, this procedure made it easier to get the notes, but sometimes made it harder to get the over-all feeling. Also, I felt pretty intimidated, even out and out frightened by his appearance - I hadn't had much contact with blind folks, up till that point in my life...of course this was mixed up with my long-standing admiration for his music and feeling honoured to be able to take lessons with him. I was 20...maybe even 21. I should have paid more attention to detail at those lessons. I'd learned a bunch of his pieces already from records or from Stefan Grossman and I thought that I knew more than I actually did.

The only other recollection that pops into my head was being invited, as many of the students were, to a birthday party of Gary's. I was very naïve, and decided to give him a bottle of good champagne for his birthday...I really couldn't think what else to give him. Well, Mrs Davis just pounced on that bottle. She made us (I was there with my girlfriend-at-the-time) take it with us when we left. She was very sweet about it and said: "You youngsters drink that yourselves!" I was extremely embarrassed.

Nick Katzman
2007

•

I was 13 or 14, and I'd been hanging around the fountain at Washington Square on Sundays as often as my parents would let me. I fell in with a crowd of young (well, young to me now, though they seemed old then) guitarists, and somehow one of them took me up to Gary and Miss Annie's home in the Bronx. The fellow who took me seemed a little fazed at going up there; when we first got on the subway, there were a lot of different colors, I wasn't worried; I was living in East Orange, New Jersey, where I was one of four or five white kids in the school system.

I already loved Gary's guitar playing; I'd read an interview with Dave Van Ronk praising him and had grabbed all his records from the local library. To be allowed into his house was, I felt, a great privilege. I wasn't so much interested in learning his guitar pieces (though I did try) as learning his songs, and think that endeared me to him. His wife, who I always called Miss Annie, liked me because I adored her chicken stew. It was the first time I'd had chicken fricassee, and I think I disgraced myself by asking for seconds, then thirds. From then on, whenever I came over, she'd feed me.

Gary was blind, but like most blind people I'd known, he didn't make a deal of it. He always had a "lead boy" when Miss Annie couldn't be there, a student who'd act as his eyes while he manoeuvred around the city. And manoeuvre he did! Always

impeccably dressed, we'd make our way down to Washington Square park with his long big Gibson J-200, and crowds would gather to listen. He testified as he sang, which again wasn't new to me; living in East Orange, almost everyone I knew sang, in and out of church, and most of my friends' grandparents considered music a form of worship.

I wrote more songs, my parents moved to New York, and one night Miss Annie and Gary decided they'd had enough of my babbling about wanting to play a "real show". He was playing at the Gaslight Café that week, and invited me to come along and open the show. When we arrived there, it turned out that no one had thought to discuss this idea with Clarence Hood, the owner, or his son Sam Hood, the manager. Mr Hood (the elder, I never heard him called anything else) was not pleased. He took one look at my under-age self and informed the Davis's that it wouldn't be possible.

Reverend Davis protested, Mr Hood insisted. After a few rounds, Gary, appearing to give up, shrugged and shuffled a few feet away. He appeared to be lost in thought. After another few minutes of Miss Annie and Mr Hood arguing, I likewise moved away, and the Reverend called for Annie to come over. She came, there was a whispered consultation, then she went back to Mr Hood and gravely informed him that The Reverend was not feeling well, and likely wouldn't be able to go on...

Needless to say, I did go on that night, opening for The Reverend Gary Davis in front of a packed house. After my set, I met a fellow who took me to a lawyer who took me to a producer, Shadow Morton. We cut "Society's Child" a few weeks later.

I owe my career to Reverend Davis and Miss Annie.
Janis Ian
2007

•

The Children of Zion

I remember reading somewhere that when he was asked about having never fathered children Rev. Gary Davis replied, "I have many sons and daughters". Whether Rev. Davis ever said these words or not, truer words have never been spoken. I am sometimes struck by the fact that though I never got to meet this man, his music is now such a big part of my life. The fact is that Reverend Davis actually has many grandsons and daughters.

When I first heard one of Rev. Davis' recordings my reaction was probably the same as many others, "Can all this sound be coming out of one guitar?" How can he keep a sophisticated bass line, a chopping middle and an accurate melody going simultaneously? I simply racked up Rev. Davis' playing alongside Lonnie Johnson's and Blind Blake's as "impossible" and moved on. However, life is strange. With time I began to meet and listen to some of Davis' students. About 20 years ago I attended a workshop with Roy Book Binder. He showed us the finger-breaking Gary Davis "G7" chord and I came away with a little bit of "Buck Dance". I met Larry Johnson and I came away with a bit more of Rev. Davis' guitar wisdom. Jorma Kaukonen and I discussed aspects of his playing, and I absorbed as much knowledge as I could from Davis' students like Ernie Hawkins, and Andy Cohen. I learned

becomes his way of duplicating what he is experiencing. The sound of a black church service might start with a sister singing a simple pentatonic melody, but she will soon be joined by other voices, some beautiful and some discordant. Someone will bring in the percussion of clapping and foot stomping, and at some point perhaps the Holy Spirit will bring in the ecstatic sound of "speaking in tongues". Rev. Davis simply had all of these sounds at his disposal. They were in his guitar.

He also conveys the call and response that occurs between the preacher and the congregation in his singing. Notice how Rev. Davis's vocals interact with the guitar. He often chooses keys that seem to stretch his voice to the breaking point; this is what the preacher does in the sermon. This screaming-singing sets the emotional timbre of the song. Like Blind Willie Johnson's gruff vocals, Rev. Davis' singing interacts with the guitar in a way that preaches the song instead of singing it. If you listen to his essentially one chord song, "Sun Goin Down", you'll hear an apocalyptic warning being shouted as a warning to an apathetic world. "There's Destruction In This Land Somewhere" is a sermon reminding us of our own mortality, and Davis' unsurpassed "Crucifixion" is a gospel sermon without many equals.

A lifetime dedicated to exploring the musical possibilities of the guitar gave Rev. Davis a facility and a storehouse of techniques that few contemporary artists could ever hope to match. Rev. Davis was apparently a man of strong opinions. He didn't like slide guitar but "Whistlin' Blues" proves that he was a slide master too. Davis preferred the sound of a Gibson J-200 but his 1935 recordings show that he would've made a National sound just fine. Even though Rev. Davis' music was as serious as his love of scripture he also showed a sense of humour and playfulness in many of his songs. In other words, I think that he enjoyed that art of making the guitar a vehicle for his insights and thoughts.

When I was called to pastor the Sweet Kingdom Missionary Baptist Church in Detroit, Michigan I found myself looking for music that was appropriate to my calling and yet challenging as a musician. The recordings of musicians like Blind Willie Johnson, Joshua White, Elder Roma Wilson, and Sister Rosetta Tharpe started to take on new meaning for me, but nobody's music started to speak to me more than that of Rev. Gary Davis. I think that is when I started to develop the confidence to try Rev. Davis songs in public. Now, when I play his songs I play them my way. Just like in preaching, you're telling a story that has been told millions of times. You'll never tell it better than your predecessors will, you'll just tell it your own way. I don't think that Rev. Davis wanted any of his students to become carbon copies of himself. I think that he wanted them to take his chord shapes, his syncopated bass line, and his driving rhythms as a guideline to what the guitar was capable of. This allowed him to set the highest of standards for even future generations of musicians that he would inspire. In fact, when I started using some of Rev. Davis' chord shapes and techniques as templates for songs (even in songs that he never recorded), I discovered that even the most mundane songs started to sparkle. Some of Rev. Davis' direct students even began to tell me that my playing actually reminded them of the Reverend's. Well, I still don't quite believe that, but I am encouraged by it. There was and will be, ONLY ONE Reverend Gary Davis, but I am

a great deal from all of these players and over time I came to appreciate that Rev. Davis' playing was not impossible, it was just impossible to duplicate.

Eventually I came to realize that Rev. Davis's style could not be duplicated like classical music, in part, because his music represents a living style. Forget about trying to play his stuff, note for note. You'll never get it! Even if you get the notes right, you'll never get the feel. When I stopped trying to figure out the tons of tablature that I had collected, I began to appreciate that Davis was about the business of being open to music that God had given him. The Holy Spirit is always fresh in the way He speaks to us, and Rev. Davis seemed always fresh in his approach to playing.

However, this doesn't mean, "slap it together any way you want". While Davis' playing is always open to variation and improvisation it is also a highly disciplined style. Rev. Davis' chord shapes are among the most challenging things about playing one of his songs, but tied to those shapes is the idea of replicating the sound of the Black Church. The Black Church is polytonal, multi-rhythmic, spontaneous experience. The sound of traditional black church worship is charismatic and has to be open to change. In Rev. Davis' playing is the sound of a man caught up in the Holy Spirit. Also, Rev. Davis' right hand technique, using usually only thumb and forefinger, creates a rhythm that is always strong and driving. Gary Davis music has the characteristic of being chordal and melodic, at the same time! So, as he moves through the song the guitar glad and honoured that I can count myself as one of his many grandsons.

Rev. Robert B. Jones Sr
2007

●

Rev. Davis as a Teacher

Rev. Davis not only played the guitar, he played several other instruments - harp, piano, five and six string banjo. Consider the breadth and depth of his repertoire, the amount of techniques he invented and mastered, his soulful singing and the fact that everything he ever recorded is still in print, from his duets with Blind Boy Fuller to his last Biography recordings. Consider that he founded three churches, and that he was an important lynchpin in the Civil Rights Movement. Consider also that he had a self consciousness about his music that applied a due importance to it, that he recognized it was part of an ongoing tradition, and that the tradition of music making was important, and he knew that.

Now, consider that he was virtually alone both among blues and gospel players in being a self conscious, vocational teacher of the material that he played. As far as I'm concerned, that raises the stakes a notch right there. Rev. Davis did not want his music to go away when he did, and to that end, perhaps without realizing it, he taught his way to immortality as much as played his way there.

Davis the teacher; he taught his older brother to play. He taught for his tuition at the Spartanburg School for the Blind. He undoubtedly exchanged licks with those around him - Willie Walker in Greenville (from whom he learned "Slow Drag", "Make Believe Stunt" and "South Carolina Rag"); Walt Phelps (who learned Candy Man from him); Blind Boy Fuller, "who would have been alright if he had stayed under me"; the Trice brothers (who said "He could play five hundred chords to your two. He never let a string be still"); and Lead Belly and Brownie McGhee. These last two are important, since he taught at the apartment of the one and the school of the other.

Rev. Davis moved to the Bronx in early-mid 1940's, it is not clear exactly when. Almost as soon as he got there, he fell in with Lead Belly, Lead's wife Martha, and his niece, Tiny Robinson. Tiny told me one time that the "white boys were lined up out the door", at Lead Belly's Harlem apartment the days Davis taught there. Indeed, it would be interesting to examine whatever records were kept of those lessons, but there probably weren't any kept. Several years later, from 1948 to

Cambridge Folk Festival, UK, 1971, Nigel Luckhurst

1950, he taught at Brownie McGhee's School of the Blues, also in Harlem.

Teaching was a way of life for Rev. Gary Davis, and many people whom he taught, themselves became teachers. It is more than a way to shore up a meagre living made playing music; it was a mitzvah, a mission, a way in, an open door. I don't think Manny Greenhill ever worried when he handed the Reverend off to someone - bus, train, private car, airplane, horse and buggy - because he knew Davis would get to where he was going, there would be some guitar playing kid on the other end who would be only too happy to sanctify Davis's coffee and sit at his feet, absorbing every lick he could possibly remember.

The net result is that Davis found a school of playing, one student at a time, through his Socratic teaching methods. Hundreds, if not thousands, of his students continue to play, to gig, and to teach his word and methods along with his repertoire. At this point, Gary Davis has not only students, but grand students, great grand students and a few great-greats. It is why I was able to put together a tribute CD for him, which involved a couple of 78's and eighteen other people, some of whom weren't born when he died (Gary Davis Style, Inside Sounds 0508). More than any bluesman or gospel singer on record, Davis left his style in the hands of those who loved and cared for him.

Andy Cohen
2007

•

There was a club called the Golden Vanity in Boston where I used to play, and the Reverend Gary Davis did, too. Carl Bowers, the proprietor, had an interesting sense of business ethics and paid Gary one night with one dollar bills, telling him they were twenties. The next day Gary and his cane came tap-tapping down the sidewalk and in the door. "Where's Carl?" "He's in the office". Tap tap tap. Gary found the office, pulled his pistol on Carl (yes, the Reverend routinely packed iron) and got paid properly. I believe it was the last time he played there. (circa 1961)

Tom Rush
2007

•

Funny how life unravels before you and chooses your path. It was 1961 that I passed by the Folklore Center in Greenwich Village. I headed in and heard the fellow behind the counter playing a tune that grabbed my ears. I asked what the tune was and he said it was "Goin' Sit Down On The Banks Of The River". I asked where he had heard the tune and he said Rev. Gary Davis. This was a new name to me.

The next day I was talking to a friend of mine, Bob Fox, and he suggested I try getting lessons from a blind preacher that lived in the Bronx named Rev. Gary Davis. I was surprised that the Reverend's name had popped up twice in two days and I asked Bob for Rev. Davis's telephone number. I called up after speaking to Bob and a husky voice answered the phone. I asked if this was Rev. Gary Davis and he replied yes. I asked about lessons and he said sure "just bring your money, honey". He gave me his address and reminded me that each lesson would cost $5.00.

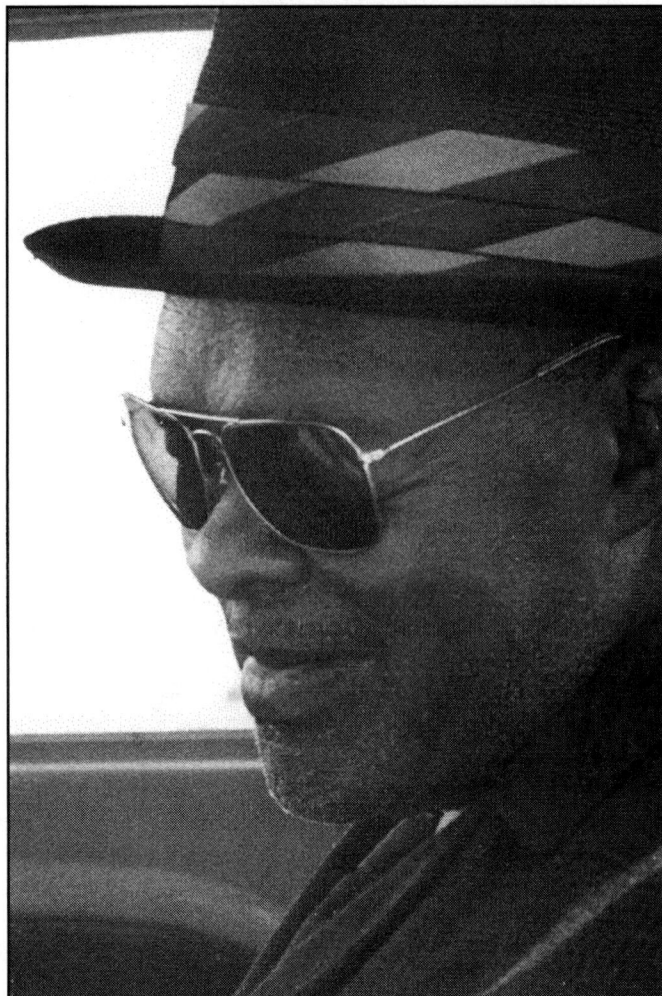

Jersey, UK, 1971, Peter Misson

I mentioned to my folks that the next Saturday I would be going to the Bronx to take a lesson from a blind guitar player. Without dropping a beat my Dad said that he actually had to buy a pair of shoes in that part of the Bronx and he would drive me from our apartment in Brooklyn.

Saturday arrived and we drove to the Bronx. My father was well acquainted with all the neighbourhoods in the five boroughs of New York City as he had a business that delivered laundry supplies to Laundromats. After a good hour drive we approached the street. It was lined with tenement buildings with windows broken and garbage in the streets (reminded me of Kurt Vonnegut's description of Dresden after the Allied bombings that he described in Slaughterhouse Five). I checked the address from my notes but could not find it. I asked a lady hanging out of her first floor window and she directed me down a set of stairs and then through a dark alley and then up some stairs to a shack that stood between the buildings. My Dad walked with me in to this "new world" for this bright-eyed teenager. I knocked at the screen door and a face popped out. It was Rev. Davis. I was taken aback at first as he was not wearing his sunglasses and I could clearly see that one eye had only white while the other seemed to have a bulbous cataract. But Rev. Davis immediately set the tone and asked if "I had brought the money, honey" and invited me inside and told my Dad to come back in a few hours. To this day I have no idea where or what my Dad did for those few hours as there were no shoe stores in that neighbourhood!

This started a long and wonderful relationship. I would travel to Rev. Davis' house each weekend, always by myself or with friends, and would sit taking lessons for hours upon hours at a time. I would lug my heavy Tandberg tape machine to his home, church or to concerts whenever I could to record songs, stories and preaching. If I had love problems I would confide these to Rev. Davis and he would give me advice and even tease me with a song. I would tease him back trying to get him to play, sing and record songs from his childhood that included blues, folk tunes, bawdy songs and the likes. Annie Davis would smile when I was doing this and would say I was the "devil's child" but she loved me just the same.

Rev. Davis had so much music to hear and document and even today, over 40 years since studying with him, I continue to discover new performances by Rev. Davis that I've never heard. A truly amazing musical genius.

Stefan Grossman
2008

●

My memories of B. Davis are as vivid today as they were then. I think about how much patience he had with teaching me and how proud he was as a teacher. We would sit for hours playing a song endlessly until I could just about almost play it. Then he would sit and listen to me struggle with it, jump in with his booming guitar sound and play it again and again until I could almost just about play it again. He would continue the drill until my hands would give out. He was so proud to pass along his amazing music. He'd always say "when you're ready and go out into the world you tell them that I'm your teacher".

My lessons would be full day affairs and a lot more than guitar sessions. There were the stories and advice. One time I wascomplaining about a problem I was having with the principal of my school; "…well, sometimes there's only one thing to do with people like that– I would just whop him up side the head to make him understand. If that doesn't work, just have him call me and I'll take care of it! ". I asked him his advice on how to write music; …"first you take the whole note, then the half then quarter, and the rests - and then you just put it all together…now the melody…well that's another thing."

I taped all those lessons and recently listened to them again. Like it was - Davis playing and singing at full volume, Annie crashing dishes in the background while she is singing along, the neighbors coming and going stepping over the microphone on the floor -.then a lot of laughter.

Presently, I am working on a documentary film about Davis. The more I get into the project I realize again just how original a voice he was as a musician. Being original was important to him. At the time, I thought I was learning guitar tunes. But the main lesson I learned was something he would often say; "…Play what you know… play just what you know…"

Woody Mann
2008

●

Me And The Reverend

So there I was, face to face with the legendary Rev. Gary Davis. We shook hands. His was as soft as a baby's. All he did most of his life was play the guitar. He had no sunglasses on… his eyes were clouded over. I had never looked into a blind man's eyes before. It was definitely spooky, but he seemed to be a friendly old man.

"You got your guitar with you?" he asked. "Yes I do sir," I replied. "What kind of guitar you got there?" "I have a Gibson, a J-200," I told him. "Let me see that thing," he said in an inquisitive high voice. I handed him my jumbo sunburst Gibson. He ran his fingers over the body, the neck and the strings, before strumming a big six finger chord that I had never seen before. "That's a fine guitar you got there," he said. "Go over to that closet and get Miss Gibson out of there," he instructed me. I did so and took it out of its case as he asked me to. "Let's hear what you can do with Miss Gibson," he ordered. I was nervous for sure. I played him some of his "Candyman" song. "Good God Almighty," he exclaimed, "You sound like Dave Van Ronk." He laughed. This was the greatest compliment that I had ever received about my guitar playing!

"I'll straighten you out, don't worry about it," he said. "I never could get Dave Van Ronk to play it right," he told me. Well, we monkeyed around with "Candyman" for hours. The Rev. was very patient, but I was hanging on to the way I played it, it was after all, my best song! I finally learned a few tricks from Gary that I to this day think snazzed up my version of the song, but I do believe neither the great Reverend Davis or my first guitar hero Dave Van Ronk ever approved of my arrangement…but like I always say, "They're both gone, and I'm what's left."

Quite a few hours went by. I was trying to learn "Slow Drag," one of the amazing instrumentals in the Reverend's bag of tricks. He patiently played each small part very slowly and I tried to duplicate the sound. "E string, E string he'd say…that's it. You got it….now play this…" Finally Mother Davis called us up for supper! I knew something was brewing in the kitchen, I was not thrilled with the smells. Dinner was turkey wings and a big pot of 'greens' with big old ham hocks and God knows what else was in there. I was a "vegetarian" of sorts, didn't eat any four - legged animals and forced myself to eat small pieces of meat cut up into tiny pieces, washing it down with lots of water. I never got into the 'soul food' that Mrs. Davis cooked though I did enjoy her fried chicken. Others are still raving about every meal she served!

After dinner, the Rev. stoked up one of his Hava-Tampa cigars and we continued with my lesson until he started dozing off. I excused myself and rushed back to my apartment to see if I remembered my lesson.

I played guitar for hours that night. I couldn't sound like Rev. Davis, but I had gotten down a nice instrumental ragtime tune 'in the style of' Gary's. That night I realized that I would never be able to play like my mentor, and decided that was alright. There were plenty of 'students' who could duplicate his music note for note. Like Dave Van Ronk and my other heroes, I wanted to play it my way and create my own arrangements.

The next day after my school class, I was back at the feet of the master. I informed Mother Davis, that I would have to leave by five. I really wasn't ready to sample another supper from her kitchen yet. The lesson went well. After the Rev. straightened out my "Slow Drag" some, we moved on to "Devil's Dream". My goal was to learn all the ragtime numbers from his Prestige album, The Guitar & Banjo of Rev. Gary Davis. This was my favorite album at the time. I didn't have much interest in learning his "Christian" numbers. I just didn't think that I could perform them with conviction, as they were so dependent on his fiery vocal attack and his belief in God! At this time, I knew that I was going to pursue a career as a guitar playing 'blues guy', in the folk music scene.

By the end of the week, I was back at 109-42, 174 St., taking my third guitar lesson from "Brother Davis." On my way out, the Rev. said, "Don't be comin' by for the next few weeks, I won't be here. "Where are you going?" I asked. "I'm going out on a tour, my manager's sending me out to Detroit to play the Chessmate and to marry up Lorring and Sue and then to Chicago to play at the Quiet Night for a few days. Then I'm going to the Buffalo Folk Festival back in NY and then to Maryland to do a concert at John Hopkins University," he explained.

"I've got fifty dollars saved up," I told him, and "Maybe I can go out on tour with you." Rev. Davis chuckled and said, "Fifty dollars ain't gonna get you very far these days." After struggling through his "Buck Dance" for hours, I was headed out the door when Brother Davis said,"If you wanna go with me, you be here tomorrow morning at 6:30. Bring your $50 and I'll carry you the rest of the way. It's gonna take some time to straighten you out playing that guitar." Without hesitation, I knew that I was going to be there, that I was going on the road with Rev. Gary Davis! I thanked him and headed back to my place, hardly believing that this was not a dream.

Of course it did briefly enter my mind whether dropping out of school and giving up my G.I. Bill benefits was such a smart move. I didn't get much sleep that night and I was packed up and ready to go at the crack of dawn. When I got to Gary's, I knocked on the door. Finally Mrs. Davis answered, "What in the world are you doing here so early in the morning?" she asked. "Rev. Davis said to be here at 6:30 if I wanted to go on the trip," I told her. She laughed and informed me that the train didn't leave until 6:30 at night and that Brother Davis was still asleep. "Well, you come in and I'll fix you some breakfast," she said. Lord, have mercy I thought….

Rev. Lawrence was to take us downtown to Penn Station where we were to catch the 6:30 pm train to Chicago. He showed up around 3pm for lunch. Before we left the house, we all joined hands and a prayer was said for Jesus to watch over us as we made our way West. Promptly on time, the train eased out of the station and me and Gary were headed out on our adventure.

Our journey was expected to take about thirty six hours.

"You can't be makin' up no sermon on Tuesday for next Sunday, it might not hold true, you understand?"
-The Reverend Gary Davis

We were seated in regular seats in a non-smoking car. Rev. Davis, of course wanted to head to the 'smoker' where he could light up one of his favorite cigars. I left him down there, puffing away from time to time throughout the trip. We slept some in our seats as we chugged across the country throughout the night.

During the next afternoon, I left Rev. Davis in the smoking car and headed out to get some coffee. Upon returning, I could hear a heated discussion coming through the smoke filled room.

"Good God Almighty," Rev. Davis shouted, "A man can't go to no college and learn to be no preacher……You can't be makin' up no sermon on Tuesday for next Sunday, it might not hold true, you understand?" He was going at it with a uniformed porter. "Rev. Davis, you better calm down," I said. "Let's go back to our seats." I was worried that he might have a heart attack or something. "Don't hush me up!" he shouted at me……Well, I could take a hint, so I eased myself out of the smoking car, leaving the two of them to finish up what they started.

When we finally got to Chicago, we were met by a kid that drove us over to 'Old Town'. That's where the Quiet Knight was located. We met Richard Harding who owned the club. He and Rev. Davis had worked together before a few times. "Is there a phone call for me?" he asked the boss. "Yes there is Gary", answered Richard. "Long distance?" he wondered. "No Gary, it's just a local call. " "Well let me have it" he said, and then, Richard poured a little whiskey into a glass and handed it to the blind Preacher. Gary said hello into the glass, sniffed it and proceeded to drink it down. After that first gig, I figured out that I was responsible for handling all the "phone calls" for Reverend Davis while we were on tour.

We were shown upstairs to Henry Moore's apartment, which was where we were to stay for the week. After resting up some, we went down the street to get some dinner. The restaurant was just a corner joint with a counter and about ten small tables. The waitress brought us menus. I looked over the menu and read it to Rev. Davis. When the gal came back to take our order, I ordered a chicken sandwich with fries and a coke. "And what will you have sir?" she asked Gary. "I'm gonna have the pork chops," he replied. "Would you like peas or carrots?" "Are the peas greasy?" he inquired. "Absolutely not!" she told him. "Well, I'm just gonna have the carrots then"…… As the waitress leaned over the table, Gary nipped at her arm! She walked away in a huff. "Just wanted to taste the meat," he said to me…a waiter brought us our dinner!

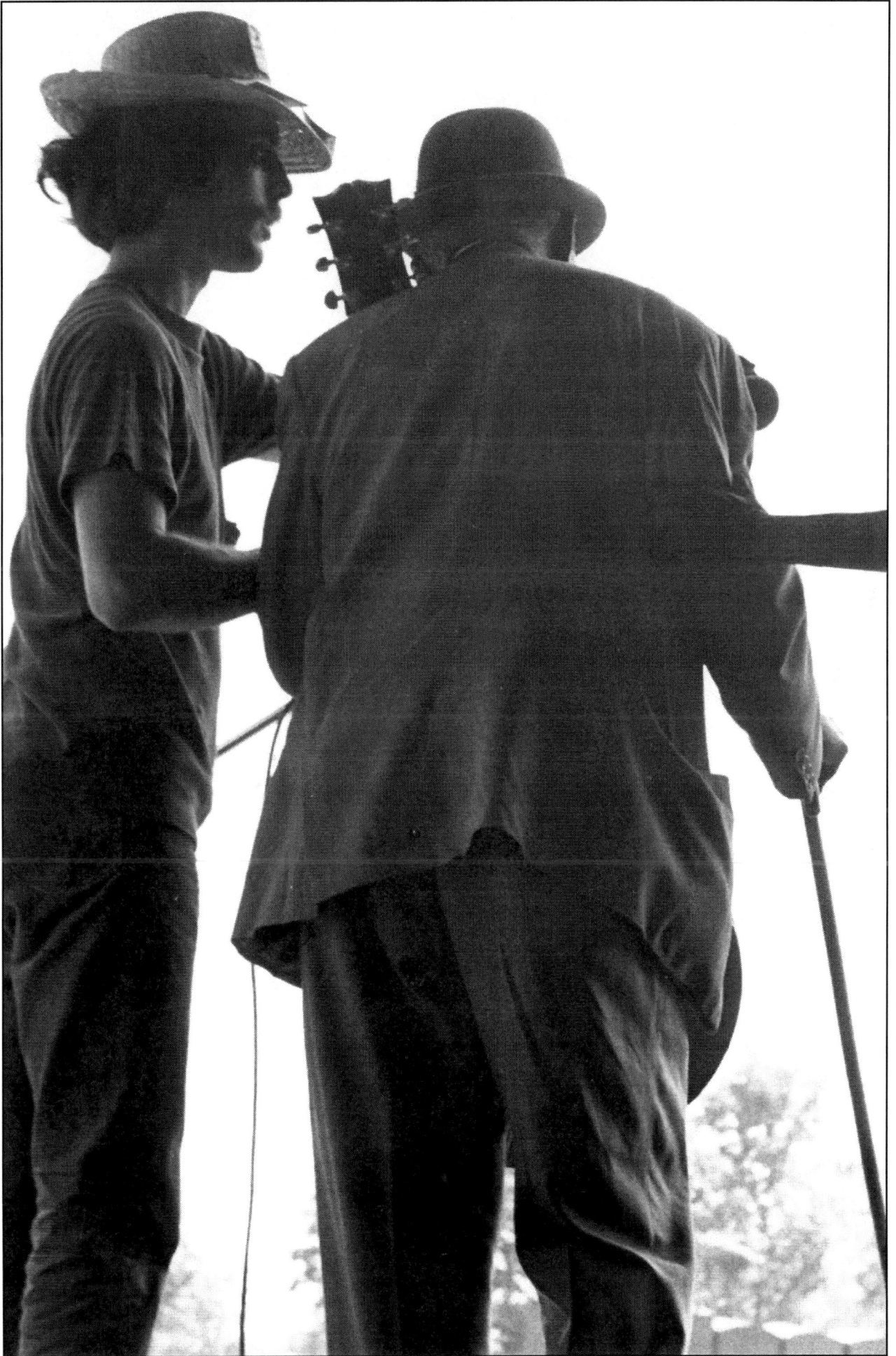

Unknown Festival, circa 1968, Stefan Grossman

USA Festival, circa 1968, Courtesy Hans Theessink

California, 1968, Alice Ochs

Sister Davis had instructed me to not let B. Davis eat greasy food, to make sure that he got plenty of rest and that he wasn't to sleep in his suit! Gary was not big on taking off his suit before he went to bed. On the second day, I reminded him to put on his Brown suit for the Saturday night show. "B. Davis", I said, "Sister Davis said to change to your other suit on Saturday Night." "Where is Sister Davis?" he said to me. "She's back in NY". "That's right, and you remember this lesson.......when we're on the road, we're on the road and when we're home, we're home! You understand that Roy?" "Yes sir Rev. Davis, I understand."

One night at The Quiet Knight, a young fan asked me if Rev. Davis would like to try his new 12 string guitar. Knowing already that Gary loved guitars, I brought the kid and his new Bozo guitar back stage. He took to it like a fish to water. The more he played it, the more he wanted it. The boy said that Rev. Davis could use it on stage if he liked and he did. After the show, Gary teased the kid that he was not going to give the guitar back to him. The owner was freaking out a little bit and starting to worry about ever getting his guitar back. Finally I got it back for him, promising B. Davis that we would go visit Bozo the next day and he could order one for himself.

The following morning, we took a cab over to Bozo Podunavac's shop. He was a very nice man and offered Rev. Davis a discount because he was a famous musician. "I don't want no discount," Gary said. "I want to have a guitar built about this big in the waist and about this big over here", he went on and on. And so, the guitar was ordered. For weeks after, every time I spoke with B. on the phone, Gary would say he's waiting for the UPS delivery truck to bring his new guitar. It was big excitement the day "Miss Bozo" arrived.

I recently ran into Mr. Podunavac at The Orlando Vintage Guitar Show, down here in Florida where I now live. I asked him if he remembered me. He looked at me for a while and I said, "Rev. Gary Davis." Bozo shouted excitedly, "You're the boy, the boy who brought the famous blind guitar player to my shop."

Forty years had passed, but we shared a wonderful memory.

Next stop on the tour was Detroit. We stayed at the home of Lorring and Sue Janes. They were to be married by Rev. Davis later in the week. Lorring was a fine local guitar picker. With B. Davis staying there, we had an endless stream of his guitar picking friends stopping by for a lesson or just a hello. There were some excellent players among them and I hardly touched a guitar the entire week. I was taking it all in though.

On the opening night of the gig at The Chess Mate, things were pretty quiet. It was a Thursday night and Lorring and Sue were both working. After the sound check we were sitting backstage waiting for show time, when the manager called me aside, "Doesn't look like anyone's coming tonight, it'll be better tomorrow. You better take Rev. Davis back to where you're staying." Talk about an awkward moment for me. "Rev. Davis, nobody's here and the man said we should come back tomorrow", I told him. "Oh, well, oh, well," he said, and we packed up and drove back to the house. The highlight of this leg of the tour was the wedding.

Friends and family gathered on the Sunday. The living room was full. The couple's regular minister was there and Rev. Davis sat in a big armchair holding a bible. I don't believe it was one he could read. At home he had, not a Braille bible, but one that was in New York Point (The NY system for the blind), later replaced by Braille.

The two ministers said their pieces and the couple were married. The wedding certificate was placed in B. Davis' lap and a pen in his hand. After a quiet awkward moment, with everyone watching B. Davis, I put my hand over Gary's and guided the pen to write Rev. Gary Davis. I always say that I was responsible for their marriage being legitimate.

Lorring and Sue stayed married until she was stricken with cancer and passed away many years later. I still get to see him from time to time when I work in Michigan. His new wife is also named Sue.

The Folk Festival at The University of NY at Buffalo was our next stop. We were assigned a dorm room at the college. I got the Rev. settled in and decided to head down to the student union for a coffee. Some of the students who noticed Rev. Davis and I checking in together stopped by my table to talk. "You're with Gary Davis aren't you". "Yes I am", I replied. "After the show tonight, we're having a party, it would be so cool if you could bring the Rev." I said that we might be able to make it, being casual and aloof and one guy gave me the address of where the gathering would be.

When I got back up to our room I excitingly told Gary, "I got a party for us to go to after the show," knowing that he would be delighted and he was. The concert that night was super. The New Lost City Ramblers, Rev Gary, and a host of others played to a packed house.

Rev. Davis changed so many of our lives. We were all lucky that he was so willing to share his life with us. Last time I visited Rev. Davis was in the hospital just before he passed. I remember saying to him, "...beside the music Rev. Davis, you gave me all my closest friends." He said "I know that Roy, I know I did." I have so many stories of those days and so many memories. Someday I just might have to write a book!

Roy Book Binder
2008

With Roy Book Binder, Buck's Rock Camp, Conn., 1969, Bob Carlin

Berkeley Blues Festival, 1970, Veryl Oakland

Part Three

Selected Concert Reviews

**with Quotations from Rev. Gary Davis
(The quotes are in bold)**

Love is just like a vein in a spring (a drinking spring):

Keeps you with supplements to cherish up what you have.

●

I'm going to do this song about before this time when another year I may be gone. You all sitting down here and laughing and talking and thinking and we're right here together and we may look in one another's faces no more.

(Sings)

**Going away, How long,
Going to stay, How long,
I ain't coming back, How long,
To Judgement Day, How long,
Oh will I get to Heaven, How long,
Sitting right down, How long,
Ask my Jesus, How long,
Of the Starry Crown, How long
Oh will I get to Heaven, How long,**

New York City, c.1954, John Cohen

**I want you meet me there, How long,
Going to have a good time, How long,
Singing and shouting, How long,
I'm going to tell my Lord, How long,
About this old world, How long,
About the trouble I had, How long.**
Extract from tape by Dr. Ellen Steckert, 1952

●

Sometimes I can't behave myself. I wants to get me five or six people sometime when you come here, sometime, and make me a sermon. Just a short sermon about four minutes and a half sermon. Let you carry it away. Not today so you needn't ask for it!
(plays "Get Right Church and Let's Go Home")
Extract from tape by Dr. Ellen Steckert, 1952

●

Always keep the other party guessin'. Never let a man know - even think - what your next move will be. If you're goin' to that door and that person know you're goin' there, walk to some other door first. Only way to survive.

●

The Reverend Gary Davis is a thin, slightly stooped man. His bald head and sunken cheeks give him a somewhat ascetic look, which makes his gold-rimmed dark glasses seem a little incongruous; like many street singers, he is blind. He hardly resembles the 1956 photographs which appeared in the Record Changer. There he had much more hair, a fuller face, and gave the appearance of stocky exuberance. In his Boston concert last December he was withdrawn and reflective. A lot must have happened to him since 1956, not much of it good.

The Reverend has a small voice which doesn't carry as well as his six-stringed guitar, and which sounds a little strained in the lower notes. When he moves from a low note to a high note he breaks into a growl, which he uses to good rhythmic effect. He sings, "Blow Gab'rel, blow Gab'rel", the accent furnished by the growled "Gab" lending an extra emphasis that is quite thrilling. The remarkable thing about his voice is that, despite its small resources, it doesn't become monotonous over a number of songs. It has a certain subtle timbre, difficult to describe further, which maintains the listener's interest.

But it is his terrific guitar playing which makes me consider him one of the great jazz performers. He employs thumb and finger picks with considerable digital dexterity to draw an astonishing variety of sounds from his instrument. He varies his playing style from piece to piece to suit the tune, in some of which he slaps the box with his palm, taps the neck of the guitar with his fingers and gets many other percussive effects. These are not mere stunts but are used sparingly and are always completely integrated into the melodic line of the song or guitar solo. The same thing is true of the occasional verbal punctuation of "Oh My God" and others. There is constant interplay between his vocal line and guitar line, the whole adding up to a marvellous art.

The concert itself was not too successful. The cold audience of young "folksong" enthusiasts never did warm up to the Reverend, and he himself never got completely loosened up.

With Sonny Terry, London, UK, 1964, Val Wilmer

Too much of the time was given over, not to Gary Davis, but to a singularly insensitive "folk-singer" and banjo-picker. As a "folk-singer", Barry Kornfeld wore an open khaki shirt and corduroy jacket. Reverend Davis wore a quiet, light brown suit, starched shirt, and four-in-hand tie. However, as a chance to see in action a performer I had only expected to hear on records, the concert was an event not to be missed.

The Reverend's first number was an instrumental spiritual in two strains; he did not know the title. It was a tune he had heard a brass band play down South. He knew how it went alright, he just didn't know its name. "You can be on a road, you know, and you may not know the name of the road, but you know where you are". As a warm-up tune, it showed little of his virtuosity and a lot of the effects associated with banjo rag music. But with the singing of "Right Down Here" his brilliant guitar work began to appear. There was more of it with the singing of "Blow Gabriel" and "Samson and Delilah" (the same tune Blind Willie Johnson recorded as "If I Had My Way"). There were some stunning breaks, in some of which a single string would be left vibrating while the others were completely stopped. Percussive discords would be followed by sparkling runs, "blue" slurs would be followed by stinging chording, a piece would seem to come to a dead stop, only to be taken up again by the moving voice and ringing guitar. The well-known "Twelve Gates to the City" was accompanied by beautiful sonorous chords, and the voice, for all its smallness, sustained the long melodic line wonderfully.

The Reverend changed his guitar tuning to "Hawaiian" and he used a bottleneck, sliding up and down the strings to accompany a narrative about a trip he had taken to Los Angeles. "I was proud to be in California. I forgot I was broke". "I was happy as a pig in the sunshine". He told of how a girl followed him, how she bought Gordon's Gin and Bottled-in-Bond - "that gal didn't buy nothing except something to drink" - and how they ended up in her place, which had a piano; there was a striking imitation of the boogie-woogie piano on his guitar. That proved to be, for me, the last piece. After intermission, the "folksinger" came back. It was pretty late by that time - the

concert, a very chic one, began at 11.00 p.m. - and when he started to talk about blues on the banjo, I left.

According to Kenneth Goldstein, Gary Davis was born in 1896, in South Carolina. As a young man he was a blues singer, but after becoming blind he turned to religion and was ordained in 1933 in North Carolina. He has recorded for Perfect in 1935, with Sonny Terry for Stinson in 1954, and in 1956 for Riverside. Like the gospel singer Georgia Peach, the Reverend is a one-record singer, and like Peach's, that one record should be issued in England. The recording balance on the Riverside was carefully arranged so that the voice is given its proper volume in relation to the guitar, something that is not possible without amplification. It might be argued that this is electronic tampering with nature, and so not Art, but as Goldstein reports: "As soon as we played back the first recording, Gary broke into a huge grin. There was no doubt about it, he was listening to himself the way he wanted it to sound".

It hardly needs mentioning that street singing of the Reverend Gary Davis kind is dying out, and with it a marvellous guitar style. Like many of the early jazz instrumental styles, it seems ideally suited to the instrument, and like them it has expressive resources not realised before or since. But the young "folk" guitarists can't begin to master it, and indeed they seem curiously unaware of how thin they sound compared with the Reverend's playing. As for the modern jazz guitarists - just how the post-Charles Christian single string style, with its endless succession of quavers, represents a development beyond the Reverend Gary Davis's astonishing playing, only they can explain.

J.S. Shipman
Jazz Journal
March 1959

●

Folk Music: Old and Young Stars at Town Hall
Mr. Davis, a bent, and tired looking preacher and former street singer, offered moving gospel songs in a rasping, gravely voice. A stern beat and strutting guitar figures gave his style a blues tincture. His words were not always audible, but the forceful conviction of his song-sermons shone through.

Robert Shelton
New York Times
September 1960

●

They're all alike to me. They're all my children.
(Asked what his favourite song was.)

●

The Rev. Gary Davis is an extraordinary performer. A balding, slightly stooped brown man of 67, he is totally blind, has to be led on stage and placed at the mike. When caught after a plane trip from his Harlem home (he was born in South

Chicago Folk Festival, 1962, Tom Paley

Carolina), he told the audience, "I've got a misery in my short ribs that pinches off my breath," and it took three or four hymns (he sings little else) to warm up. But while doing so he got the sophisticated, largely university audience singing, "That Old Time Religion" with him. (All signs of breathing difficulty had vanished when caught again another night).

When he did warm up he sometimes sounded, in a high tune called "Beautiful City", like the late Bessie Smith in, e.g. "Bleedin' Hearted Blues". Another of his finest was a blues hymn, "In This Land", which he sang in a rich strong voice, with accompaniment full of warmth and feeling on his guitar - on which he's highly skilled and inventive. He's also a harmonica whiz and did one tune on it.

Rev. Gary Davis chats with the audience as he would to a friend, with some amusing remarks at one point - but mostly, as he said, "I don't clown around; I sing". That he does, and there aren't many like him at his best.

Le Hibou, Ottawa, Canada
Variety, November 1963

•

When I came along the old folks, you know, didn't care about the guitar. You better not bring no guitar in no church! They thought it was wrong. After I got to reading after the Bible to find out what the Bible said about instruments. I played guitar anytime, Sunday and anytime. No harm in playing music, but it is what you play. I find it a great thing to play. Everybody can play it. It is a great thing.

I played a guitar for my grandmother and she said, "Oh put that thing down! Or the devil will get you! Put that thing down or the devil will get you. That thing will carry you to hell. "

There ain't nothing going to carry you to hell but what you want to carry you there. If this thing had carried me to hell I would have been there a long time ago. So if anything carry you there it will be something else, not a guitar, that's right.

I've been playing a long time since I was seven years old and I ain't got to hell yet! That's the truth! I know I ain't going there.

1964

•

The "Folk Blues and Gospel Caravan" at present touring the country came to rest last Sunday at the Odeon, Hammersmith, and provided some inspired vocal moments. Some of the artists - like Sonny Terry and Brownie McGhee, Muddy Waters, Otis Spann, and Sister Rosetta Tharpe - are familiar to British audiences, but they all sang well in their particular styles and were welcomed like old friends. Even Sister Rosetta's melodramatic gestures and flashing eyes that made her look as if she had heard that the Almighty himself was sitting up in the gods didn't detract from the power and sincerity of her voice.

The newcomers, Cousin Joe Pleasant and Blind Gary Davis, were impressive - Pleasant's humorous approach contrasting with Davis's fierce, earthy style - and between them they gave an indication of the vast range of expression possible within the blues idiom.

Daily Telegraph
May 1964

•

You know when you see you ain't got a little time you have to bite and bite pretty hard while you bite because you ain't got long to bite, you know. I ain't got but just a little while. I have to do like a cod fish biting and jinking on at the same time. So if I don't get no bait I'll grab on the hook!

Thank you for this grand opportunity of which I'm not so worthy of! But how it be the case I'm here in your midst as a black man, like a fly in buttermilk. It ain't how a thing looks though. It's what it is. Ain't that right?

UCLA Concert
March 1964

•

To play blues on a guitar I'd teach them to play the guitar like a piano.

•

Now as I tell you when I was coming up you know, I was a courting boy, the girl would follow the boy to the porch and kiss him. She runs her neck way out like this, you know, and kiss him. When she wouldn't get close and get him by the hand like I am by you all. So she got him to begin to feel cherry rose like did mine. She wanted to hug him, well I did too. So I had hug and kiss this girl, you understand. I tried, I went down in the woods by a pine tree and I tried some tricks to see if I could play my guitar right on and hug this pine tree! And I played the guitar with one hand and hug that pine tree. I said now this here, this ought to work. This girl's mother was crazy about music, didn't care nothing about what it was. She was crazy about it. So when I got ready to hug her, you understand, that's when the old woman done turned her head off. I get chance to hug her. Come a little closer, (talks to the girl he is holding), I ain't going to hurt you ... keep your eyes on your boyfriend and tell him to get his hand off that pistol and so you know what I did? I wouldn't wait till the next night to go to this girl's house, went there that night. So I had to spellbound her old lady before I could hug this lady, this girl.

Must show you how I spellbound the lady.

(Calls up a girl from the audience to help him and plays, "Kissing the Girl and Playing the Guitar at the Same Time")

Did you see that boyfriend? (Voice from audience: "I had my eyes on you all the time"). I know you did because I had your girlfriend up here! Listen, don't you all be fighting and scratching back home, going way back home because I don't mean no harm. I don't want nobody's girlfriend. Please! Don't slip in my room and kill me in there, you see. If you happen to come in the room I tell you what to do. You bring me something to do me some good, you understand. You do that won't you? Uh? You hear me, answer me! Will you do that? I got to get a real direct answer. Will you do that? You would give me nothing to kill me? Uh? If you want to kill me, shoot me, don't you put nothing in nothing to kill me you understand. I don't want your girlfriend. I just want to show you something about her, you understand. (Voice from audience: "I understand"). Alright now!

What's your name? Uh? Charlie Cots? When you get on the cot you sleep don't you? Then she has to pinch you and stick you with a pin ... Charlie, Charlie, Charlie (imitates a woman's voice) ... you see, but if you ever to get awake, you awake but they had to do something so much to get you awake. You know what happened about that? You see there is so much chloroform in them hugs and kisses, you understand. You have to stop awhile before, so you can wake up.

With Sonny Terry and Brownie McGhee, London, UK, 1964, Peter Dyer

Berkeley Blues Festival, 1970, Veryl Oakland

Once a woman let you lay on her arm, you understand it's ... (snores) ... all like that kind of stuff.

That's the truth, that goes for me too. No sooner has she put her arm under me I'm ... (snores) ... Brother Davis, Brother Davis, Brother Davis ... she quick calling me, Gary, Gary, Gary.....

... Uh, Uh, Uh ... you see. See that's a woman's arm. That's a chloroform to a man, see. Somebody kill you dead before you wake up good. That's bad too and it's dangerous for a woman to put her arm around you, you understand. Do you melt down like butter in a hot pan, you see, and she's not on letting me calling me honey too much, you see, because a thing I ain't going to do she make me do it anyhow, you understand. I done told her a lie and said I wasn't going to do it.

What makes you all women like that? Tell me that! You all won't tell us the secret but you kill us dead, won't you? I try my very best to let a woman put her arm on me but I can't save my life and I know there ain't anything but death you see. I love that little sweet thing but I declare if every time you kiss one you near death, you see.

Indiana University
February 1st, 1964

●

It would be difficult to imagine a more distant extreme of gospel singing to that of Rosetta Tharpe than the music of Blind Gary Davis. In style and approach he belongs to the street evangelists of the earlier part of the century and at times, especially in, "If I Had My Way", he sounded like a reincarnation of Blind Willie Johnson. Blind Gary is not a man who has changed with the times and it seemed most incongruous as this blind, elderly man with his acoustic guitar fervently chanted his hell-fire songs to a packed modern concert hall. It could be faith, integrity, habit or a perverse kind of showmanship which has preserved this remarkable style beyond its natural time and habitat, but make no mistake Davis is an archetypal figure in Negro song. Here for a few fascinating moments we were taken to the very fountain head of our music; it was a unique and memorable occasion.

G. Lambert
Jazz Journal
June 1964

●

Now, I'm going to play a piano a little bit. You would all like to hear a piano? I been picking the guitar a long time but I'm going to play the piano now.

(Plays Twelve Sticks)

●

I saw, heard or was present at four concerts in all, in fact the last four in a row, and the variety of things done by each artist makes writing up the events a trifle difficult. Blind Gary, for example, could be pretty erratic, as at the New Victoria second house when he played two instrumentals under great strain, then had to be led off stage by Sonny Terry in a state of near collapse, apparently quite overcome

by his reception. Anyone who saw that show probably thought they had a bad deal, but to expect a genuine street singer to turn out any sort of professional performance is to destroy all the good things that are good in the blues and gospel idioms. If you were lucky, and apparently you had an 80% or better chance, and saw Gary at his very fine best, as I did for 35 minutes at Brighton, then I'm sure you'd agree that Gary Davis on stage can produce the most wonderful country gospel music any concert stage is ever likely to see. His moving and beautiful rendering of "Pure Religion" was one of the most wonderful things I have ever witnessed: and Muddy Waters, following on, broke his usual silence to pay a sincere tribute to "the Reverend".

Simon Napier
Jazz Monthly
July 1964

●

Now I'm going to give you a little taste of "Maple Leaf". Just showing you all how you all must do with a guitar. Don't you let a guitar do you. You outdo it! Let the guitar know that you bought it and you are the best man or the best woman.

Since my time is rushful I got to be rushful with the time. I ain't got time to do what I would like to do but I hope I leave enough here for you not ever to forget.

(Sings "Oh What A Beautiful City")

●

I just want to show you all a little about a guitar. If you happen to come to New York. If you happen to come there look for 3826 Park Avenue. If you want to learn how to play guitar don't come calling me "Honey", bring your money! And then I teach you how to play. I don't promise to give you no brains. Now if you ain't got no brains don't come to me because I'm too big a fool myself. You see and if you come with some brains then you and my brains get together then and help me be able to teach you what you want. It ain't but five dollars, you see, and I guarantee you that it'll be worth ten dollars to you. Come to me. I'm asking you to come to me because I got what you need. I ain't got what you want but I got what you need, you see. Because some of you all want to come out in life, get out of life in music and if you come to me I'll take pain to teach you. I don't teach for five dollars an hour but bring me five dollars and I guarantee you that you will know something before you leave if it's no more than I took your money! That's right. I'm be sure that you tell somebody that I took your money. You tell somebody that. But I'm going to be sure to do something for your money if I take it, you understand. How about that?

Indiana University
February 1st, 1964

●

All regular Ford ain't going to do nothing but run that's full of gears. It ain't going to do nothing but run,

you understand. Because you going through the woods, you ain't got no road, you understand, and that Ford's going to break down trees and keep on going, you understand. See what I say? But these other cars have struck a tree, you understand, they'll choke up and, you understand. You know what I know a Ford will do, it will run into a Cadillac and tore it all to pieces and just stood there and Cadillacing right on, you understand. It beat that Cadillac Cadillacing you understand. That Cadillac was torn to pieces and this Ford stand up there and wasn't hurt, this Ford stand up there Cadillacing right on. Well, this you think about it. This Ford is a tough car. Then you go across mired ground and that car won't stop. That Ford won't. So you get that when the cops get at you now down there making that stuff in the woods down there, you see. Now here's where you start to get away from them you see.

(plays "Buck Dance")
Indiana University
February 1st, 1964

•

One of the more pleasing aspects of the current pseudo-blues-based hit parade has been the rise in popularity of the genuine blues and negro folk performers, and the opportunity to see them perform in person.

Last year we had the highly successful American Negro

London, UK, 1964, Val Wilmer

Blues Festival and on Sunday at the Fairfield Hall the Blues and Gospel Caravan proved as popular as its predecessor.

Many forms of blues were sung and played - the "travelling" blues, the humorous and bawdy and the more up-to-date City blues - their simplicity of lyric being moulded by voice tones and phrasing into astute comments on everyday life learnt largely from life itself.

Shouting and stirring Gospel songs were provided by Sister Rosetta Tharpe whose infectious personality carried itself through her songs to a highly appreciative audience. "This Train" and "Didn't it Rain" were particularly well received.

Another Gospeller, the Rev. Gary Davis, showed how a simple lyric sung with faith can carry its message with great impact. In "When I get to Heaven" the fact that some of his words were inaudible was of no consequence - the mood had been established by his gravel-like voice.

The partnership of Sonny Terry and Brownie McGhee has flourished through the years into today's leading blues duo, and the unsophisticated presentation of their act personifies good blues singing. Their "Walk On" and "Been Treated Wrong" were the highlights of the concert.

Blues in the modern manner were performed by Muddy Waters and Cousin Joe Pleasants, the latter's sly laugh and humorous lines in "Evil Man" establishing him as a firm favourite with the audience. Waters was in any case assured of a warm reception, as apart from being the No. 1 Rhythm and Blues artist, his influence on the current influx of beat groups is unrivalled.

Croydon Advertiser (U.K.)
May 1964

•

Now I want to show you how to get away from the police! I don't know how this country is, I don't know what they make up in this country. What do they make up here? Uh? Moonshine! Do they! Well I can talk with you then can't I? Well, if they make that Moonshine, the Moon will always shine!

You know! Well listen, take my advice don't go in the woods with no Cadillac and don't go in the woods with no Dodge and don't look at a Plymouth at all. You know what to get? You get something that ain't got nothing but gears and a seat.

Listen, this is the way, I quit picking the guitar and comes to play the piano, you understand. Here I comes playing this piano.

(plays a Rag)

Thank you good friend. Do you hear me talking to you? (whispers) Alright then, listen. I ain't going to tell no stories yet and I ain't going to tell no lies but I might do the best thing I can while I'm here on the platform. I want to leave something here for you to think about.

(plays "Oh What A Beautiful City")
Indiana University
February 1st, 1964

•

Now I want to sing you a song that people are always after me to sing. I hardly ever sing it but I hardly ever think to sing about my condition either. I used to keep my head down all the time. When did anyone care a thing about a blind man but something raised my head up one day and I can be just as much as anybody. I don't care if I was blind. I had a woman ask me one time, you see, "Reckon you'll ever marry?" Another said, "Oh no. What would he do with a woman him blind and can't see. She'll have to take care of him. I wouldn't want that responsibility". I cried over that many times. I want you all to hear me, please listen to me, I cried over that. This song come to me and I sing about it.

(Sings "There Was a Time When I Went Blind")
UCLA
March 1964

•

Good evening people. I want to say to you all I have different feelings and I am very glad you all brought me on the programme like this you know. I love this kind of stuff and I can't get loose as far as I want to get loose in there and it's kind of hurting me because I love it. And the more I do it the more I love to do it. But it be the case since I ain't got but just a while to be with you I try to do my best to try and sing you something. Well I hear these songs it makes me feel like something.

Anybody would like to know how to play a guitar and don't know how? While I'm here I can teach you in less time than a week how to play a tune and you know it before you leave. But be sure to bring your money Honey! That's what keeps the horse a running.

UCLA
March 1964

•

Now after Jack Elliott's come up I got to come back again and I'm going to try to do the best I can. In all of my sets, see, I never play more than four or five songs to a set but since this here my first time coming here I'm doing my best to get my stinger in, you understand. Once I get my stinger in I know I get you into coming back again, you understand.

Indiana University, 1964

•

He is a genuine original and at the same time part of the authentic tradition rather than being a singer who has assumed its attribution. He is now sixty-nine years old and in his life has witnessed many social and musical changes and has packed into his years more drama and incident than most men could wish.

Gary has an unexpected line of wit. One enthusiast called for "Twelve Gates To The City" but, said Gary, "that's a Judgement number. If Gabriel called for you to go you wouldn't be ready; and I know I ain't". And he didn't play it.

Paul Oliver
Jazzbeat
August 1965

•

How many of you all can lift up your feet tonight? Would you like something put on your heels to make

London, UK, 1965, Steve Rye

you feel like there is fire on your heels?
(plays "Make Believe Stunt").

•

Having spoken to Gary earlier, I hoped he was going to play us some harp; Joe Boyd forewarned us by letting it be known Gary was doing secular stuff and he did have his harps. Not to be sad to say, Gary was on for 45 minutes but never looked like matching his performance at the same venue last year. He talked and strummed away the first ten minutes and suddenly started on "Tennessee Waltz". Patti Page considered it wasn't too bad. Next he asked for a girl's name. It took five minutes to get one, then Davis played a piece on it. He followed this with a quite superlative guitar solo which brought Charlie Turner's "Kansas City Dog Walk" to mind. If the programme so far was unpredictable it was soon to become incongruous. Gary sings, "She's Funny That Way" but it wasn't funny any old way. But the next unannounced number was a narrative on bootleggers which was most entertaining: it was his last number but neither the crowd or Gary were satisfied so willing hands were thrust aside and Davis reached out once more for the mike; "just an old guy but full 'o fun, y'know" he announced in broadest Nor' Carolina. The encore was a version of "Candy Man" and once more we were treated to some beautiful picking. This time he was almost carried off stage. Still, Jack Elliott had to go on sometime I guess. Didn't see him either, but he proved himself a most likeable person. And I wouldn't mind Pete Seeger playing if he followed Bukka White I guess. Altogether an entertaining evening if not memorable.

Extract from :- American Folk Blues Tour Concert, Brighton 1965
Simon Napier
Blues Unlimited 24 (U.K.)

95

If you got a dog, you don't want him to run around: you know the next thing you do is tie him. Sometimes God has a way of fixin' people ... Those He love He chastise ... And sometimes, you know, when God takes a man's sight He gives him something greater.

●

I never was shy around none of those guitar players.

●

Wouldn't hire him for a dance.
(of Skip James)

●

Hollered like someone was hitting him all the time.
(of Blind Lemon Jefferson)

●

I ain't never heard anybody on a record yet to beat Blind Blake on the guitar.

●

Simmie Dooley, he was just as good as any man I ever heard playin' a guitar, him and Willie Walker.

●

He was a good guitar player. He played on the orders of Blake on some things but he didn't have a bass like Blake. But he was tolerable good – awful good!
(of Big Bill Broonzy)

●

He got further than I did after I taught him a few things.
(of Brownie McGhee)

●

Get along there boy, this rag of mine is too tight. Makes your heart beat tight! He meant to play the guitar though and he played good. Nobody tell you that Blind Blake don't play guitar, yes he did!

●

On Stage at the Free Hall Manchester June 4th
After a few remarks about trouble in its various guises Gary

Buck's Rock Camp, Conn., 1969, Bob Carlin

moved into a slow blues with the accent on the guitar. Biting phrases on the treble strings underlain with ominous bass figures in a timeless tradition. "Cocaine Blues" came next and Davis gave a tremendous version of one of his better known numbers. There followed the high spot of the evening – an instrumental which displayed Davis's absolute mastery of the guitar. In the course of approximately six minutes Gary must surely have utilised almost every note, every chordal phrase, every trick of technique available on a six-string guitar. His dazzling elaborations on the basic theme displayed an endless fund of ideas and a supreme ability to translate them into music. The earlier numbers had gone down well with the mainly folk-orientated audience and this breathtaking tour-de-force received tremendous applause. The only Gospel number of this set followed, a vigorous "Children of Zion", after which there was a pause while Gary fumbled in his pockets eventually producing a suitable harmonica. I had never heard him blow harp before and was duly amazed at his prowess on the instrument. Sounding very much like Sonny Terry – whoops included – Gary performed a very creditable harmonica blues. This was to have been the climax of his act but in response to considerable applause he was brought back for an encore – a short untitled instrumental. He left the stage to a tremendous ovation.

Bob Groom
Blues World
July 1965

●

Sometimes our brain gets filled up with cocaine and we haven't took a sniff. Sometimes you get tied up in love, and you got cocaine a plenty and you don't have to sniff none. Ain't that right?"
(Plays 'Cocaine Blues')

●

The New Lost City Ramblers, who have done so much to create an atmosphere where a traditional performer feels welcome in a city auditorium, weren't lax either and they really enjoyed their time on stage, with plenty comments to spare. Reverend Gary Davis, with all that was going on, took over the stage and masterfully sang "Death Don't Have No Mercy" to a stunned, hushed audience. The next thing you heard was the good Reverend saying, "Kids, that's where it's at". And they all agreed that they had learned something.
Sixth Annual University of Chicago Folk Festival

Israel G. Young
Sing Out!
May 1966

●

When the blind Rev. Gary Davis was helped on stage at a "First Generation Blues" concert at the Electric Circus last month, a doubtful murmur stirred the audience.

Davis, 73 years old, appeared awkwardly out of place as he was led painstakingly through a jumble of electronic equipment to the microphones.

He wore a full-length overcoat buttoned to the neck, a brown derby hat, and glasses with black lenses. The strap of his heavy 12-string guitar cut into his neck. For nearly a full minute he stood wordless in front of the audience, swaying slightly.

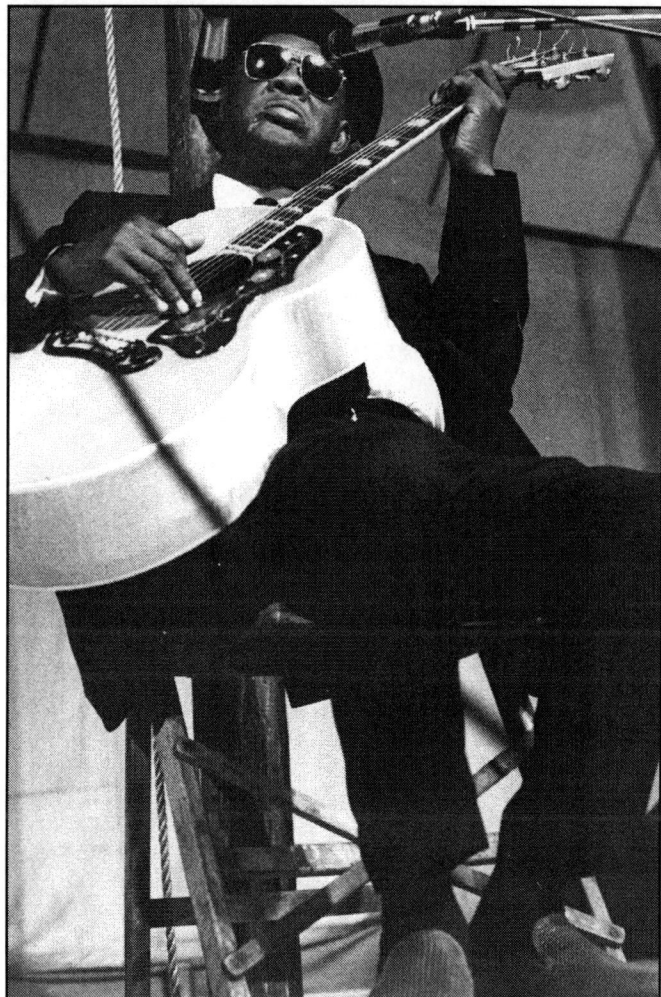

Cambridge Folk festival, UK, 1971, Nigel Luckhurst

"My God, this is terrible", whispered a teenage girl in a see-through blouse, "What if he can't do anything?"

Davis groped for the microphone, and when he found it said almost inaudibly: "Now I don't want you gettin' to expectin' about what I'm doing here. It ain't much."

He began to play, his calloused fingers working the strings. The guitar's twanging, ringing, cutting voice filled the room with feelings of agony and loneliness.

And over the eloquence of the 12-string guitar came Davis's rasping voice. Usually grave, then soaring to high notes and becoming more powerful before subsiding into a low murmur.

And, when he finished, the girl in the see-through was on her feet with the rest of the audience. She was clapping hard, and, she was crying.

Tim Ferris
New York Post (Extract)
June 1969

●

Now, people had different feelings, you understand. He worried about a woman, or worried about a man, something like that. Get all stirred up in a cauldron. Thing like that is the blues.

●

The setting was an art studio.

The music was folk, "Greensleeves", and classical, with the

UK Tour Poster 1964

Poster 1964

wedding march from "Lohengrin" on a harp.

It was the wedding of Detroit guitarist and folk singer Lorring Janes to Susanne Mosher, 21, who is herself a pianist and flautist.

The pastor could not see the handsome Janes, 26, in neatly trimmed beard, nor Miss Mosher, in long flowing locks holding a bouquet of daisies.

And the Rev. Gary Davis, nationally known black guitarist closing out two weeks at the Chess Mate, could not tell their colour.

But he knew they were white. Blind since infancy, the 76 year old musician said he can tell colour by speech.

He has performed many weddings, he said, but most of them white. "They just seem to know my guitar playing and want me to do it", he said.

"We visited with him a number of times in New York", said Janes.

"Most people regard Gary as a guitar player, and not a minister. And being a guitar player too, we thought it would be great to be married by him".

In the ceremony Davis talked about the sanctity of marriage.

Janes is a member of the Holy Cross Lutheran Church 15301 Grand River, and Miss Mosher of the Church of the Holy City (Swedenborgian), 10840 Curtis.

The Rev. Herman Burkett of St. Mark's United Methodist Church, Southfield, was on hand to sign the marriage licence. Janes is a scoutmaster in the St. Mark's Church.

The blind guitarist recited from 1 Peter 3 "wives be in subjection to your husbands" and "ye husbands give honour unto the wife, as unto the weaker vessel".

Asked if he was best at being a minister or playing a guitar,

Mr. Davis said: "God put his best into a person when he calls him to be a minister".

H.H. Ward
Detroit Free Press
February 1969

●

To see him at first is almost frightening. He's old. Not the way 35 is old, but old, 75 years old. And he's blind ... we want him to see us and he can't. His face isn't all that friendly either; it's foreboding, in a perpetual scowl. We're afraid to speak to him, afraid we'll say the wrong thing. He asks and answers questions bluntly, without hesitation. He's different, very different, and he knows we're afraid of him.

We had all known he was coming, Reverend Gary Davis. Our excitement had been building up for over a week, hearing every other person say, "He's coming, Gary Davis is coming".

It was strange once he arrived, and Roy was showing him and his wife around the camp. There was an ever-growing crowd following him and what seemed like hundreds of cameras clicking simultaneously. We crowded out of the shops to see him, coming closer but keeping distance, everyone passing the word, "He's here, Gary Davis is here". We were all very tentative, even cautious. We wanted him to like Buck's Rock. We wanted him to be impressed.

Then he was up on the lawn in a chair, the rest of us on the grass around him. He began to play ... rich, warm, incredible music, beauty all its own. "He's playing, Gary Davis is playing". Gary Davis, still the name, not yet the person. More cameras

98

With Mother Annie Davis, Buck Rock's Camp, Conn., 1969, Bob Carlin

clicking, tape recorders going, microphones held as close as we dared. We can't take our eyes off him ... watch him, look at him, he's Gary Davis. Scarcely breathing, scarcely moving. He's talking to us ... answer quickly, enthusiastically. Laugh, laugh when he jokes, be sure to laugh at the right times. It's Gary Davis. Please play some more, but we don't dare ask him. Wait...

Listen, listen to the music, listen to that guitar. It's real, simple, direct, pure music that he plays, that he sings in a deep, guttural, rough voice. There are fewer cameras now, fewer microphones. Relax ... not too much, just a little ... lean back. Beginning to listen, beginning to hear it. Still watching him though, he's smiling now as he plays. Relax a little more. The cameras have stopped. The music is all, all-encompassing. We're listening, hearing it, touching it with all our senses, feeling its beauty, his beauty. The music becomes the man, direct, basic, warm, real. Our initial fear becomes very distant, unimaginable. He jokes with us, asking us to sing with him, letting the music bind us together. We burst into roars of applause after each song, in gratitude, in thanks. And when he has sung the last song, we rush to shake his hand, to kiss him.

After he left that evening, the feeling he had brought and shared with us remained. He's part of us now, he's part of Buck's Rock.

Francis Camper
Student, Buck's Rock, Conn., 1969

●

All of you that want to take a pattern at me after I'm gone, want you to get close around where you can hear well. Taking notice of the way at the chords that I change. I do not mind nobody learning how to do what I am doing because some of you may not be able to get where I done got anyhow. And Lynn and I don't want you get far from me. I want you to catch this here and carry it home with you. Uh? I told you Lynn and I want you to catch this and carry it home. First thing I want to sing to you is, "Talk on the Corner". You know men love to get on the corner and talk about the good women they have, you know. You hear one fellow said, "My gal don't care about where I go as long as I bring it in when I come ... the money!" Yeah! Another fellow, you understand, one that had no money, you understand, you better bring it in, you understand. He can't get nowhere for she's a jealous woman. This is the story he tell about his girl...

(plays "Talk on the Corner")
Buck's Rock Camp, 1969

●

Berkeley Blues Festival
Reverend Gary Davis, composer and singer of "Holy

Author's home, Jersey, UK, August 1971, Robert Tilling

Blues", sermonised that he had come to "get Berkeley" because he heard about its troubles, then drove the point home with a song warning the audience, "You better mind how you use your knowledge as you live". Bukka White's stories were so tangled and interminable that it was hard to tell where a song began and a story left off, and Furry Lewis, a 77 year old, wooden-legged street sweeper from Memphis, told the audience that when he got married he had 15 cents and his wife had 25. "Then the next day she left me flat, sayin' I had got her just for the money".

Michael Lyndon
New York Times
April 1970

•

I want to kiss the prettiest girl that ever walked in California when I get off this stage. That'll make me sleep better and live longer, you see!

•

Now, here's something I'm coming down to now. I want you to listen at me and give me the answer. There come a time when you like to have company. Ain't that right? And there come a time when you wished people would stay at home? Ain't that right? Uh? That happen more constantly that so when you'd love to have company. Ain't that right? Some people wait till you get your dinner on the table or breakfast or what it is. Leave their house, sit down and eat you out and got more to eat than you got! Ain't that right? Somebody always got a window open that leads right to your kitchen door, you understand? First thing you see is them with their nose turned up smelling your coffee, come on. The woman look at her old man and says you tell them folks to stay home. You tell them. Well you don't know where you will need a person again, you understand, you can't tell a person to stay away from your house. You wished to God they would though sometimes. No use me telling you how to do it. I'm here to tell you to sing it to them, you understand. Go to the house and sing it to them. Now you do not know what to sing and I'm here to tell you. I want you all to repeat right behind me. Are you ready?

Come down and see me sometime
Come down and see me sometime
Eat your breakfast before you come, bring your dinner in your hand
Get out before suppertime.

Now you tell me what that means. It means you don't want to give them a bite to eat. Ain't that right?

•

Listen, there come a time that we people ought to get together till God gives us this cover. We ought to

Cambridge Folk Festival, UK, 1971, Nigel Luckhurst

get together. Now if you mean to get together you're going to have to help me with this song about, "Let Us Get Together Right Down Here", and there ain't no use waiting to get to Heaven to get together. Guess some of you folks say, "When I get to Heaven I'm going to sit down", and all that stuff. If you ain't done no sitting down now, you understand, you ain't going to have time to sit down when you get to heaven. I bet some of you would tear heaven up, you would be so glad to get there. Uh? This reason God taking his time letting you get there, I want you all to help me sing this song.

Let Us Get Together Right Down Here
Let Us Get Together Right Down Here.
Cambridge, 1971

•

Davis: Preaching at St. Pancras
The Rev. Gary Davis converted London to his rich warm brand of religion on Sunday. To be more precise, he converted 500 Londoners in the first folk concert at the new Shaw Theatre in St. Pancras - and that number included a fair sprinkling of Rev. Davis followers who had hitched and hiked from remoter parts of Britain to hear him.

In reviewing what he achieved, you've got to start with religion because that's what the man does. Oh, it's a deeply human kind of religion, which happily embraces guitar-picking and woman-hugging as part of life. As Gary pointed out at one stage, what he was saying came direct from God, not out of any book. Then he went on to sing a song which was the antithesis of the pie in the sky doctrines of so many religions "Let's Get Together Right Down Here".

You have to pinch yourself sometimes to remember that this incredible man is actually in his 76th year. Despite his blindness and a bad leg which had been giving him trouble throughout this too brief, hardly publicised tour, his fingers seem to have lost none of their agility and his voice none of its remarkable power and flexibility.

What distinguishes most black singers from even their cleverest white imitators is this flexibility, the use of the entire dynamic and harmonic spectrum of the voice, one moment resonating deep in the chest cavities, the next pulling back the lips into a hoarse shout which kills all the subsonic tones, and emphasises the 'top' characteristics then rounding the voice out into a rich falsetto.

The fact that what Rev. Davis does comes right from the heart - as it undoubtedly does - shouldn't blind us to the considerable technique employed to do what he does. That goes for his guitar playing too, for though the effect sounds simple, it is in fact extremely complex, even sophisticated.

This should not really be surprising, for his music has recognisable roots in the great pre-slavery civilisations of West Africa, where sophistication and surface gloss were not confused with each other, and whose music had taken a completely different path from the decaying traditions of European classical music before the slavers came.

The survival and strengthening of black music in the interim, and the continued decay of white European music is a small indication of the power of what the white man found in Africa, and sought to destroy with whisky and Bible-pounding religion.

Yet even these degenerating influences are transformed in the mouth of a consummate craftsman like Rev. Gary Davis who takes the humanistic core of Christianity and throws away authorization and establishmentarian dross that has clung round it for centuries, who takes the instrumentation and harmonic structures of white music and penetrates to the basically sound 'Africa within' still to be found there somewhere, communicating a rich, passionate involvement with life and music which is immediately appreciable.

Romford, UK, 1966, Steve Rye

All this is a long way round method of trying to convey the remarkable transformation Rev. Davis wrought in that stuffy little theatre on Sunday night. He touched our souls, and by some strange magic, as we left the theatre, it did seem for a moment, as if the whole of smoky London had indeed been converted.

Karl Dallas
Melody Maker 1971

•

Now here's another short one. I want you all to have a good time you understand. Sometimes you slip off from your boyfriend going to these dances, you know, your boyfriend comes catches you there. He's so mad he can't tell you to come out. He grab you by the head and drag you out! He's so mad and you see he's mad and you try and square him up. "I just sort of..." (Imitates a woman's voice) Wop! And he done hit you. "Me and Sally..." Wop! He gets you outdoors, you understand, and he hit you six blocks and kick you twelve. That's some kicking ain't it? Then when you get to the house you got about eighteen or twenty steps to go up to get up on the porch and he set his foot under you and when you get down, you understand, you're sitting in the living room on the floor. He's on you before you can get up Wang Gang! "You going to kill me honey?" Womp! Womp! "O Lord, you going to kill me honey? I didn't mean no harm". Womp! "I didn't mean no harm". You get up like a fool and laugh about it. Hah Hah! You know my man like he killed me last night. There ain't nothing to laugh about you be certain of it. You're so sore you can't put your clothes on. He would have stomped your livers out you see, that's right. You need a doctor so bad so when you come in, you understand, you have one hand on the frying pan trying to cook and the other on your stomach. He said, "What you doing with your hand on your stomach child?" "You know where you stomp me last night". "Get your hand off that stomach and put both hands to that thing and cook me something to eat! " You be so bad. You be so weak you're ready to fall out. I'll give you places, you understand. I didn't tell you not to go!

Now, I don't know how you all been. I didn't come here, I didn't come here to meddle in anyone's business. I come here with my head on my body and I want to go back with one! Some of you all may be bootleggers. I don't know that you is but I just come here to give you a lead on being a bootlegger and to give you good advice. Don't go down in them woods with no Cadillac, you understand, making that stuff. Don't take no heavy car down in the hole. If you do you going to have to leave it down there, you understand. Time you think you're down there by yourself you got all the police in town down there with you. You got to come out and down there, then you take a car to carry you away from down there. You get an old Ford. I don't care if that Ford ain't got no body. If it got a good engine and a good transformission. May not have no good seat but you pack that seat full of overcoats so the springs won't come up and stick you! Then you hold to the steering wheel and I'll tell you what a Ford'll do. It will climb up a tree and keep on going and it won't turn over. Then if anybody want to ride with you, you ask then if they got any nerve and if they ain't got no nerve don't carry them along with you. Because they cause you to get excited and they get killed, you understand. And you know that Ford will jump a gully. It will jump over you understand. If you fooled that Ford it will swim, see, and it'll go across ploughed ground. Don't have to have no smooth ground and when you come down there and you're trying to get away from that man here is what you do...

(Plays "Buck Dance", Cambridge, UK 1971)

•

Gary Davis in Bristol

Rev. Gary Davis, frail and looking extremely old, could only promise a 45 minute show. So, on his one date outside the Cambridge Folk Festival (actually he went on to play Brighton and London - ed) he was preceded by one and a half hours of contemporary folk singers a la Joan Mitchell, James Taylor et al.

We were all a little dubious about the Reverend's ability to perform for even the allotted time. He was so much older in every way than on his last visit, and all of us who know and love his music were concerned that anticipation could easily become an embarrassment. But not only did Rev. Gary give a stunning show, he also gave a very surprising one. His guitar work was slightly stiffer, the sparkling runs and antiphonal responses - 'Talk to me, Miss Gibson, just talk to me' - were a little slower. But that immense, powerful, gritty and abrasive shouting voice was as overwhelming as ever.

The first part of his recital was the expected - "You gotta move", "Samson and Delilah", "Keep Your Lamp Trimmed And Burning" and other well worn favourites. Despite waning fervour in the guitar accompaniment, the message came across as strongly as ever.

Then came the surprise. Gone was the Rev. Gary Davis, street preacher, and in his place sat Blind Gary, the blues singer and entertainer who once played with Blind Boy Fuller and Bull City Red. We had an intricate "Candy Man", a hilarious country song called "She wouldn't say quit" which became increasingly bluer verse by verse and even the old ballad "She's Funny That Way".

Add a couple of his famous buckdances and the audience

With Maddy Prior, Romford, UK, 1966, Steve Rye

was completely in his hands. This was a side of Gary Davis I had always thought vanished with his sight those many years ago, although he has been persuaded to re-record some of the dances. He needed no persuasion in Bristol to run the gamut of blues eroticism and it was an experience I wouldn't have missed for anything. A marvellous concert and one to remember alongside the British debuts of Son House, Skip James, Bukka White... for in its way this was a debut too - the first time any of us had seen what Gary Davis must have been like thirty years ago.

Rumour has it that this was his last British tour. Not surprising at his age, but like Son House, the frail old man led onto the stage bore no relation to the fiery entertainer that followed.

David Harrison
Blues Unlimited 1971 (U.K.)

•

Now, since I am here, I try to come to tell you about a little of everything and there isn't time to tell you about a little everything. I can't do one thing too long so I am going to tell you about a little of everything. Uh? You got to hit a lick out of some things and got to hit some things. And that's the way it is. Now I want all you girls to tell me something about this I going to tell you about, I ain't asking none of you men about her, I'm asking these girls to tell me something about this girl that I going to sing about ... (plays ... "I Got a Girl Who is Crazy About Me").

Now I'm waiting for some of you women to tell me what's the matter with that gal, please! Mam' be nice and tell me what's the matter with her. Now won't you all tell me what's the matter with her? Now if there's something about that girl you won't tell me there is something I would use. You kind of like that. I'm going to tell you men what to do with your jealous

Keele Folk Festival, UK, 1966, Brian Shuel

women. You know you've got to work some time and if you be five minutes late you come in, you come in, she got her mouth run at you, you understand, the way you stop her mouth running at you, you don't have to hit her in that mouth! Just come home and sit down and say, "I ain't gonna work no more, now you do the work!" Then tell her that this here daddy got to love and can't go to work, you understand, and because I be a little behind time and your raising cane as if I just come from another woman's house when you just come from your work. You just go home, quit sitting down and go home and lay down! You understand, you let her go get it. That's the jealous kind of woman you understand. And just call for everything that you think you want, you understand, if you think she won't get it, she'll get it. You know, if you think she won't kill you too. She'll do that, uh? Because she doesn't have to do much to keep you, you understand. It ain't going to take much to kill you, you understand, she found out you ain't going to do her no good. She make away with your brother uh? You have to know how to handle a girl like that, you understand. She's jealous!

•

Now tonight I ain't going to try and give it to you in one night. For you wouldn't know what to do with it no how! If I give it all to you in one night you

wouldn't know where none of it was at. So I am just going to give you just a little bit to let you know where some of it's at!

Cambridge 1971

•

The American guests – Mimi Farina, Tom Jans, Rev. Gay Davis and Jean Ritchie – were all superb. I suppose Gary was the showpiece of the entire festival – and the old master showed no signs of deterioration. His timing and co-ordination are still excellent, although his playing has slowed down slightly, which is inevitable.

Gary delighted everyone and took an active part in the Festival. He even appeared at the guitar workshop and treated us to a few gems such as "Buck Dance" and "Sun's Going Down". In his various sets he displayed great showmanship and great intensity with such classics as "Marching Song", "Candy Man", "Maple Leaf Rag", "Let's Get Together", "There's a Destruction", "Pure Religion" and "Samson and Delilah".
Extract from Report of Cambridge Folk Festival, 1971
Jerry Gilbert
Sounds

•

Always keep the other party guessin'. Never let a man know – even think – what your next move will be. If you

104

goin' to that door and that person know where you're goin', walk to some other door first. Only way to survive.

(On others stealing his guitar playing ideas)

●

The Rev. didn't make an appearance until Saturday afternoon, by which time he had quite a reception committee. Most of his audience, brought up on a diet of Davis admirers, must have expected a digital wizard with a voice weakened by time. In fact, Gary Davis's voice was incredibly strong, while his guitar playing was understandably not so fast as the younger guitarists who have acted as missionaries to some extent – spreading the word of the master.

His Saturday afternoon open-air performance was good without being sensational, but in the seclusion of the marquee in the evening he scored a major success with harmonica and guitar. Throughout Sunday he established himself not only as a musician but as an emotive character. Laced between the three numbers he played – "Let Us Get Together", "Death and Destruction", and "If I Had My Way" – was a persuasive dialogue with Davis conducting a campaign of racial harmony and judging women by their cooking rather than their looks.

Davis's repertoire was by no means devoted to the religious material that he preferred at one time. One wondered what he thought of John James who played one set at a guitar seminar as sensitively and skilfully as ever.

Andrew Means
(Extract from report of Cambridge Folk Festival, Melody Maker, 1971)

●

Now you all expect me to do like the other fella but I have to do like Reverend Davis. If I do like Reverend Davis I might do well but if I try to do like the other person I might play hell. So I ain't gonna try and do like the other fella!

●

I ain't done nothing to nobody and I ain't going to do nothing to nobody. I don't want nobody to do nothing to me. If I got anything you want before you leave here I want to give it to you. And when you leave here I don't want you coming back to me, you understand, or nothing, whether it be good or bad. I don't want you coming back.
Cambridge, 1971

●

The electric guitar, you're just playing the electricity.

Cambridge Folk Festival, UK, 1971, Stefan Grossman

If you get where there's no electricity, you ain't got no guitar!

•

It's just a mess! (Talking of Rock and Roll).

•

Reverend Gary Davis in Jersey

Reverend Gary Davis visited Jersey this year and although it was only a short stay, its impact was incredible. On 5th August he played in front of a full house of over 250 people and showed that he is still a magnificent musician.

On his first set he played his fifteen-year-old 'Miss Gibson' and startled all the guitarists in the room with his amazing skill, speed and unorthodox style, picking with only two fingers and fretting with the flat of his fingers. During this set he played three instrumentals and told a story about bootlegging: "You need an old beat up Ford that will climb trees to get away from the cops!" In between each number he told stories and talked of his belief, "When you got nothin' nobody wants you, and when you got somethin' everybody wants you!" He was, of course, referring to his music and he also told us how he bought homes from "Just pickin' guitar", and he was

rightly proud of this. He ended his first set by singing his old favourite, "Right Down Here": we all joined in the chorus and it went on for some time!

His second set was like a dream. He used his twelve-string 'Miss Bozo' and to me he showed that he is still the world's greatest twelve-string guitar player. He opened with "Candy Man", which is even more exciting on a twelve-string. At the end of the set we saw him at his greatest, playing "Whistling Blues" with a huge pocket knife, on a borrowed Martin. I have never heard him play this piece and it brought the house down. Two more encores followed and the atmosphere was electric.

At the end he was cheered out of the room right out onto the street and I am certain if he had played all night no one would have left. He had everyone completely spellbound.

Afterwards at my home we had a party with just a few admirers and he went on singing and talking. He played his mouth harp and I asked him why he did not play it at the concert and he said, "I just knew there was something I had to do!"

For a few wonderful days I had this truly great man staying with me and it made me realise even more what a sincere and gentle man he is.

Robert Tilling
Blues World 1971 (U.K.)

Jersey, UK, August 5th 1971, Robert Tilling

●

I have no children but I've got many sons.

●

Some people think it don't take you no time to get you anywhere. You don't get nowhere in one night. Some people never get that far because they get impatient - too hasty with themselves.
(On learning to play the guitar)

●

If you got a dog and you don't want him to run around, you know the next thing you do is tie him. Sometimes God has a way of fixin' people. Those He love He chastise, and sometimes, you know, when God takes a man's sight he gives him something greater.

●

My motto's always been to bring out something somebody else hadn't heard before. I always loved to do things different than anybody else did.

●

You know you can't give a two week old baby peas and cornbread. You've got to give it what it's able to eat. Lot of people come here wanting me to teach them things but they're not able to stand up to it. I'm subject to mistakes. All of us are.

●

Here's a song that I heard my grandmother sing. This song is five hundred years old! I asked her where did she get it from, and she said that her grandmother's mother sang it ....way back yonder. I kept it in my memory as a child coming up and I decided when I learn to play guitar I am going to learn that song.
(1968) (plays Children of Zion)

●

Sometimes you're going east but you're actually going west. That's the way it happens with all of us sometimes. Mistakes is the best stop in life. You know too much you understand, then you done made a mistake already. You be too perfect then the mistakes been already made. But you go try to do a thing and make a mistake to start off with, then that's the best start in life. It gives somebody a chance to correct you.

●

I'm sleeping now!
(Makes a fake loud snore! – while playing a blues instrumental during a lesson with Woody Mann)

107

New York City, 1961, Don Schlitten

Part Four

Selected Record, Compact Disc, Video, Book and DVD Reviews

HARLEM STREET SINGER
Bluesville 1015

The disk is a major contribution to understanding the evolution of gospel song. For here the curious juxtaposition of "sinful" music with sacred words is just what flocks of gospel groups are practising today.

While the sincerity of some people in the gospel movement can be questioned, the Rev. Davis cannot. He is foremost a distinctive, imaginative country-blues guitarist and his singing voice - rough, rude and primitive - is capable of the most excellent type of statement.
Robert Shelton
New York Times, March 1961

•

BLIND GARY DAVIS
Pure Religion And Bad Company 77 LA 12/13

This is a magnificent record by the blind street singer who still sings on the Harlem Streets. A superb guitarist (and every other track is a solo) he literally breathes blues into every line and every solo, which isn't surprising as Davis was once a blues singer, but when he turned to religion he gave up secular songs. Quite one of 77's best issues.

Blues Unlimited, March 1965

•

REV. GARY DAVIS/SHORT STUFF MACON
XTRA 1009

The Rev. Gary Davis has already had a whole LP to himself, Pure Religion and Bad Company on the '77' label. He was also one of the high-spots of last year's Blues Caravan, extraordinary, moving, a living fossil, one of the last blind street singers. His guitar playing is sweet and raggy, his voice hoarse and urgent. The contrast between the two is as delicious as melon eaten with ham. On this record all his material is religious, but there is no impression of trying to `sell' it. The feeling behind the music is blues rather than gospel.

Short Stuff Macon is almost unbelievably primitive. He uses his material to suit himself, or fails to escape from within his limitations, it's often hard with country singers to decide which is the case. The opening track, "My Jack Don't Drink Water", has three notes in it, but the spacing of the vocal phrases thrown against the repetitive rhythmic patterns is the opposite of monotonous, "Corina", a beautiful blues-inflected pop song, of Witherspoon's version, is robbed of its melody and melted back into the material from which it derives. It all

sounds very African and archaic, and yet Macon is only 38 years old. In the blues it's not when or where you were born, but what happened to you later, Davis was born in 1896 in South Carolina, but he kept moving, whereas until very recently Macon had never left his native Crawford, Mississippi.

George Melly, Jazz Journal, March 1965

•

REV. DAVIS 1935-1949
YAZOO -1023

Current research suggests that Gary Davis, at one time, considered as a side-product of the Carolina 'blues school', was in fact one of its most influential figures. It appears that Blind Boy Fuller learned guitar from Davis and though Fuller eventually had more imitators this was probably due as much as anything to the complexity of Davis's playing which was beyond all but the very best guitarists. Davis, of course, had become a religious singer by the mid-thirties and rarely performed blues again for thirty years. With a couple of exceptions these titles have all come from his three-day session for ARC in 1935.

One or two titles have been reissued before, but these copies are unusually clean. "Hallelujah", for instance, coming over like a recent recording. The combination of rapid picking, rhythmic swing, recitative vocal and whining blue notes in this item typifies Gary Davis's brilliant unequalled musicianship. The unerring proficiency, with every note clearly stated, sets up a scintillating contrast with his rasping strained voice. Davis chanted his vocals, interspersed vocal comments, hummed, muttered to his guitar "talk to me" hollered and croaked while his fingers rolled out the notes as though they belonged to another being. Listen for the interplay of voice and guitar on "I Am The True Vine", or the incomparable, "Twelve Gates To The City". The latter has been a `standard' in his repertoire for many years and it is remarkable to note how perfectly formed it was at that date. Mention should be made of Blind Gary's blues, in which both his links with, and differences from, the other Carolina musicians are more evident. Two titles were

Adelphi recording session, NY, 1969, John Townley

made in 1949 though I find these less exciting than his earlier, (and later) recordings. An interesting note by Stefan Grossman analyses the musical structure of Davis's work, adding to the pleasure to be gained from this exceptional issue.

Paul Oliver, Jazz Journal, c.1969

●

RAGTIME GUITAR
Transatlantic TRA 244

This is the second LP to be devoted to the purely instrumental talents of the Rev. Gary Davis (the first was Prestige 14033) and it is 34 minutes of pure joy for all lovers of his brilliant guitar and banjo stylings. "Cincinnati" is a familiar theme in Gary's repertoire under the title "Slow Drag". "West Coast" (properly "East Coast Blues") is a rendition of the Blind Blake tune played on a six-string banjo. "Buck" is a very old rag - Gary shakes off its cobwebs in this lively interpretation. "Tickle" flows along with Gary producing several interesting variations on the basic theme. The "Two Step" and "Waltz Time" versions of "Candy Man" make for interesting comparison with his usual presentation of this blues (different to John Hurt's but equally great). One misses the vocal but both have their own charms although the 'conventional' treatment is the most effective I feel. "Walkin' Dog" presents some unusual changes based on pre-war blues piano playing and at times resembles "St. Louis Blues". "Italien" is a sprightly piece performed on a twelve-string guitar. Gary's humorous approach to it comes bubbling through. "C" is a fairly straightforward piano rag impeccably played. "Make Believe", although at times similar to "Maple Leaf Rag", is a unique creation overall which once again demonstrates the genius of Gary's musicianship. These recordings were made between 1962 and 1970 by Stefan Grossman (who also provides the sleeve notes) and he promises further LP's in a

Adelphi recording session, NY, 1969, John Townley

series devoted to the songs, stories and instrumentals of Rev. Gary Davis. If they are all as good as this first set then we can look forward to some exciting listening in the months ahead.

Blues World No. 41. Winter 1971

●

CHILDREN OF ZION
Kicking Mule 101 / Transatlantic TRA 249

Although this is a nice album overall, it does present rather a mixed bag of Davis; despite Stefan Grossman's assertion in the sleeve note that these recordings find the Reverend at his peak, there are some guitar goofs; the fast instrumental, "Twelve Sticks", is raggy in more than one sense of the word, and, "Come Down" and "Tipperarary" are concert funnies that don't stand up to repeated playing at home. However, the latter demonstrates Davis's sophisticated musicianship very well; the correct harmonies are diligently adhered to and a comparison between this version and Mance Lipscomb's is interesting if inconclusive.

The religious numbers are all superb and Gary sings with overpowering conviction over his own beautifully intricate accompaniments; his presentation of a song like "Twelve Gates" doesn't differ in essentials from any of his previous versions but his constant deep involvement in the material ensures that his performances are never perfunctory.

"Buck Dance" although off-recorded is nice here because of Gary's asides and the audience participation, and his satirical piece "Soldier's Drill" is a satisfying climax to the album. In these relaxed concert surroundings Davis evidently felt justified in going on a bit and although the track is a shade too drawn-out at 6.5 minutes, it remains an extremely witty piece of guitar playing. The almost frighteningly hip audience respond accordingly, roaring with laughter in all the right places.

In keeping with Transatlantic's current policies, the album is a lovely production job; Grossman's note is on the inner sleeve with a clutch of recent pics of the Reverend, and the cover has two excellent colour shots of him at last year's Cambridge Folk Festival.

Ron Brown, Jazz Journal, 1971

●

LORD I WISH I COULD SEE
Biograph BLP-12034

Half a dozen years older than Son House - he was born in 1896 - Reverend Gary Davis has continued to be active to a remarkable degree. It's hard to believe that these recordings were made when he was seventy-five years old. But it must be admitted that his abilities are waning a little; his voice is not very strong, though made more powerful by recording than it actually is in live performance, and his fingers are not as fantastically nimble as they were in say, his 1956 recordings made by Kenneth Goldstein for Riverside. That's to be expected of course, but it should be noted, for I found some of the tracks a little disappointing. "Eagle Rocking Blues" by way of example, is an odd, very slow item which is more notable for being a blues from this source than for any intrinsic qualities

Adelphi recording session, NY, 1969, John Townley

it may have. Gary Davis has long played blues, but has only recently taken to recording them again. For the most part they are very traditional items like "Crow Jane" or the more well-known of his secular songs like "Candy Man" which I recall Rory McEwan singing and playing, having learned it directly from Gary Davis, back in the mid-fifties when his music was professedly only religious.

Of the religious themes, "You Better Get Right" is notable, with fingerwork which really gives the lie to my statement above; is incredibly well played. "Lord I Wish I Could See" is a disturbing reminder of his sightlessness and makes a poignant companion to the closing title "I'll Do My Last Singing" in which Gary Davis is clearly aware that he is in the late autumn of his life. It's a touching, somewhat wistful album which may not be the Reverend's best, but is still a reminder of his exceptional powers.

His has been an undeservedly hard life and we're all culpable for having taken him a bit for granted.

Paul Oliver, Jazz Journal, 1971

●

BLUES GOSPEL, VOLUME ONE
Biograph BLP-12030

Unfortunately I didn't see Gary Davis on his recent, brief visit to England; if he'd been on form anything like this it would have been a tremendous experience. On these 1971 recordings he sounds in finer fettle and rather less old than he did on certain of his recordings of some years back. Comparison with those records, and with the Yazoo reissue

of his earliest session which I reviewed recently, show that Davis has never ceased reworking his material, although not so drastically as to alter the character of his pieces. In addition he has incorporated recent compositions into an already wide repertoire which harks back to early years of the century and beyond. "How Happy" and "Soon My Work" are examples of such recent compositions, the latter has a haunting melody but the slow tempo adopted is not particularly well suited to Davis's vocal style. "Samson and Delilah" was learnt from Blind Willie Johnson's recording "If I Had My Way" and is now a familiar Davis piece. He has transferred the emphasis from the almost entirely vocal presentation of Johnson and worked out a virtuoso guitar accompaniment, integrated with the vocal line. The other two spirituals here ("Angels" and "Children", both older pieces), show effective use of a minor key, considered by Davis "lonesome sounding", and certainly creating an ominous effect on "Angels".

Davis's too rarely heard blues are like nobody else's, and five tracks are riches indeed. The four secular items with guitar are all delivered in a semi-talking manner, producing a mellow effect in comparison with his rather strident spiritual style, and although "Sally" and "Hesitation" have elements in common, these four show well the breadth of his talent. "Hesitation" occurs surprisingly widely in the blues, country, popular and jazz traditions, but it is doubtful if there is another version as beautiful as this.

"Whistling", learned in 1917, has fine bottleneck passages, and shows interesting affinities with Willie McTell's "Travelling Blues" - narrative over riff interspersed with bottleneck passages in imitation, and so on. "Talk" has a charming Blind

Adelphi recording session, NY, 1969, John Townley

Blake-style raggy double-tempo break.

As this is called Volume 1 there is presumably more to come: I hope it reaches the same high standard.

Bob Yates, Jazz Journal, 1971

●

AMERICAN STREET SONGS

Riverside LP 148/12-611

This album, which has never been made available in Britain and is apparently even rare in the States, was originally issued as RLP 12-611 and was subsequently remastered in 1961 and re-issued under its present number. It forms part of the long deleted Riverside Jazz Archives series. The editor of this fine series of documentary albums was Kenneth S. Goldstein and it is interesting to learn how this album came about. Goldstein wanted two singers, one to represent the secular tradition and another to represent the religious tradition. The former was no problem - as Riverside had in its archives ten or twelve numbers recorded by Pink Anderson at a fair in Virginia back in 1950.

Goldstein had already met Gary Davis, who he had recorded for Stinson (SLP56) with Sonny Terry in 1954, so here was the obvious choice for the "holy blues". A session was arranged for 29th January, 1956 and the results are a delight to hear. Gary was in great form, playing nine numbers (most of which were first takes and eight are issued). All the numbers are full of the usual Davis trademarks; the dazzling guitar breaks between verses, the slurred vocal and instrumental lines and those amazing exchanges between voice and guitar. All the songs here are of exceptional interest, several of which he had recorded at the first session, for ARC, twenty odd years earlier, with almost identical arrangements. "Blow Gabriel" was not one of these and Gary never recorded it commercially again. The lyrics here are straight from Revelation, with shouted references to "Rocks a'melting, trees a'blowing and the moon is bleeding". This is real hellfire and brimstone stuff. In contrast, "Oh Lord, Search My Heart" is a beautifully controlled, rather sedate piece, with a haunting melody, somewhat reminiscent of a Lonnie Johnson tune. "There Was a Time That I Went Blind" is rather unusual and not related, I think, to the traditional spiritual, as has been suggested elsewhere, either melodically or lyrically. The words are very much Davis's own - not concerned in general terms with man searching after the truth, but very much with his own handicap.

There was a time that I went blind, (x 2)
It was the darkest day that I ever saw,
It was the day that I went blind.
Nobody cares for me, (x 2)
`Cause I lost my sight and I have to be led,
Nobody cares for me.

Steve Rye, Blues Link, c.1974

●

LET US GET TOGETHER

Kicking Mule 103

There are at present 9 readily available albums by the

Peterborough, UK, 1971, Courtesy: Peterborough Evening Telegraph

Reverend, and although on this release we hear his usual mastery, it does not tell us anything new. It is an interesting album, with one or two songs that are no longer available elsewhere, but none of the tracks are anywhere near his best. This is good Davis, though (was he ever bad?!), and an interesting mixture of blues, gospel, harmonica and guitar instruments.

Side one opens with one of his favourite songs, followed by his famous "Cocaine Blues", here sung and played right through, unlike previous recordings which were only partly sung, or purely instrumental. For me one of the highlights of the album is "Death Don't Have No Mercy", a beautiful rendition; the guitar break is among his best, "Let Us Get Together" was one of Gary's concert favourites, and he often had the audience singing along, but it does not have the same impact as a solo. It is good to hear "There's Destruction In The Land", lyrically one of his most moving compositions.

The other highlight opens side 2, when the Reverend plays behind a lady singer, whose name is not given, but who I suspect is one of the Davis's friends from their chapel. Gary's fine playing well complements the strength and conviction of the lady's singing. The two guitar instrumentals, "Georgia Camp Meeting" and "Blues in A", are full of originality and are always impressive Davis runs, but marred a little by the recording quality. The harmonica solo "Fox Chase" (over 6 minutes) drives as much as ever, and no one plays harp quite like the Reverend! The final track shows us some of the Reverend's humour when he imitates crying.

All in all, a pleasant album, and very desirable for the many Davis fanatics, but not an album on which to start a collection of his work. It should be of interest to all guitar students. The sleeve notes are a conversation with the Reverend about his playing, etc., and good reading.

Robert Tilling, Blues Link, July 1974

LET US GET TOGETHER

Kicking Mule SNKF 103

This is the latest in a series of records produced by Stefan Grossman designed to illustrate the many vocal and instrumental techniques of the Reverend Gary Davis, and follows on from "Ragtime Guitar" and "Children of Zion". This album is a collection of "rags, blues and religious tunes", and therefore concentrates equally on voice and instrument.

The selection of tracks is generally a happy one, though as far as I can see "Georgia Camp Meeting", is the only piece which could be classed as a rag - a version which, in fairness, depends a little too much on the listener's imagination in some of the trickier parts. However, the success of the album is in presenting the singing Reverend in relaxed mood, rather than striving for perfection in a recording studio. This was achieved by selecting tracks from sessions recorded in Davis's home and the office of his publisher, the recordings being spread over a number of years. Thus the dynamism of Gary Davis is brought over well - particularly in "Oh, Glory, How Happy I Am", my personal favourite, "Blues in A", and "Let Us Get Together", the title track.

The producer of the album deserves credit for the obvious care which has gone into putting this record together. Although a fine collection which I would recommend to any Gary Davis fan - if such a recommendation were needed, to those who do need an introduction to the Reverend Gary Davis, however, a word of advice. Try not to be too critical of the occasionally out-of-tune string or bungled left-hand passage. His is a taste truly worth acquiring.

Douglas Gordon, Guitar Magazine, 1974

WHEN I DIE I'LL LIVE AGAIN

Reverend Gary Davis Fantasy 24704 (Double Album)

This double album is a re-issue of two of Reverend Davis's superb early 60's Prestige/Bluesville recordings and presents in its entirety "Harlem Street Singer" and "A Little More Faith".

Throughout both discs Davis is in magnificent form, his strong vibrant voice shouting out the message of his wonderful "Holy Blues". His breathtaking guitar playing is always to the fore, seeming to grow and grow in prowess, and it punctuates the vocal lines with his usual brilliance and sensitivity.

Most of the tracks are in religious vein, such as "A Little More Faith", "God's Gonna Separate" and "Lo, I Be With You Always". Many are basically church sermons set to music, full of emotional intensity: Davis's great faith and sincerity shines through.

His blues-based guitar style is more evident on such

Adelphi recording session, NY, 1969, John Townley

numbers as "I'll Be Alright Someday" and "You Got To Move", the latter being a showpiece for his remarkable guitar technique. Unlike many of his later albums, which feature 12-string guitar, Davis here plays only his beloved "Miss Gibson" 6-string.

The recording quality and layout are first class, and these records represent an invaluable insight into the styles of one of the finest gospel singer/guitarists ever.

G, Bready, Guitar Magazine, 1974

•

O, GLORY
Adelphi AD 1008

I wrote in Blues Link with great enthusiasm about the recent Reverend Davis release on the Kicking Mule label and I can only write with the same enthusiasm about the latest Reverend Davis album on the Adelphi label! The two albums in fact complement each other in as much as they show aspects of Reverend Davis's music that are unique to his recording career.

On this latest Adelphi release Reverend Gary plays and sings with his wife Annie, the Apostolic Family in chorus, and is accompanied on four tracks by Larry Johnson playing harmonica ... and surely that is enough to tempt all Davis admirers to get this album without reading further! For me the most exciting aspects of this album are the two tracks, "God Will Take Care Of You" and "Out On The Ocean Sailing". On the latter title Gary plays five-string banjo which he has not played on record previously and the instrumental is also new to me. On "God Will Take Care Of You" we hear him playing the piano and backed by the Apostolic Family Chorus, which is made up of John Townley, Monica Moscia, Jerry Novac and Bobby Brooks. This is a simple tune and Gary's piano playing is direct and basic but the overall impression is quite dramatic and I feel that Gary is playing and singing with great emotion. I am sure this song must have been a favourite at his Baptist Chapel.

It is good to hear both Gary and Larry Johnson together on an album, for Gary regarded Larry as one of his best students and fondest friends (It would be good to hear Gary and Larry playing guitar together!) Of the four tracks where Larry backs Gary on harmonica I feel that "Lo, I'll Be With You Always" is the most successful with them both really working together well and helped with the odd comment from the Reverend. "Help me harmonica, come on in". I am certain that Gary would have been pleased to have this album out with Larry on it for I feel that Larry Johnson is a fine musician whose albums do not really do him justice and I hope he will soon record again and give us a tour here.

For many reasons Gary's song "Soon My Work Will All Be Done" is among my favourites and now on this album to hear his wife singing as well makes it even more exciting. Annie was a fine wife to Gary and they were married for over 30 years. She always makes people welcome in her home and always encouraged Gary to play and sing and often when she went along with him to concerts she would sit at the front and sing along with him! She is still living in New York and in good spirits and working as hard as ever for her church.

The album was recorded in 1969 and produced by John Townley who also wrote the short but sincere liner notes and this album is a must for all of Reverend Davis's admirers. It is not perhaps the best record on which to start a Reverend Davis collection but it is well worth a listen and it still shows him to be a giant among musicians.

The design and layout are of the highest standards and the front cover, in particular, is beautiful by any standard. I cannot congratulate John Townley and Gene Rosenthal enough for the superb album and we should look forward to further releases from Adelphi with great anticipation.

Robert Tilling, Blues Link, 1974

•

LO, I BE WITH YOU ALWAYS
Kicking Mule SNKD 1

Without a doubt, Lo I Be With You Always is the definitive Rev. Gary Davis album, a double live presentation which takes up where the earlier Stefan Grossman productions for Transatlantic left off. In fact, I suspect that two of the tracks on side three, a couple of gospel numbers, are from the same sessions that produced "Children of Zion", since like that album they are acknowledged to Manny Greenhill. Actually, if I wanted to recommend the album to all lovers of Rev. Davis's music I would merely have to whisper one word "Candy Man". For while we've had variations on the basic song, a two-step instrumental and a three-four version in waltz-time, this time Stefan has come across with the basic song, which he describes in his notes as "the best one I have heard from him - it shows everything about the tune from the spoken introduction to the guitar improvising". Actually such a breadth of technique, humour and that elusive characteristic known as soul is crammed into the song that it's hard to credit that it runs for a mere five seconds over three minutes from the spoken introduction, mentioning briefly how he learned it in 1905, to the heavily strummed final chords. For me, however, it is not this old, old favourite that sticks in the memory but the two tracks that follow, recorded at the Mariposa Folk Festival in 1959 with the Georgia Sea Island Singers, which may give us some idea of what things were like when the Rev. Davis used to hold forth in his storefront church in New York. It is sometimes too easy to forget, when we are listening to the performances of a man like this, that in a sense when we take him out of his environment and put him in a concert hall and (worse) into a recording studio, we are falsifying his music, making it something it was not, and losing much of what it was. But in the almost a quarter of an hour when he is singing "I Got Religion, I'm So Glad" and "I'm A Soldier In The Army Of The Lord" his music enters a new dimension that puts things back into contact. Of course, things like the sly "The Boy Was Kissing The Girl While Playing The Guitar At The Same Time" which I remember him doing with a very co-operative beauty at the Shaw Theatre shortly before his death, or the spontaneously improvised "Please Judy", are important aspects of his music, too, but without an understanding of the gospel foundations the thing begins to float away into abstraction and become less meaningful. And on a purely technical level, despite the somewhat mediocre recording quality, it's fascinating how when he is really rocking on down, the Reverend keeps the guitar playing much more interesting stuff. It would have been so easy to just chunk out the basic rhythm in chords, but all the time there's the most beautiful little things happening without in any way interfering with the rhythm. A lot of young white guys have taken up the musical torch lit by Gary Davis from Stefan himself to Ralph McTell - even Bob Dylan has done a version of one of the songs on his album - but these are the roots from which their music sprang. Don't ever forget it.

Karl Dallas, Sounds, 1974

•

I AM A TRUE VINE
Interstate Music (Heritage)
HT CD 07 (CD only)

I Am A True Vine is a new compilation of remastered tracks from Grossman's archive of his mentor - Rev. Gary Davis. Recorded between 1962-63, the emphasis is distinctly upon Davis's picking skills. The selection includes previously unissued tracks including "God's Gonna Separate", "Soon My Work Will All Be Done", and a version of "Cocaine Blues" which leaves nothing whatsoever to be desired (except perhaps a peek at the rest of the big G's archives). Recorded in his late 60's, Davis's voice occasionally let him down but his guitar

Jersey, UK, August 5th 1972, Robert Tilling

playing is consistently outstanding. It is a pity that he recorded so little twenty years earlier when he was at his peak.

Stephen Quilley, Folk Roots, 1991

•

DELIA -
LATE CONCERT RECORDINGS 1970-71
American Activities UACD 103

It is good to see a recording presented with such loving care and affection as this one is. The outward appearance is enough to tell you that the producers take both pride and pleasure in offering this to the public; and the little note that Reverend Davis's wife will get appropriate royalties tell us that their hearts are in the right place.

There has to be more to a record than honourable intentions, though, but the Reverend Davis can be relied upon to deliver the goods. There are two separate live performances here - one in Connecticut in August 1970, the other in Jersey (the Channel Islands) about a year later. Of the songs he performed at the first, only two are repeated at the second - one of which is the inevitable "Candy Man" - which gives a small indication of the breadth of his repertoire.

There are many highlights, for Davis's was a many-sided talent. "Mountain Jack", "Walkin' Dog" and "Whistlin' Blues" are superb blues, while on the ragtime instrumentals like "Buck Dance" and "Cincinnati Flow Rag" his playing is always a salutary reminder that this is music to be danced to, not just a set of showpieces to be listened to and admired (though they are surely that as well, and the very title "Make Believe Stunt" suggests they are meant that way). It may be on the religious songs, though, like "Samson and Delilah", "Pure Religion" and "I Am A True Vine", that you see Davis's full genius at work; the beautiful melodic guitar work providing the perfect complement to his passionate, declamatory singing. At his best on material like this, he could produce some of the most captivating of all American sacred music, it has to be said that Davis was getting old by this time, and that amazing voice had lost a little of its consistency and authority, and while his playing is pretty near as good as ever, there are occasional rough edges in that department as well (slightly dodgy tuning, buzzing strings). Also, not the Reverend's own fault, but on the Jersey concert, the sound is occasionally wobbly. Nevertheless this is still a delight from the start to finish, and while there are probably better Gary Davis records, I don't think that anyone who buys it will regret doing so.

Ray Templeton, Blues and Rhythm, July 1991

•

PURE RELIGION AND BAD COMPANY
Smithsonian/Folkways SF 40035 Compact Disc

I am particularly delighted to see this set re-appear after many years of deletion. It first appeared in the UK nearly 30 years ago on Doug Dobell's `77' label and before that it was released on the Folk Lyric label in the USA. The running order and the titles are the same as the original release but with the added attraction of having two extra songs, "Time Is Drawing Near" and "Crucifixion", recorded at the same session in 1957.

I cannot recommend this outstanding set enough for here we have the great man at his VERY BEST. This was the first album on which I heard his song, "Candy Man", and although it is one of his more simple tunes, it is for me still quite infectious, and from the moment I first heard it I was hooked! I have listened to these recordings many, many times and never tire of them. His guitar instrumentals on "Mountain Jack", "Buck Dance", "Devil's Dream" and "Seven Sisters", are as inventive, superlative and as commanding as any that can be found in the history of American folk music.

As Bruce Bastin points out in his knowledgeable and informative sleeve notes, Rev. Davis was "a deeply religious performer", and here we have some of his most emotional songs including the moving "Bad Company", telling of a young man who has committed murder and is awaiting the electric chair. None of the sacred songs quite have the power and gusto, particularly in the vocals, that can be found on the equally exciting double Fantasy album (Fantasy 24704), recorded during the early 1960's but they are just as entertaining and enjoyable.

Three of Rev. Davis's most requested songs, particularly when on tour in the UK, are performed here as instrumentals, "Candy Man", "Hesitation Blues" and "Cocaine Blues".
I think this was a time when Rev. Davis did not want particularly to sing - at least not in public - any of his blues

lyrics. At the time this recording was made in New York City (by Fred Gerlach and Tiny Robinson, Leadbelly's niece) Rev. Davis was not yet performing very much for white folk audiences.

Although many recordings of Rev. Davis's music are easily available at the moment this re-issue is still very welcome. It will only enhance his highly respected reputation.

Robert Tilling, Blues And Rhythm, September 1991

•

COMPLETE RECORDED WORKS, 1935-1949
Document Records DOCD-5060

Even within the blues, a tradition known for its guitarists, South Carolina's Gary Davis stands alone. As the biographical notes for this CD point out, Davis's talents were of such magnitude that they transcend any particular musical style or era. Building on the early Piedmont tradition of contemporaries like Willie Walker and Pink Anderson, Davis created a unique guitar style. His inventiveness and technical skill are not surpassed by any other guitarist of any genre or time. To this day Davis's playing presents one of the ultimate challenges to acoustic guitarists.

This recent release from Johnny Parth is a joy. It collects

all Davis's commercial recordings, rendering obsolete Yazoo 1035, whose 14 cuts are all present on this CD. It is interesting that Davis occupies such a seat of reverential awe within the blues community, since his commercial recordings include only two blues. Much of this has to do with his central role in forming the blues of the Piedmont, his association with Walker and Blind Roy Fuller, and the fact that many of the gospel songs which make up the bulk of this CD are done in standard blues form - twelve bars and three chord changes.

The bulk of the material here (15 out of 18 cuts) is from Davis's initial 1935 New York session with Fuller and washboard player/guitarist Bull City Red. Davis, already by the time concerned about the propriety of recording blues, performed two instrumentally astonishing blues the first day, but refused to record any more for the remainder of the session, although he did accompany Fuller on several of his. The 13 gospel songs recorded over the last two days of the session (one an accompaniment to Red's vocal) sealed Davis's reputation for all time.

Although he recorded brilliant music of all types well into the 1970's, he rarely again equalled the combination of musical brilliance and religious fervour captured on these sides.

Rounding out the CD are three recordings from the 1940's. 1945's "Civil War March", which in later years he would record as "Soldier's Drill", is a five and a half minute masterpiece that hints at the breadth of Davis's repertoire. (In later years the only music Davis would refuse to play was blues; aside from that caveat, his programs would include marches, Tin Pan Alley tunes, country dance songs and rags, along with gospel songs). The final two cuts, a sacred pairing from 1949, represent his last recordings for the black market, and mark the first appearance of the large-bodied wooden guitar which would become his trademark in place of the steel-bodied National he had used since the 1935 session.

Highly recommended, this CD is as important to any serious blues collection as the recordings of Robert Johnson or Lightin' Hopkins. While Davis's shouted and exclamatory vocals are in sharp contrast to the elegance and polish of his guitar work (and may, for some, be an acquired taste), his role in shaping America's approach to the acoustic guitar cannot be overstated.

(One little quibble: Why does the title of his CD refer to Rev. Blind Gary Davis? Neither his single blues 78, nor his gospel recordings, ever referred to him by that name. His 1935 recordings, both blues and sacred, listed him as Blind Gary, and many of his later recordings listed him as Rev. Gary Davis. Reissue record companies should not make up new names for artists to suit their own purposes or marketing convenience).

Peter R. Ashoff, Living Blues, January 1992

•

BLUES AND RAGTIME - SHANACHIE 97024
Peg 'n' Whistle Red - Biograph BCD125

The Gary Davis comes from a series of recordings made by Stefan Grossman on what sounds like a variety of equipment and in venues between 1962-66. It isn't an instrumental set as I had hoped - not because the vocals are bad because they are not; but there is a need for more albums devoted entirely to

Cambridge Folk Festival, UK, 1971, Nigel Luckhurst

Davis' amazing skills as a guitar player.

You get plenty of that here, complete with weird tunings and even a slide showcase on *Whistlin' Blues*. One track, *Twelve Sticks,* is a genuine tour de force, easily the equal of anything the Reverend recorded elsewhere and there's a lovely laid back tribute to Blind Boy Fuller on *Baby Let Me Lay It On You.* Some of the tracks he recorded elsewhere *(Cocaine Blues, Bug Rag)* but never quite like this, for Grossman obviously gave the old man his head. That also lead to a twelve-minute version of *Hesitation Blues* which rather outstays its welcome and a very curious rendering (I use the word advisedly) of *She's Funny That Way. Candyman,* one of his specialties, is fairly awful, sung in a mock falsetto out of time with the delightful guitar accompaniment. But at its best, this is a brilliant showcase of Davis's skills as a player although the vocals are peculiarly soft and often spoken rather than sung. The biggest drawback on many tracks is a dreadful audience who applaud every minor joke and crow with delight when they recognise a tune. They might have inspired Davis' very relaxed performance but they are a pain on repeated listening. Guitarists will find a 30-page tablature in the booklet but check if you already have a Gary Davis CD on Heritage - I think some tracks may be duplicated.

David Harrison, Folk Roots, October 1993

•

THE COMPLETE EARLY RECORDINGS
Yazoo 2011

Because he lived in New York, Reverend Gary Davis was teacher to the early acoustic blues revivalists. Dave Van Ronk, Roy Book Binder, Stefan Grossman, Jorma Kaukonen, and dozens of others studied with Davis and hailed him as the greatest of ragtime blues fingerpickers. Oddly, their opinion has been borne out; the work of all the interesting guitarists of the '20s and '30s is now available, and Davis sounds as good as ever. Blind Blake may challenge him for pure right-hand speed but not in all-around musicianship, and there are few other players whose recorded work compares to Davis'.

One reason for Davis' instrumental primacy is that he spent little time playing blues. Working with the more complex harmonic structures of gospel music pushed him to expand his musical vocabulary beyond what he would have needed had he stuck to blues or his showpiece ragtime instrumentals. Davis was a guitar evangelist, a gospel musician - the "holy blues" rubric attached to him in the '60s was only a marketing device. Of course, he was capable of playing fine blues, but the two secular numbers on this early session are its weakest moments.

The religious songs are among the greatest guitar pieces available in any style. Davis' wide, vocal guitar tone and incredible accuracy and speed serve perfectly to frame and echo his preacher's shout. The arrangements are virtually the same as those he played in the '50s and '60s, but he never again equalled the precision and technical virtuosity of these sides.

His singing is wrenching and strong, though he is a bit stiffer and hoarser than on his best later recordings. Still, his vocal power is impressive, and the way the voice and guitar work together is a marvel. Davis' many imitators tend to sound as it they are singing over excellent arrangements; Davis himself sounds like a unified musical whole, the voice and guitar equal

At Home, circa 1963, Stefan Grossman

parts of a homogeneous creation. Showy as the guitar work gets, every lightening run serves the voice rather than distracting from it. Call it blues or call it gospel, this disc is indispensable for anyone interested in great fingerpicking and singing.

Elijah Wald, Living Blues, 1994

•

REVEREND GARY DAVIS - LIVE AND KICKIN'
Justin Time Records JAM 9133-2

Also to be highly recommended is the Gary Davis album which documents a concert he gave, also in 1967. I was fortunate enough to experience a Davis concert and this record brings back fond memories of that occasion. Those of you who did not catch Rev. Davis live will find this CD gives a pretty good impression of what his shows were like. Apart from the expected dazzling "raggy" guitar picking, you also get a harp number and some of the chat, the overall package also giving an indication of the warmth, humanity and humour of the man. The recording quality is superb and you get a nice cross-section of typical Davis material, such as "Twelve Gates to the City", "Maple Leaf Rag" and "You Got To Move". According to Bob Tilling's excellent book on Gary Davis, these would appear to be newly discovered recordings, so completists will want to snap them up. However, you don't have to be a completist to enjoy this brilliant release, just a lover of good music.

Michael Prince, Blueprint, 1997

•

DEMONS AND ANGELS/THE ULTIMATE COLLECTION
Shanachie 6117

Unlike most of his contemporaries - Bukka White, Son

House and Mississippi John Hurt come readily to mind - Reverend Gary Davis (originally from South Carolina) didn't have to get 're-discovered' as the sixties folk revival took hold. He had never laid his beloved Gibson guitar down - basically making his living as a street musician his entire life; first at chitlin' struts and parties in the South ('I was a 'blues cat' then, Davis savours) and later up on New York City's Harlem sidewalks. He'd lost an earlier chance at fame and fortune in the thirties when a former pupil, Blind Boy Fuller turned his transfixing style into a string of best-sellers but, still at the top of his game (while old enough to collect Social Security) Davis' amazingly virtuosic dexterity, off-the-cuff wizardry and fascinating repertoire finally won him a measure of the success he deserved.

As Stefan Grossman, the producer/compiler of this excellent sounding, three-CD extravaganza, accurately puts it, Davis' panoramic musical genius makes him the equivalent of 'the Stravinsky of the acoustic guitar.' His organic song-bag not only stretches back to the turn of the century (with hokum, ragtime and traditional strains) but encompasses pop and gospel standards, medicine songs, cakewalks, country dance tunes, vaudeville, hymns, marching band riffs and, of course, the country blues. All 58 selections were 'culled from over a hundred hours of studio, concert and home recordings made by those who loved his music best - his student, Grossman, an accomplished folk guitarist, among them. During these years (1958-66), Davis was also an instructor at Brownie McGhee's Home Of The Blues Music School, worked as a singing preacher and cut the odd album for independents like Riverside, Prestige and Stinson.

The first disc emanates from a series of concerts Davis gave at Columbia University, circa 1958-59 and, in many ways, is the most revelatory of the three. Davis, on the brink of becoming a celebrity, is brimming with equal parts bravura and passion, hi-jinx and spunk. From the opening song, an ancient dance tune,

At Home, circa 1963, Stefan Grossman

featuring some libidinous moaning and groaning, it's obvious Davis has spent a lifetime fluidly fusing a spontaneous East Coast rag technique with his own complex genius – creating an extended lexicon of tunes full of technical flash, nay, kinetic wonder, containing ear-opening side-pockets of improvisational amazement. Other near-instrumentals ('Slippin'', 'Soldier's March' and 'Square Dance Verses' are similarly expansive, while he conjures the idea-rich momentum of modern jazz pianist Art Tatum on the likes of 'Twelve Sticks', a prankish variation on 'The Dozens'.

Also included are re-vamps of Davis' sole thirties 78 rpm release, 'I'm Throwin' Up My Hands' and 'Cross And Evil Woman Blues', as well as expository gospel songs like the harrowing 'Crucifixion', 'Keep Your Lamp Trimmed and Burning' and 'I Am the Light.' Davis' nearly toothless, cigarette-worn voice had eroded slightly, due to his years outdoors, but still possessed an earnestly rough (if strained at times), angular edge - always intensely emotional, often dramatic, even poetic on occasions. Songs such as 'I'm So Tired' and the chordal-voiced 'Don't Know Where To Go,' along with the various untitled blues and rags are, simply, timeless.

The magic continues on the succeeding CDs. Disc Two is a sampling of various home-recording sessions from 1946-66 and the third features concert material from the same folk-boom period. As the set's title implies, Davis was the master at dressing up gospel in the clothes of the blues - 'Sportin' Life Blues' is followed by 'God's Gonna Separate' (a rare, challenging, key of F tune) while the careening, old-timey snapshot 'All Night Long' preceded 'Who Shall Deliver' and an impassioned 'Jesus Met The Woman'.

Other spotlight efforts, often accenting Davis' idiosyncratic, rapid-fire thumb/forefinger picking approach (his fingers would characteristically blur together after he got warmed up) and 'talking' or 'crying' passages include solos like 'Devil's Dream', yet another run through of 'Twelve Sticks' ('I'm gonna play a piano a little bit,' Davis announces prior to the latter) and 'Lord, Stand By Me' - later secularized by Ben E. King. Plenty of Davis' influential chestnuts are also offered - 'Cocaine Blues' (complete with sermonizing), 'Twelve Gates To The City' (perhaps his most recognized arrangement) and 'She Wouldn't Say Quit' among them. Rarely performed obscurities ('Lord, On Your Word') abound, along with 'Whistlin Blues', the sole live bottleneck recording currently available by this American music master.

Davis was always learning new material and expanding that songbook, not relying on re-hashes of his hits like so many of his peers, and continued performing (he played numerous Newport Folk Festivals as well as Carnegie Hall) until the end. He died of a heart attack, aged 76, en route to a Newtonville, New Jersey gig in 1972. For all those who think that Ray Charles or James Brown is the apex of gospel-infused soul music – here's the real deal.

Gary von Tersch, Blues and Rhythm, May 2001

•

REVEREND GARY DAVIS - LIVE AT NEWPORT
Vanguard VCD 79588-2

These performances come from the 1965 Folk Festival, and

the old LP, to which two titles have been added, has long been one of my favourite Davis albums. It captured an afternoon when the Rev was on top form, despite a cold that accounts for the intermittent sniffing, and was clearly feeding off the crowd's enthusiasm. They applauded themselves at the start of 'Samson' for knowing the Peter, Paul and Mary version, but their reaction at its end springs more worthily, from amazement at Davis's mastery of his instrument.

He was also a master of this audience, artfully blending the ferocious emotional commitment of the spirituals with humour of songs like 'Lovin' Spoonful' and 'She Wouldn't Say Quit'. The tapes from which the old LP was drawn were exceptionally well-recorded, and careful sound restoration for CD enhances the listening experience. My only reservation is that the bonus tracks have been tacked on without much thought for their effect. 'I Will Do My Last Singing' is so obviously a valedictory set closer that 'Soldier's Drill', brilliant though it is, slightly spoils the balance of the disc. The problem is compounded by 'Cindy', which features banjo, and a tune that I don't think Rev. Davis did elsewhere on record. When he plays his subsidiary instruments, it's always a bonus (there's harp on 'I've Done All My Singing'), but unfortunately 'Cindy' finds him in the company of his pupil Barry Kornfeld, on guitar and most of the vocals. (When he does sing, Davis is rather distant from the microphone.) Kornfeld's knowing, self-satisfied delivery makes for a jarringly disappointing final track. Until then, however, the CD is a transfixing experience. If it's pointed out that, 'Cindy' apart, all the songs are available in other versions; my response is that, while it's nice to own one Faberge egg, the opportunity to acquire more should not be missed.

Chris Smith, Blues and Rhythm, 2001

●

REVEREND GARY DAVIS
THE GUITAR AND BANJO OF...
Original Blues Classics OBCCD 592-2

Actually, it's the guitar, banjo and harmonica of...but not the voice, on this particular release. That's a pity, in one sense, as nobody could sing like the Reverend Davis, but on the other hand it means that it's wall-to-wall instrumental fireworks, and he was on absolutely stunning form on that March day in 1964 when he was recorded. On this straight reissue of an original Prestige Folklore album, we have him showing off just what he could do - astonishingly imaginative and dexterous finger picking on guitar, frailing on a banjo, and on the one track, the standard coon hunt/fox hunt impression (not that it sounds 'standard' in Davis's hands). There's a pretty well definitive reading of the one Davis tune that every wannabe finger style guitarist in the world must have had a go at, 'Candy Man' - beautiful, almost hypnotic playing.

There's an amazing arrangement of a march tune, in which you can pick out the various parts that would have been allocated to instruments in the military band. And there's a good selection of the rags that enslaved so many listeners at the time - Davis working the piano arrangements into guitar format and executing them with style and panache. Everything he turned his hand to, from blues like 'Can't Be Satisfied' to traditional dance tunes like 'Devil's Dream' sounds extraordinarily accomplished.

Time is rather short, at a couple of minutes short of forty, but its retail price should reflect that, and with the sleeve facsimile on the front of the booklet and Chris Albertson's original notes inside, you can transport yourself back to the days when this music was still fresh and new, and knocking out all those young guitarists from New York to New Malden. Some went on to make a career out of trying to play like this, but none had the character and the genius of the Reverend Gary Davis. Highly recommended, especially to guitar freaks.

Ray Templeton, Blues and Rhythm, March 2002

•

IF I HAD MY WAY: EARLY HOME RECORDINGS
Smithsonian Folkways Recordings SFW CD 40123

In B&R 176 I reviewed with great enthusiasm a new release of late fifties material from Rev. Gary Davis (World Arbiter 2005), and within no time at all we have yet another very exciting collection of previously unreleased material on the market. This time it comes from the highly respected John Cohen, who is, among other things, a filmmaker, historian, producer, photographer, artist and a founder member of the acoustic trio The New Lost City Ramblers. All but one of these tracks (a very clean version of the c.1945 recording 'Civil War Parade') were recorded by Cohen at Davis' home during 1953, and include a number of titles that have never appeared elsewhere. The growing army of Davis aficionados need not read on any further but just rush out and buy this highly recommended set now!

Fortunately there is only one title that appears on both the World Arbiter and on this set - here it is called 'Marine Band' and on World Arbiter 'Two Step' - it is a highly paced marching band tune performed with tremendous energy, and has only ever appeared on these two albums. Nine of the tracks, recorded by Cohen on a quarter inch tape, reel-to-reel Penton machine, have never appeared elsewhere, which adds greatly to the interest of this very welcome release.

The accompanying booklet is excellent with some photographs by Cohen that I have never seen previously, including a beautiful shot of an immaculately dressed Davis walking alone on a Harlem street. The very informative notes, also by Cohen, are personal, knowledgeable and thorough. The song notes are particularly interesting and include fascinating and informative comments from the noted gospel historian Horace Clarence Boyer. Considering that these informal recordings were initially made just for Cohen himself, the sound quality is very good with just the odd slight distraction here and there, which in no way hinders the enjoyment of this set.

By the time of these recordings Davis had only appeared in one or two public concerts, including the Leadbelly Memorial Concert held in New York City in 1950, and spent much of his time preaching at his storefront church and playing on the streets of Harlem. Most of the time he performed on the street alone but occasionally, during 1950-1955, he was joined by singer-guitarist Rev. McKinley Peebles, later also known as 'Sweet Papa Stovepipe' who, during the seventies, made a number of concert appearances.

Fortunately on one of the days that Cohen was recording Peebles turned up, and he recorded them performing together, along with one solo track from Peebles.

This set opens with 'If I Had My Way' a song that Davis recorded many times later in life, which I regard as one of his greatest titles, and the guitar playing is as confident as I have ever heard. Although at times the magnificent guitar work is a little raw it is highly inventive, and I know of no other guitarist that has come close to Davis' articulate and highly individual skill. Although Davis recorded some titles many times, the great joy is that every version is different and all of the previously released titles here contain interesting changes and surprises.

There are four titles on which Davis and Peebles work together, and on 'The Uncloudy Day', they respond to each other very naturally, no doubt after many hours working on the street together. Peebles has a natural gospel feel to his vocals and on his only solo title, 'Give Me A Heart To Love', his guitar playing is confident and straightforward. Sister Annie Davis adds some delicate and distinctive vocals on a couple of titles, very much as she did with her husband in church every Sunday.

As you would expect there is some quite outstanding guitar picking throughout and, in particular with 'He Stole Away' (later titled 'I Did Not Want To Join The Band') and 'I Belong To The Band', his guitar work is superlative, consummate, breathtaking, captivating...I have finally run out of words! It is particularly interesting to hear his guitar technique at this point in his career, which for me is very appealing with its more raw and expressive energy. As Cohen suggests in his notes perhaps with so many young players calling in for lessons and advice he sharpened up his playing techniques even more to always be one step ahead of his admirers!

The vocals throughout are clear, strong and as passionate as ever. Davis always played from the heart whether it be a gospel song, a ragtime tune or a blues, and this first rate release only confirms my great belief that he is one of the finest musicians in the history of twentieth century popular music.

Robert Tilling, Blues and Rhythm, April 2003

•

REVEREND GARY DAVIS THE SUN OF OUR LIFE: SOLOS, SONGS, A SERMON 1955 - 1957
World Arbiter 2005

This CD is something of a surprise, over 70 minutes of previously unissued material by Reverend Gary Davis from the mid -1950's. All were recorded in informal circumstances, some

Philadelphia Folk Festival, circa 1969, Bob Patterson

New York City, David Gahr

REVEREND GARY DAVIS
FROM BLUES TO GOSPEL
Biograph/Short Factory DK 34007

Material by Rev. Gary Davis (1896 – 1972) is easy to find these days, and these two highly recommended discs make excellent additions to the growing list of first-rate releases. Recorded 36 years apart, these discs represent his first and last studio recordings. During late July 1934 Blind Gary (as he was known then - he was not ordained until 1937), guitarist and singer Blind Boy Fuller, and washboard player and singer Bull City Red (George Washington) were driven from Durham, North Carolina, to New York City by talent scout J.B. Long for a recording session at the American Recording Company.

This was the first time that any of these musicians had been into a recording studio, and for three days they produced out-standing music that has been admired ever since. Davis recorded fourteen solo sides, five as second guitar to Fuller, and two backing vocals for Bull City Red. On **The Vintage Recordings** we have all of Davis' solo titles from the 1935 session and one of the titles with Red. All these titles have appeared elsewhere and Document released the same set back in 1991; but this latest release has a new cover photograph, the original notes by UK blues authority Chris Smith, and cleaned-up sound.

The fourteen solo tracks include only two blues titles, 'I'm Throwin' Up My Hands' and 'Cross And Evil Women Blues', all the others are religious. The guitar work is outstanding in its accuracy, speed and invention. On all of the titles Davis plays a National Duolian metal guitar, using only the thumb and first finger of his right hand to pick the strings. The guitar work throughout these first recordings is breathtaking. The vocals are often hoarse and strained, but considering this was his first time in a studio, he sounds confident and controlled.

All of the early songs are superb, but 'I Am The True Vine' and 'I Belong To The Band' are exceptional in their passion and power. Bull City Red's vocals on 'I Saw The Light' are not as strong as Davis', but he is not daunted by Davis' blistering guitar picking. After these historical recordings, Davis did not return to the recording studio for another fourteen years. He fell out with Long over money, and over time his records sold poorly.

Davis left Durham in 1944 to live in New York City, and soon after his arrival he recorded (possibly in his home) the instrumental 'Civil War March'. The song is a beautifully crafted showpiece played on an acoustic guitar.

Two titles, 'I Cannot Bear My Burden By Myself' and 'I'm Gonna Meet You At The Station', were recorded in 1949 in New York City - Davis' first studio work since 1935. His vocals are mellower and constrained while his guitar picking is as strong and as captivating as ever. This set proves that Davis was one of the most consummate guitar players of his generation.

The beautifully produced **From Blues To Gospel** was first released on Biograph Records in 1971 and last appeared on a disc about twelve years ago. It is good to see it released

---

probably at someone's home (a train can be heard passing on one track) and the remainder at a store-front church. Despite this, the recording quality is excellent. This CD's subtitle neatly summarises the contents: 25 minutes of solos, 25 minutes of songs and 20 minutes of a sermon. With minor exceptions that's how it's sequenced. Apart from 'Candy Man', sung in falsetto, and 'Cigarette Break', the first 10 tracks are guitar solos. All of them display Davis's usual formidable technique but sometimes, particularly on the four improvisations, one does have the feeling that he is showing off this technique purely for the sake of it.

More to my taste are the four religious songs that follow. The lyrics and Rev. Davis's hollering voice give these songs a meaning and intensity that mere instrumental virtuosity can never attain. 'My Heart Is Fixed' is particularly fine, a longer and more committed performance than the version on the pure 'Religion And Bad Company' CD on Smithsonian Folkways. The next few tracks were recorded in a store-front church. The sisters in the congregation (and one brother) sing 'Hold To God's Unchanging Hand', accompanied by an unknown pianist. Then Rev. Davis joins them as lead singer for the charming and heartfelt 'My Home Is On High', one of the highlights of the CD. I'm not qualified to judge Rev. Davis's abilities as a preacher, but I can say that during the 20 minute extract from one of his sermons, which appears to be a stream-of-consciousness improvisation, he gradually builds the intensity, helped by responses from one of the ladies in the congregation. For all that, I doubt that I shall play this track again.

For reasons which should be apparent, this is not a CD for the newcomer to Rev. Davis. Nevertheless, any existing admirer who buys it is sure to find something to astonish and delight within its varied contents.

Juke Blues, June 2003

●

REVEREND BLIND GARY DAVIS
THE VINTAGE RECORDINGS (1935-
1949) Document Records DOCD-5060 (UK)

once again with new notes and a stunning cover photograph. The thirteen titles were recorded on March 17, 1971, and are taken from Davis' last studio session, when nineteen titles were recorded in all. Most of the titles are performed on a twelve string Bozo guitar, and although his playing is slower and less powerful, it lacks none of his creativity, and the vocals are as passionate as ever.

The first six titles are secular and were probably part of his repertoire from his earliest times as a musician. Highlights include a beautiful instrumental version of the traditional song 'Crow Jane' another instrumental, 'Eagle Rocking Blues', the timeless harmonica solo 'Lost John' and his masterpiece 'Samson and Delilah'. The final song, 'I will Do My Last Singing' ends the set on a high note.

Robert Tilling, Living Blues, 2004

•

REV. GARY DAVIS - LIVE MANCHESTER FREE TRADE HALL, 1964

Document Records DOCD 32-20-14

Rev. Gary Davis (1896 – 1972) was admired in the UK long before his first tour during spring 1964, and although his recordings were fairly hard to find at that time his songs such as Candy Man and Cocaine Blues were being regularly performed around the folk club circuit. He first visited the UK touring with "The American Blues and Gospel Caravan" which also included, among others, Muddy Waters, Otis Spann, Sister Rosetta Tharpe, Joe Pleasance, Sonny Terry and Brownie McGhee. They performed to much acclaim in a number of major concert halls including performances in London and Liverpool, and it was on May 8th in the northern city of Manchester that this recording was made.

The tour, and Davis in particular, had rave reviews in the press and he was greatly admired by his fellow travellers; often on stage Muddy would refer to him as "My Reverend". At the start of the tour Sister Rosetta Tharpe was not too keen on some of his offstage behaviour but by the end of the tour she was one of his most ardent fans. There were times on this tour that Davis was not at his best, due to the long hours of travelling and perhaps a little too much partying, but on this eleven title set he is at his most sparkling.

Many Davis fans thought that he may not play any non secular music on this tour as there were rumours that he no longer played blues in public, but at every concert he performed a mixture of blues, ragtime and gospel music to the delight of all. The two opening titles You Got To Move and If I Had My Way get this highly recommended disc off to a terrific start. The guitar craftsmanship, as you would expect, is as expansive and complex as ever, while his vocals must have convinced the huge crowds that he was on top form.

There is just one title Sun Is Going Down where Davis invites harmonica maestro Sonny Terry to join him on stage, which happened frequently through the eleven date tour. Davis and Terry recorded an album back in 1954 but have very rarely recorded together since then, in fact, I only know of one other similar track from a 1998 release (Groove CD GJ97006), which was probably recorded during the same tour. They really kick up a storm together powerfully expressing their

huge individual personalities and leaving me wanting more of this exhilarating material.

On Coon Hunt Davis shows off his own harmonica skills, an instrument that he first played as a young child living in South Carolina, and it is one of the most highly charged of his rare harmonica recordings that I have heard. There are four guitar instrumentals and I Got A Little Mama , Sweet As She Can Be and Sally, Please Come Back To Me find Davis at his most creative, spontaneously moving all over the fret board with ease and fluidity. His much recorded, and emulated, Cincinnati Flow Drag is crisp and strident while his version of the classic ragtime title Maple Leaf Rag really does put him in a distinctive class of his own.

There were no doubt very few people in the audience who had ever seen such a magnificent acoustic guitar performer, for apart from Big Bill Broonzy, a few years earlier, there had been no one of Davis's stature touring the UK previously – for many, including myself, it was quite a revelation and I treasure the concert programme to this day.

The sound quality at times has some interference but certainly not enough to distract from this forty minute long performance and the heartfelt notes by the British blues authority Bob Groom greatly add to the enjoyment.

Robert Tilling, Living Blues, 2007

•

LIFTING THE VEIL: THE EARLIEST BLUES GUITARISTS

World Arbiter 2008

Rev. Davis's titles, recorded in 1956-57 by Tiny Robinson and Fred Gerlach, seem to be overmatter from the 'Sun Of Our Life' (World Arbiter 2005). They are wonderful performances, well-recorded, some of them extended ('Mountain Jack' is seven minutes), and played by a musician in peak form; as with the Leadbelly, the titles are familiar, but the swaggering, swinging 'Lost John' appears to be his only released version on guitar rather than harmonica.

This material will be essential to fans and students of Rev. Davis; so will the booklet's extracts from a 300+ (!) page oral history, documented by Elizabeth Lyttelton Harold (Alan Lomax's first wife) in 1951. It would be gratifying if the complete document were made into a pdf, or otherwise published; meanwhile, what we have here is significant, among other things because his interlocutrix drew Davis out on the effects of blindness and racism in his life. ('We belong to the white people. If we fool with a white woman, they'll kill us. We ain't got no law. We belong to them. It was a long time 'fore I got myself tamed to white women. If I just brush up against one, I know I was looking for somebody to lynch me.')

(Part review)

Chris Smith, Blues & Rhythm, April 2008

•

REV. GARY DAVIS - LIVE AT GERDE'S FOLK CITY – FEBRUARY 1962

Stefan Grossman's Guitar Workshop CD SGGW 114/5/6

As Stefan Grossman tells us in his heartfelt notes he

Possibly Newport folk Festival, circa 1965. Photographer unknown

125

London, UK, 1964, Peter Dyer

was encouraged by Davis's manager and friend, the charismatic Manny Greenhill, to record Davis whenever he could. Over the years Grossman has collected a wealth of Davis material, recorded informally at Davis's home and live in various concerts, and this three disc compilation finds Davis in concert and on sparkling form.

The energetic Davis was sixty five years of age at the time of these recordings and was at the height of his powers, and all of his impressive skills are captured on this very highly recommended set. There are many surprises including a number of titles that have not been released elsewhere , alongside some of his most popular titles such as Say No To The Devil, Death Don't Have No Mercy and Soon My Work Will All Be Done.

The thirty six titles were recorded during a week long booking, 3 - 10 February, at Gerde's Folk City, the legendary club in Greenwich Village, New York City. The venue had presented over the years a long string of legendary performers including Roosevelt Sykes, John Lee Hooker, Sonny Terry and Brownie McGhee, Ramblin' Jack Elliot and Bob Dylan. Davis sounds relaxed and obviously enjoying the attention of the highly appreciative audience and Grossman, who recorded this set on a heavy Tandberg recording machine, has included a number of fascinating song introductions and anecdotes all adding greatly to the enjoyment.

By the time these recordings were made Davis had quite a following and had appeared at a number of major clubs and festivals including the Newport Folk Festival and the Mariposa Festival. He had in the previous two years recorded two, must have, magnificent albums for the Prestige Bluesville label which show him at his very best, and here he is on equal form. His vocals, in particular, are powerful, committed and totally commanding while his guitar picking is as inventive and as consummate as ever.

There are startling versions of the show - stopping guitar instrumentals Twelve Sticks and Buck Dance, while the recording of Lord, Search My Heart, the only title included here from Davis's first recording session in 1935, is one of the best versions that I have ever heard. One of his most popular songs Candyman has high falsetto vocals and comes from his earliest days as a performing musician and includes a stunning guitar passage. Another song I Am A Pilgrim, which I have never heard on record previously, and as Davis informs us, comes from the time that he was first learning to play the guitar at the turn of last century. Another of the previously unrecorded songs People That Used To See, Can't See No More has a guitar melody that is very similar to another of his most popular songs Cocaine Blues and is one of the standout moments of this intriguing release.

Of the other never previously recorded titles that I particularly enjoyed is Working On The Building a song which I am sure was very popular in his church congregation, with a guitar break that is as inventive as ever. The other three new

With Roy Book Binder, Buck's Rock Camp, Conn., 1969, Bob Carlin

titles Just A Closer Walk With Thee, Lord I Won't Go Back In Sin and Tesse all add tremendously to the fascination of this set. On two titles Soon My Work Will All Be Done and Oh Glory, How Happy I Am Davis is joined on stage by the New World Singers, (Gil Turner, Happy Traum and Bob Cohen), who shared the bill with Davis for the week, and there is no doubt that everyone is having a good time.

There are very few recordings of Davis playing the harmonica and the titles here Oh Lord and Right Or Wrong are certainly among the fine moments with Davis creating tremendous tension and atmosphere. This is an exceptional release and thanks go to Grossman for releasing this important collection. His tremendous sense of humour is obvious alongside his committed Christian beliefs and he performs with passion and integrity. This is an absolute must for established Davis fans and if you have none of his material start here and you will not be disappointed.

Bob Tilling, Living Blues, June 2009.

Book Review

EIGHTY OF REV. GARY'S BEST

Devotees of the brilliant Harlem street singer, the Rev. Gary Davis, will be pleased to know that a book containing eighty of his best religious songs has just been published, entitled "Rev. Gary Davis: The Holy Blues" (Robbins & Chandos).

The book has been beautifully produced with some exciting pictures of the blind Baptist preacher who is now well into his seventies. Photographers David Gahr, Jean Hammons, Julius Lester, Lenny Schechter and Arthur Tress have included some exciting poses of Gary Davis at home with his famous guitar "Miss Gibson" and wife Annie Davis.

It is only in comparatively recent years that the songs and music of Gary Davis, laid down with a brilliant mixture of contrapuntal and freely improvised playing have got the recognition they deserve.

But further comment on the importance of the Rev. Gary Davis is redundant in view of Stefan Grossman's excellent eulogy at the front of the book.

Stefan Grossman has spent much time with Gary Davis as has Georgia guitarist Larry Johnson, and by virtue of this, these two head the field today in the hand-me-down East coast style of playing.

Much of Davis's early work before he "got religion" was in the ragtime style, but his religious songs show the same kind of musical exuberance.

The book prints the musical notations, words and chords of the songs. What it cannot do, of course is to detail the little runs and traits of the Davis guitar style; neither can it include all the "Good God Almighty" phrases which Davis throws into his songs.

Stefan Grossman has compiled a more advanced book of tablatures for the avid disciple of Davis, but the value of this book is that it is as relevant for the beginner as it is for the more advanced guitarist with an admiration for such songs as "Trying To Get To Heaven In Due Time", "Twelve Gates To The City", "Say No To The Devil" and "Death Don't Have No Mercy". The last two songs in particular, stand up quite easily with the use of the old fashioned flat pick and a rhythmic strum. Alternatively the guitarist can adapt his own picking to the songs.

The important thing is that the wealth of Gary Davis's songs should be sufficient to inspire anyone. The book illustrates the chord shapes in tablature form, and lists a discography of Gary Davis's records at the rear; and although it is difficult to obtain his records on Prestige/Bluesville and Fontana, 77 Records (Dobell's) have produced a very good example of his work, and Yazoo are in the process of issuing an album of his early material, which will be available in England through the usual outlets.

J. Gilbert, Sounds, November 1970

Video Review

REV. GARY DAVIS AND SONNY TERRY
MASTERS OF THE COUNTRY BLUES
Yazoo 501 video

I've never reviewed a video before, and feel it somehow incumbent on me to write something quite different to what I'd write if this were just a sound recording - to concentrate on the visual aspects. This feeling is increased by the fact that there is no "track-listing" provided; the message is that the music as such is less important than if this was an LP or a CD or whatever. This is problematic, as what we have is a most unvisual production. Since Gary Davis and Sonny Terry were essentially sedentary performers, there is frankly not that much to see. Originally recorded for the Seattle Folk Society, at an unspecified date (my guess is the early 1960's) it features a set by Davis, sitting in a studio performing, without an audience, followed by a set of Sonny Terry doing the same. The film is monochrome, and direction amounts to the occasional switch between a few different camera angles. Davis is facially expressionless, allowing his voice and playing to do the communication, so that the visual interest lies in watching his guitar technique (perfect for students of his style

to check out the chord shapes and finger positions). There are a few highlights in this respect, like when he plays just with his left hand, while the right beats a rhythm on the top of the guitar - you certainly wouldn't get the full effect of that on a record. Terry is more physically active, using his hands and arms when talking, smiling and gesturing at the camera, and moving about a bit when he sings and plays. Somebody seeking the secrets of his playing style will find it less useful, as the harmonica is of course hidden in his hands, but the more resourceful might pick up the odd tip.

The music in both cases is splendid - Davis well up to his usual standard, and Terry on excellent form. The latter comes almost as light relief, to some extent, after Davis, whose stern, unsmiling features lend an intensity to the proceedings, even on a light-hearted song like "Please Don't Tell Nobody". There is a brief introduction (for the video, not on the original film) by Taj Mahal, from which I learnt that Durham, North Carolina, is pronounced Doorh'm, not - as I have imagined all these years - like the city in the north of England. Taj is in full colour, and looks resplendent in his garish outfit, but I have the feeling that those spectacles will come back to haunt him in later years, like a pair of loon pants on an Open University tutor.

Ray Templeton, Blues and Rhythm, April 1992

DVD Review

REV. GARY DAVIS
THE VIDEO COLLECTION
Vestapol 13111

This highly recommended, one hundred and five minute long, disc was compiled by Stefan Grossman and has brought together a fascinating collection of films all recorded during the last ten years or so of the great man's life. The life and times of Rev. Gary Davis (1896 – 1972) has been well documented and this compilation gives us just a little more insight into this charismatic and influential musician. Much of the material on this easily available release has appeared elsewhere over the past few years but it is great to see it all collected together here.

The opening film which is new to me and starts off this engaging set on a very high note. It was made during the early sixties, when the Davis was living in the Bronx, New York City and graphically illustrates the impoverished conditions that he and his wife Annie were living in. At the end of the film there is a short section showing him, playing a Martin guitar, and singing *Lord, I Feel Like Goin' On*, where he appears tremendously confident belying his harsh life and difficult living conditions. The speed and dexterity of his guitar playing is outstanding with powerful and committed singing. He is at his very best and the recordings he made at this time for the Prestige- Bluesville recording company are equally memorable and well worth searching out if you do not already own them.

There are two titles, *Children Of Zion* and *Oh Glory How Happy I Am,* from Pete Seeger's popular 1967 TV show "Rainbow Quest" where Davis is in the studio alongside a rather bemused looking Donovan and Shawn Phillips. Davis plays a big bodied twelve string guitar and looking at his most majestic, performing with total power, confidence and his vocals are at their most commanding. Here is a man that has had a complex and often tough life, and at

the age of seventy one is still at the peak of his powers.

The anthropologist John Ullman, of the University of Washington, invited Davis to Seattle during 1969 to be filmed for their archive and during his visit Davis was also informally filmed at the home of Ullman. The film quality is rather poor but the seven cuts are fascinating finding Davis relaxed and obviously enjoying the attention of his devoted admirers. There is a beautiful version of the rarely recorded gospel song *Keep Your Lamps Trimmed And Burning* and a gently lilting and inventive blues instrumental, *Hard Walkin' Blues*. There are two fascinating cuts where he is giving a "lesson" and just gives a small insight into what that experience must have been like. This section has some of his most popular and highly inventive ragtime guitar pieces including *Buck Dance, Make Believe Stunt* and *Twelve Sticks* – all performed with tremendous agility and control.

There are eight cuts from Ullman's studio session and although fairly easily found on video this is their first appeared on DVD and I for one am delighted to see them collected here. The filming really shows Davis off to his best and guitar players wanting to learn his technique and style will find theses titles invaluable. Davis is really on great form, he looks well, in complete control and his vocals in particular are at their most committed and engaging. Fortunately Davis at this session recorded some of his most well known and impressive material including *Candyman, Twelve Gates To The City, Cincinnati Flow Rag* and perhaps his most impressive of all gospel songs *Sampson And Delilah* and this memorable version is one of the highlights of this release.

I remember seeing the film "Black Roots" on British television just after it was released in 1970 and have not seen it since and it makes me even more pleased to see a small part of the film included here. The hour long film was made by the French director the late Lionel Rogosin and it is the only material filmed in colour on this release. Davis looking frail is surrounded in an informal dimly lit setting by fellow African American performers including Flo Kennedy, Rev. Frederick Kirkpatrick, Jim Collier and Larry Johnson. New York based, enigmatic and greatly neglected talent, Larry Johnson was a close friend of Davis and his harmonica playing on *I Belong To The Band* makes me wish that they had recorded more together as a duo. One of Davis's great gifts was as a story teller and often the highlight of his live performances and here he tells a complex tale of murder and revenge and when he sings his classic slow paced, *Death Don't Have No Mercy*, the women in the group are brought to tears. I believe that this intriguing film is being updated and I for one look forward to the release with great anticipation.

The last section was recorded at the wedding celebration of John Gibbons, who was one of the earliest guitar students of Davis who first met Davis in the late fifties. The film quality is very rough and made watchable only by the fine quality of the music. It is particularly interesting to hear *Spoonful* and *She's Funny That Way* two rarely recorded Davis titles and the whole release ends with the strident instrumental *Buck Dance* leaving me wanting more from this very important and influential man.

Bob Tilling, Living Blues, February 2009.

At author's home, Jersey, UK, 1971, Robert Tilling

Part Five

Selected Obituaries

ev. Gary D. Davis - Son of the late Evelenia Davis and John Davis was born in Laurens, S.C., April 30th 1896; he left this life Friday May 5th 1972. Although Rev. Davis was blind from birth, he never let it hinder him. He continued pushing himself forward in the service of the Lord. As a child he joined the Center Raven Baptist Church in Gray Court, S.C. He was also a professional player of the twelve string guitar. His music was heard throughout the world, with his fine unique style. He met and married Annie Bell Wright in 1937, after residing in S.C. for several years. They later moved to N.Y. City, where he continued with his work as a musician and minister. He also was a member of the Baptist Evening Minister's Conference and Musician's Union Local 802. He was stricken on his way to Nuetonville, N.J. He was taken off the Turnpike to a local hospital, where he suffered a cardiac attack.

He is survived by his wife, Sister Annie B. Davis, of N.Y.C., two step-daughters, Miss Ruby Wright and Mrs. Ann Pressey; three grandchildren all of N.Y. City; four cousins, Evelenia Wakefield, John A. Barksdale, also of N.Y. City; Sally Mae Govan of Columbia, S.C, and Junior Sexton of Fountain End, S.C.; three sister-in-laws and a very devoted friend, Mrs. Tiny Robinson with a host of other relatives and friends.

With eyes that were always closed and now body still,
He always did, the master's will...
So sleep on Gary, and take your rest ...
We all loved you - but God loved you best.
Sleep on Brother.
Funeral Service Sheet, May 11th 1972

The Rev. Gary Davis, a blind gospel singer and ragtime guitarist whose blues-tinted style influenced many younger performers, died Friday of a heart attack in Kessler Memorial Hospital, Hammonton, N.J. He was 76 years old and lived at 109-42 174th Street, Jamaica, Queens.

Mr. Davis had performed widely in the United States, Canada and Europe. He had been recorded and appeared also in the documentary film "Black Roots" shown here in 1970.

Reviewing his performance at the McBurney Young Men's Christian Association here in November 1970, Mike Jahn of The New York Times wrote:

"The preacher and former street singer seems more tired now than a few years ago, but still plays 12-string guitar like a young man. His songs are rhythmic, gospel music with a blues foundation, played with a casual air that nearly disguises the man's considerable professionalism".

The Funeral Service
For
Rev. Gary D. Davis
1896 - 1972

UNION GROVE BAPTIST CHURCH
1488 Hoe Avenue • Bronx, N. Y.

THURSDAY, MAY 11, 1972
8:00 P.M.

GRIFFIN'S QUEENS ABBEY, Inc.
198-20 Hollis Avenue, Hollis, N.Y.
Frank R. Griffin, Director

Interment at Rockville Cemetery
Friday AM, May 12, 1972

Funeral Sheet

With Tilling Family, Jersey, UK, 1971

131

Larry Johnson playing a banjo that belonged to Rev. Davis, one of his canes hangs on the wall, New York City, 1972, Val Wilmer

New York Times, May 1972

•

Rev. Gary Davis Dead at 76

Hammonton NY - The Rev. Gary Davis, virtuoso of ragtime blues and gospel, died May 5th of a heart attack at Kessler Memorial Hospital. He was 76.

Davis suffered a stroke and had been in and out of hospitals for the past year, but despite his illness still played occasional gigs in New York coffee houses and folk gatherings. His intricate syncopated guitar playing slowed and his voice broadened as he grew older, but he performed with innovation and excitement until the end.

Blind from his birth in 1896, Davis grew up on a sharecropper's farm outside Laurens, South Carolina. He played mouth harp and banjo from age five and guitar from age eight; mastery of these three instruments and of the piano, stayed with him all his life.

Most of his years were spent as one of the blind street singers who once were a common sight on the sidewalks of American cities. For 20 years Davis roamed the South, managing to escape the violence that killed his father, his brother and many of his fellow bluesmen. In 1935 he was ordained a Baptist minister and gave up the blues for gospel. That same year Davis made two records for the Perfect Label in New York; they attested to his reputation as one of the great blues singers but added little to his income and he settled down to singing on street corners in Harlem, his occupation for the next 25 years.

Singing above the noise of traffic in Harlem, Davis would sometimes make nothing one day and $50 to $100 the next. Thieves stole his guitar and his crystal-less watch, but years later Davis tended to look back on those days without rancour. "With street playing, you understand, you ain't sure about a thing, and it keeps you on pins", he said. "What makes it so cool and tricky is that you ain't in a place to demand anything".

The folk boom of the Sixties finally brought Davis recognition and a comfortable income. In 1964 he played a stunning set at Newport for an audience which on the whole had never before heard of him. Royalties from some of his songs - notably "Samson and Delilah" recorded by Peter, Paul and Mary - enabled him to buy a small house in Queens, where he lived with his wife Annie until his death. He toured Europe and the US and recorded virtually whenever he was asked - so often that Mrs. Davis has been unable to assemble a complete collection of his albums.

A man of high spirits, Davis relaxed his ban on blues as he got older, though he continued to preach musical sermons each Sunday and his religious faith remained unswerving. He talked and sang often about the prospect of his own death, always without sadness. The last song on his final album, recorded in March 1971, by Biograph, was his "I'll Do My Singing".

I will do my last singing in this land, somewhere
I will do my last singing in this land, somewhere
I don't know and I can't tell where

At home, April 1972, Robert Tilling

I may be somewhere sailing in the air,
But I will do my last singing in this land, somewhere.
Tim Ferris, Rolling Stone, June 8th 1972

•

I met Gary, I think it was in 1959. I came here from Atlanta, and I was livin' in Harlem at the time. I'd been playin' harmonica since I was very young, and that always put me around guitar players... and occasionally I used to hear about this blind man who could play so well. I had never heard of him, though I had heard of Blind Boy Fuller; and when someone told me that he was the one that taught Blind Boy Fuller, that was all the information I needed... I decided to find this blind man.

First I met Alec Stewart... he just passed away... in fact he passed away the day that Gary was buried. He was another old-time blues player, and he had known Gary for fifty years... I met him through Sonny and Brownie. He took me to meet Gary one night, and me and Gary hit it off from that night until he passed on thirteen years later.

That's how I met him, and he liked my harmonica playin' and I liked his guitar playin', so a friendship began. It was a long time before I got into music with him or tryin' to learn; because I just admired the cat so, it took me months of just sittin' and listenin' before I even approached him. That was a whole turnin' point in my life, because I hadn't taken music then near as serious as I do now. Gary took his music very seriously; he was a very serious man. I don't think there was anythin' that went by him that wasn't in a serious manner; because for him, if it wasn't serious, it wasn't worthwhile.

When I did get serious about music, and I started to catch on, he told me once... I was tryin' to play somethin' he played... I don't know what it was... anyway, I didn't make the

With Thelma Tilling, Jersey, UK, August 1971, Robert Tilling

Gary played on the streets of Harlem and in its churches. His presence in New York became known, and in 1949 he recorded two sides of a 78 RPM disc: and then, in 1954, he was recorded by Stinson Records. Slowly Gary became a part of the folk revival. He began giving lessons to mostly white students who would come uptown and he began playing in coffee houses. All the while, he was involved in his religion, preaching, singing and playing guitar in church on Sunday and taking part in church affairs during the week.

In 1963, Peter, Paul and Mary recorded his song "Samson and Delilah", and with the royalty money, Gary bought a new house in Jamaica, Queens. In the years that followed, he continued playing coffee houses and concerts and giving guitar lessons, and he was recorded a great many times. Despite Annie's disapproval, he began to sing more and more of his old secular songs such as "Cocaine" and "Candy Man".

In October, 1971 Gary became ill, and from that time until his death he was in and out of hospital continually, never played his guitar, but he'd still delight in hearing one of his visitors play for him. Sometimes he'd feel well enough to go to church or give a few lessons, and in April of this year he gave one concert. Then on May 5th while driving in the car on the way to New Jersey he suffered a fatal heart attack and died in hospital nearby. Rev. Davis's funeral was held at Union Grove Baptist Church, a few blocks from where he used to live in the Bronx.

Joan Fenton, Sing Out! Vol. 21 No. 5, 1972

On May 5th 1972 Reverend Gary Davis suffered a fatal cardiac attack en route to New Jersey. His death was prefaced by a long stay in the hospital earlier this year. Despite many hard times, Rev. Davis seemed to have an unusual flair for life. When he sang and played, he put his body and soul behind it and added that extra dimension that separates musicians from people who just play music. Throughout his life he taught numerous people his incredibly unique style of guitar playing – from Blind Boy Fuller on down a long, long list of students and musicians. As he said he would, he was playing and preaching until the end of his life...

"When I die I'll live again
Hallelujah, I'll live again..."
Woody Man, Sing Out! 1972

grade, and I wasn't pleased with myself in it, although he was takin' great patience with me ... and he told me, "Well, I'll tell you... it won't help you to play guitar like me, but it'll help you to keep me in mind". Every day of my life that flashes through my mind one way or another.

He was doin' the real thing... he was playin' music; he wasn't just makin' lot of noise; he was playin' music with feelin'. I didn't hear no phoneyness in his stuff; and everything I did hear was originality. I didn't hear no imitatin'... I didn't hear no imitatin' Blake... I didn't hear no imitatin' Lemon; and Gary came out of a time when this sort of thing was popular. And for him to sit down and manoeuvre himself out of style ... that was wonderful, damn wonderful.

He was a great man, a master musician; and as time goes on and Gary's music is really studied, I think that musicians will find out that Gary took guitar playin' itself a step further. My opinion is that he should be rated right up there with Segovia, because Gary utilised that fingerboard more than anybody. Gary filled up every gap; he knew all the possibilities to go to from a chord.

Did he get the recognition he deserved? No, there's not a black musician alive who ever got that, not in this country. You can go to England and be recognised there, and then maybe come back here and be recognised...

When Gary died I felt that time had done its thing. I felt that Gary was a tree, and many branches had come from that tree, and I was one of `em; and it's up to us to see what we can do with it. Brother Davis had stumbled through this world for 76 years... he was due for a rest.

Larry Johnson, Sing Out! 1972

A Personal Tribute

My last fond memories of Reverend Gary are when last April I had the great privilege of staying with him and his wife Annie in their beautiful little home in Jamaica, New York. I had admired him for many years and to be near him was an experience that I shall never forget. I shall of course remember him as one of the finest gospel, blues and ragtime guitarists and singers but I shall remember him most of all as a kind and very sincere man. He was generous, most of all with his advice and his time. No one was refused a few moments or a handshake while he was on tour and he was always willing for you to play his beloved "Miss Gibson". He told me that he was never going to part with 'her' and he was proud to say how he had bought his home, by picking his guitar, "...and not many folks can say that"!

At a concert, given in Jersey last August, he played to a packed house at the Royal Hotel, and after the show was over he was cheered out into the street. It is a performance that is still talked about and one which certainly gained him many new friends and admirers. It was easy to see how he made his reputation as one of folk music's greatest artists, for it was an experience to see him play. Even at the ripe old age of 75 he could still get around his instrument with great speed and originality. During the later years of his life he recorded mostly with his twelve-string "Bozo" guitar, and here again proved himself a master.

His recording career started in 1935 and ever since then he recorded regularly and he leaves behind a legacy of over a dozen albums. The wonder of his recordings is that they are all of a very high standard, even those recorded in 1971. A song called "Samson and Delilah" was recorded by Peter, Paul and Mary and it became one of their most popular numbers. The two songs which, in some circles, made the Rev. Gary Davis famous are "Candy Man" and "Coco Blues" which can be heard in nearly every folk club throughout the country.

He is now a legend and of the recordings he leaves behind him few if any can be faulted. He will be remembered as a patient teacher, who scolded no one, and it is his students, including Stefan Grossman, Woody Mann and Roy Bookbinder, who will carry on spreading his music.

Reverend Gary was married for over thirty years to Annie who was a great companion to him through many hard times and, it is sad to think, perhaps they did not have many comforts until his later years. But I know Gary was happy to leave his wife well cared for.

On the last evening of my visit to his home in 1971 Reverend Gary said prayers and sang two songs "Soon My Work Will All Be Done" and "I Will Do My Last Singing Somewhere" and these few moments of hearing him speak and sing will stay for ever in my memory. He was a man of great pride and compassion and this should be remembered, for Gary Davis will never be forgotten as a musician, but he will also never be forgotten as a very kind and sincere man who did a great deal for his church and his people.

Robert Tilling, Jazz Journal, July 1972

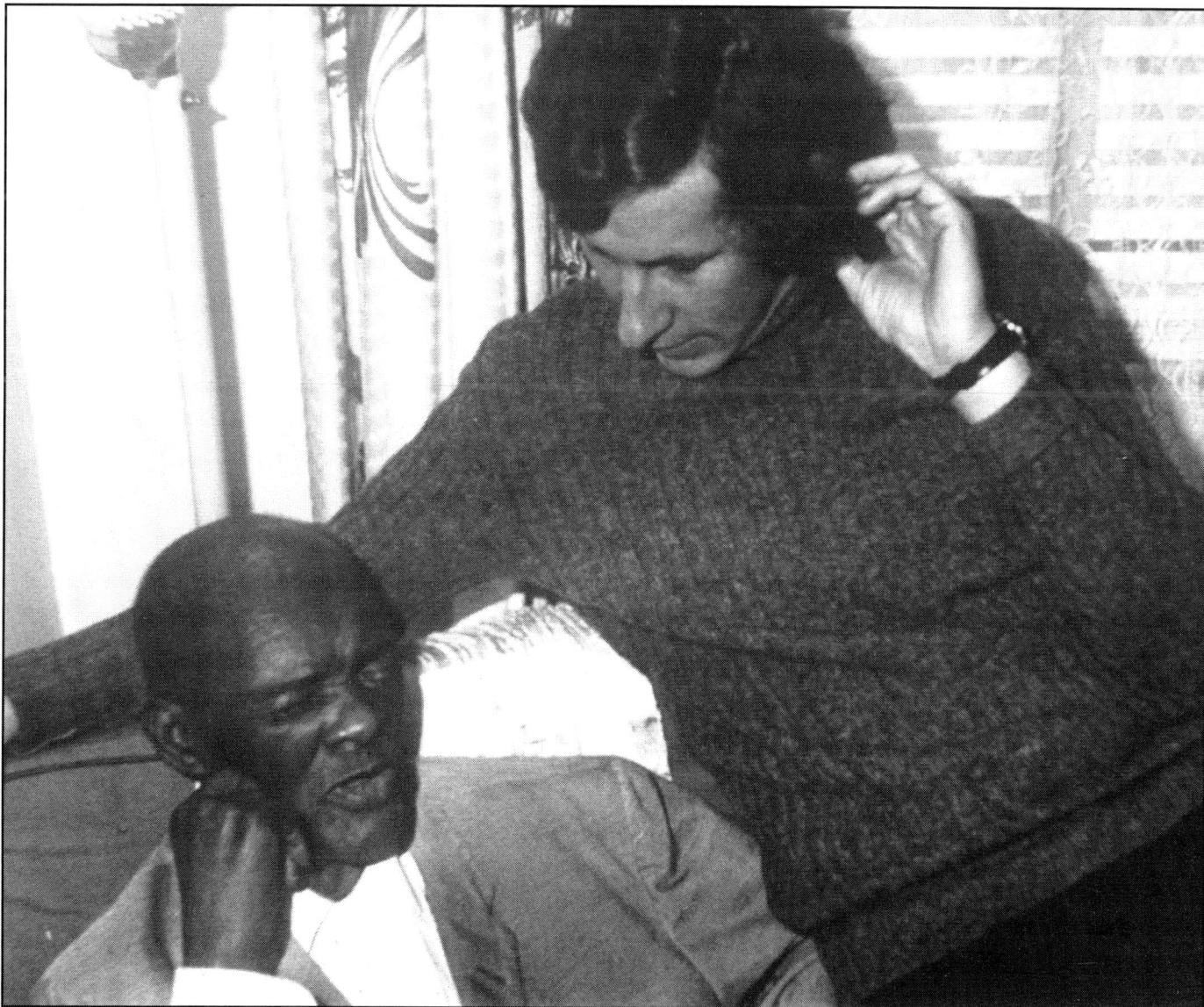

At home with author, April 1972, Roy Book Binder

New York City, 1954, John Cohen

Part Six

Discography 1935-1971

Special thanks to Bruce Bastin, Bob Laughton, Guido Van Rijn and Cedric Hayes. Also to, 'Blues and Gospel Records 1902-1941' (Storyville Publications) and 'Blues Records 1943 to 1970. A selective Discography' (Record Information Services). Where available the left hand column will show the master numbers and ending with the take number (where applicable). The right hand column will show the issue numbers of the 78 rpm's the Long Playing Records, Cassettes or the Compact Discs.

Abbreviations: v = vocal, g = guitar, v/g = vocal and guitar, g solo = guitar instrumental, h = harmonica, bjo = banjo, wb = washboard, sp = speech, p = piano, rec = records.

(The recordings from 1935 – 1945 appear on numerous compact discs, only a selection are included)

Blind Gary v/g

(On all 1935 recordings referred to as 'Blind Gary')

New York, 23 July 1935

17859-2	I'm Throwin' Up My Hands (Ain't Gonna Work No More)	ARC 35-10-16 Yazoo LP 1023, Yazoo CD 2011 Document CD 5060, Matchbox LP 168
17860-1	Cross And Evil Woman Blues	ARC 35-10-16 Yazoo LP 1023, Yazoo CD 2011 Document CD 5060, Matchbox LP 168

Blind Boy Fuller v/g (Probably Blind Gary – g)

New York City, 23 July 1935

17863-2	I'm Climbin' On Top Of The Hill	ARC 35-10-32 Vocalion 02964 Best of Blues LP 12 CBS CD 467923 Document CD 5091

(Although originally given as 'unknown guitar', it is almost certainly Blind Gary).

Bull City Red (real name was George Washington) – v/g, Blind Gary – g.

New York City, 24 July 1935

17865-2	Now I'm Talking About You	ARC 5-12-57, Flyright LP 107 Document LP BD 2030, CD 2030

Blind Boy Fuller – v/g. (Probably Blind Gary – g)

17867-1	Ain't It A Cryin' Shame	ARC 35-10-32 Vocalion 02964 CBS CD 467923 Best of Blues LP 12 Document CD 5091

(Although it does not give Blind Gary as second guitar there is a second guitar present and it is almost certainly him).

Blind Boy Fuller – v/g, Blind Gary – g, Bull City Red –wb.

New York City, 25th July 1935

17873-1	Rag, Mamma, Rag (Unissued take)	ARC 6-03-56 Vocalion 03084 CBS CD 467923 Document CD 467923
17873-2	Rag, Mamma, Rag	ARC 6-01-56 Vocalion 03084 Conqueror 30078 Conqueror 37776 Blues Classics LP 6, RBFLP 18 Best of Blues LP 12 Document CD 5091

17874-1	Baby You Gotta Change Your Mind	ARC 6-03-60
		Vocalion 03014
		Travelin' Man LP 801
		Document CD 5091

Blind Gary v/g

New York City, 25 July 1935

17875-2	I Am The True Vine	ARC 5-12-66
		Yazoo LP 1023
		Document CD 5060
17876-2	I Am The Light Of The World	ARC 5-12-66
		Truth LP 1003, Document CD 5060
17877-2	O Lord, Search My Heart	ARC 35-10-33
		Conqueror 8561
		Yazoo LP 1023
		RBF LP 11
		Document CD 5060

Blind Gary – g, Bull City Red – v.

New York City, 25 July 1935

17878-2	I Saw The Light	ARC 6-05-65
		Pirate EP MPC 526
		Truth Rec. LP 1003
		Matchbox Rec. LP 207
		Document CD 5060
		Document Blues LP 2030, CD 2030

Blind Gary. v/g

New York City, 26th July 1935

17889-2	You Can Go Home	ARC 7-04-55
		Yazoo LP 1023
		Document CD 5060
17890-2	Twelve Gates To The City	ARC 7-04-55
		Yazoo LP 1023
		Document CD 5060
17891-1	Have More Faith In Jesus	ARC 6-11-63
		Conqueror 8768
		Yazoo LP 1023
		Document CD 5060
17892-2	You Got To Go Down	ARC 35-1-33
		Conqueror 8561
		Yazoo LP 1023
		RBF LP 11
		Document CD 5060
17893-2	I Belong To The Band – Hallelujah!	ARC 6-02-65
		Yazoo LP 1023
		Document CD 5060
17894-2	The Great Change In Me	ARC 6-02-65
		Yazoo LP 1023
		Document CD 5060
17895-2	Lord, I Wish I Could See	ARC (Unissued Take)
		CBS CD 467890
		Document CD 5060
17896-1	Lord Stand By Me	ARC 6-05-65
		Yazoo LP 1023
		Document CD 5060
19897-2	The Angel's Message To Me	ARC 6-11-63
		Conqueror 8768
		Yazoo LP 1023
		Document CD 5060

Bull City Red – v/g,
Blind Gary – g.

New York City, 26 July 1935

17901-1	Black Woman And Poison Blues	ARC 6-02-56

17902-1	Mississippi River	Document LP 2030, Flyright LP 106
		ARC 6-06-55
		Matchbox LP SDR 168
		Document LP 2030, CD 2030

Notes:
ARC The American Record Company, (formed in August 1928).
The title of the Yazoo LP is 'Reverend Gary Davis 1935-1949' and the
Document CD is titled, 'Rev. Blind Gary Davis, Complete Recorded
Works 1935-1949, In Chronological Order'. All the other LP's and CD's
are compilations and have other artists included.

Reverend Gary Davis – g solo

		New York City, c.1945
	Civil War March	Asch LP 4, Document CD 5062
		Catfish CD 146

v/g

		New York City, Jan 1949
A4171	I Cannot Bear My Burden By Myself	Lenox 520, Continental LP 16003
		Yazoo LP 1023, Document CD 5060,
		Yazoo CD 2011
A4172	I'm Gonna Meet You At The Station	

g. solo.

		New York City, Spring 1950
		(Recorded by Tony Schwartz on 6th Ave
		and 46th St., New York City)
	Guitar Instrumental	Folkways LP 5581

v/g or g solo -1,
Sister Annie Davis v -2
Kinny Peebles v -3

	Home of Rev. Davis, New York City,
	1953
	Smithsonian Folkways Recordings
	SFW CD 40123
If I Had My Way	"
If The Lord Be For You – 2	"
Twelve Gates To The City	"
You Got To Move	"
We Are The Heavenly Father's Children	"
A Friend Like Lonely Jesus	"
Get Right Church	"
Marine Band – 1	"
Shine On Me	"
There's Destruction In This Land – 2	"
He Stole Away	"
The Unclouded Day – 3	"
Say No To The Devil	"
I Belong To The Band	"
Give Me A Heart To Love – 1, - 3	"
He Never Has Left Me Alone – 1, -3	"
Got On My Travelling Shoes -3	"
Civil War Parade – 1	"

v/g with
Sonny Terry, h -1.

	New York City, April 1954
Death Is Riding Every Day	Stinson LP 56
Jesus Met The Woman At The Well	"
Oh, What A Beautiful City	"
Say No To The Devil	"
Motherless Children -1	"
Bad Company Brought Me Here	"
I Can't Make The Journey By Myself	"
You Got To Move	"
When The Train Comes Along -1	Stinson LP 12

v/g or g solo -1, Unknown female v -2,
unknown p, choir, congregation -3

Various locations, 1955-1957
World Arbiter CD 2005

Fast Blues In A – 1 "
Slow Blues In E – 1 "
West Coast Blues – 1 "
Rag In A Minor – 1 "
Two – Step – 1 "
Horse Thief's Blues – 1 "
Candy Man – 2 "
Cigarette Break "
Hills And Valleys – 1 "
Seven Sisters – 1 "
Crucifixion "
I Decided To Go Down "
Sun Is Going Down "
My Heart Is Fixed "
A Church Service (Hymn, Prayer, Song, Sermon) -3 "
Coco Blues – 1 "

v/g

New York City, 29 January 1956
Riverside LP 148, 611, OBC CD 524-2

Blow Gabriel
Twelve Gates To The City "
Samson and Delilah "
Oh Lord, Search My Heart "
Get Right Church "
You Got To Go Down "
Keep Your Lamps Trimmed And Burning "
There Was A Time When I Went Blind "

(Other titles on this disc are by Pink Anderson)

v/g or g solo - 1

New York City, c.1956-57
(Recorded at Davis's Home)
World Arbiter CD 2008

Come Down To See Me Sometime "
Lost John – 1 "
Soldier's Drill - 1 "
Slow Blues In E – 1 "

v/g or g solo – 1.

New York City, June 1957
Folklyric LP 125, Dobells 77 Records
LP LA 12/14, Smithsonian CD 40035

Pure Religion
Mountain Jack -1 "
Right Now "
Buck Dance -1 "
Candy Man "
Devil's Dream -1 "
Moon Goes Down "
Coco Blues (Cocaine Blues) -1 "
Runnin' To The Judgement "
Hesitation (Hesitation Blues) -1 "
Bad Company "
I Didn't Want To Join The Band -1 "
Evening Sun Goes Down "
Seven Sisters -1 "
My Heart Is Fixed "
Time Is Drawing Near "
Crucifixion

(The last two titles were not on the Folklyric/Dobell's LP's)

v/g

New York City, 22 February 1958
Folkways LP 2512

If I Had My Way

Discography

v/g

	If I Had My Way	Location and Date Unknown
		Supraphon (G) DV 101134, (Possibly 1958)

v/g or g solo – 1

		Columbia University
		New York City, 1958 – 1959
		Shanachie CD 6117
	Buck Dance -1	"
	Soldier's Drill -1	"
	Baby, What You Going To Do	"
	Twelve Sticks (The Dozens) -1	"
	Save Up Your Money, John D. Rockerfeller Put The Panoc On	"
	I Am The Light Of The World	"
	Nobody Cares For Me	"
	Slippin' 'til My Gal Comes In Partner -1	"
	Blues (sic) -1	"
	Crucifixion	"
	Rag Blues In C (sic) -1	"
	Blues In E (sic) -1	"
	Square Dance Verses (sic)	"
	Don't Know Where To Go (sic)	"
	He's My King (sic)	"
	I'm Throwin' Up My Hand (Ain't Gonna Work No More)	"
	Cross And Evil Woman Blues	"
	Keep Your Lamp Trimmed And Burning	"
	I'm So Tired Of Being Alone	"

v/g with George Sea
Island Singers (vcl, tamb, hand claps)

		Toronto (Canada), c.1959
	I Got Religion, I'm So Glad	Kicking Mule LP 1
	I'm A Soldier In The Army Of The Lord	"

(Recorded live at the Mariposa Festival)

v/g

		Newport, R.I., 1959
	Samson And Delilah	Vanguard LP 9145, Fontana LP
	You Got To Move	TFL 6037, Vanguard CD 66224

(Recorded at the Newport Fold Festival, other titles not by Rev. Davis)

v/g or g solo – 1

		Englewood Cliffs NJ. 24 Aug 1960
	I Belong To The Band	Prestige Bluesville LP 1015,
		Fontana 688303ZL (UK) OBC CD
547-2		
	I Am The Light Of The World	"
	Let Us Get Together Right Down Here	"
	Samson And Delilah	"
	The Sun Going Down	Unissued
	Lo, I Be With You Always	Bv LP 1015
	Keep Your Lamp Trimmed And Burning	Unissued
	You Got To Go Down	Unissued
	Goin' To Sit Down On The Banks Of The River	Bv LP 1015
	Twelve Gates To The City	"
	Tryin' To Get Home	"
	Lord, I Feel Just Like Goin' On	"
	Pure Religion	"
	Great Change Since I Been Born	"
	Death Don't Have No Mercy	"
	By And By I'm Going To See The King	Unissued
	I Know I Have Another Building	Unissued
	Earth Have No Sorrow -1	Unissued

Discography

Joy To Know Him — Unissued
Don't Move My Bed Till The Holy Ghost Come — Unissued

(Bluesville LP 1015 also issued on Prestige LP 14028 and as part of Fantasy double-LP 24704, also as Prestige LP 7805 and Fontana LP 688303)

v/g

New York City, 10 August 1961
Bluesville 819, LP 1032,
XTRA 5024 (UK) OBC CD 588-2

You Got To Move	
I'm Glad I'm In That Number	"
Motherless Children	"
Crucifixion	"
There's A Table Sitting In Heaven	"
There's A Bright Side Somewhere	"
I'll Be Alright Some Day	"
You Better Mind	"
I'll Fly Away	"
God's Gonna Separate	"
When I Die I'll Live Again	"

(Also released as part of Fantasy double-LP24704 and Fantasy LP 5986)

v/g or v/h-1

New York City, 1961
Bluesville LP 1049, OBC LP 519,
XTA 5014 (UK) OBC CD 519-2

Say No To The Devil	
Time Is Drawing Near	
Hold To God's Unchanging Hand -1	"
Bad Company Brought Me Here	"
I Decided To Go Down	"
Lord, I Looked Down The Road	"
Little Bitty Baby	"
No One Else Can Do Me Like Jesus -1	"
Lost Boy In The Wilderness	"
Trying To Get To Heaven In Due Time	"

v/g or h-2, bjo -1

San Diego, C.A., 22/23 June 1962
Heritage HT CD 03

Sun Is Going Down	
I'm Gonna Meet You At The Station	"
If I Had My Way	"
Twelve Gates To The City	"
God's Gonna Separate The Wheat From The Tares	"
Get Right Church	"
When The Saints Go Marching In	"
God Don't Work Like A Natural Man -2	"
Soon My Work Will All Be Done	"
I'll Be Alright	"
Old Drunken Sally	"
Kitty Went A-Courtin' -1	"
Keep Your Lamp Trimmed And Burning	"
There's Destruction in This Land	"
Death Don't Have No Mercy	"
Near The Cross	"

(Recorded live at "Sign of the Sun")

v/g

Chicago, Il. c.1962
Wolf Records 120.915

Death Don't Have No Mercy	
Soon My Work Will All Be Done	"
You Got To Move	"
If I Had My Way	"
Just A Closer Walk With Thee	"

He Knows How Much We Can Bear   "

(Recorded live at the Chicago Folk Festival)

v/g

	Cambridge, Mass., c.1962
Little Boy, Little Boy, Who Made Your Britches?	Stefan Grossman Limited Edition Cassettes
All Night Long	Shanachie CD 6117
Paul And Silas (Who Shall Deliver Poor Me)	"
Jesus Met The Woman At The Well	"
Lord, Search My Heart	"
Lord, On Your Word	"
Let Us Together	"
Cocaine Blues	"
Devil's Dream	"
Blow Gabriel	"
Sun Is Goin' Down	"
When The Train Comes Along	"
Spoonful	"
Whistlin' Blues	"

(Recorded live at the 'Golden Vanity' Club. Cassette title "Babylon Is Falling")

v/g or g solo -1, "Suzzy" – v with Davis g - 2

	New York City, 1962
Children of Zion	Kicking Mule LP 1, Shanachie 97024
Whoopin' Blues -1	"
What Can I Do -2	"
Lo' I Be With You Always	"

(Also appear on a Stefan Grossman's Limited Edition Cassette "Lo, I Be With You Always")

v/g or g solo -1

	New York City, 1962
Get Right Church	Gospel Heritage LP 307, Interstate CD 07
Blow Gabriel	"
Slippin' Till My Gal Comes In Partner -1	"
Wall Hollow Blues -1	"
Blues in E -1	"
Piece Without Words -1	"
Whoopin' Blues	"
I Want To Be Saved	"
Talk On Death Of Blind Boy Fuller	Stefan Grossman Limited Edition Cassette

v/g

	Paoli, PA., 8 September 1962
If I Had My Way	Prestige International LP/CD B072
Sally, Where You Get Your Liquor From	"
You Got To Move	"

(Recorded at the Philadelphia Folk Festival. Other titles not by Rev. Davis)

v/g or g solo -1

	Swarthmore, PA., 1962
I'm Going To Sit Down On The Banks Of The River	Kicking Mule LP 101/152/,
Twelve Gates To The City	Transatlantic LP 249, Interstate HT CD 02
(I Heard) The Angels Singing	"
Twelve Sticks -1	"
Long Way To Tipperary	"
I'll Meet You At The Station When The Train Comes Along	"
Come Down And Meet Me Sometime	"
Buck Dance -1	"
Soldier's Drill -1	"

(Recorded live at Swarthmore College)

v/g or g solo - 1, h - 2, sp - 3,
with New World Singers – 4,
v-5

New York City, February 3rd – 10th, 1962

Stefan Grossman's Guitar Workshop
CD   SGGW114/5/6

You Got To Move   "
Intro to Come Down And See Me Sometime   "
Come Down And See Me Sometime   "
Wouldn't Say Quit   "
Oh, Lord -2   "
Announcing Guitar Lessons -3   "
People That Used to See, Can't See No More   "
There's Destruction In This Land   "
Intro to Soon My Work Will All Be Done -3   "
Soon My Work Will All Be Done - 4   "
Intro to Oh Glory, How Happy I Am -3   "
Oh Glory, How Happy I Am - 4   "
I Want To Be Saved   "
Just A Closer Walk With Thee   "
Death Don't Have No Mercy   "
Lord I Won't Go Back In Sin   "
Candyman   "
Buck Dance -1, -3   "
Samson And Delilah   "
Working On The Building   "
I'll Fly Away   "
Sun Goin' Down   "
Fox Chase - 2, -3   "
God's Gonna Separate   "
Lord Search My Heart   "
Jesus Met The Woman At The Well   "
Say No To The Devil   "
I Am A Pilgrim   "
All Night Long   "
Trying To Get To Heaven   "
Thank You Jesus   "
Twelve Sticks - 1   "
Intro to Tesse -3   "
Tesse   "
Lord They Tell Me   "
Right Or Wrong - 2, -5   "

(Recorded live at Gerde's Folk City. The members of New
World Singers were Gil Turner, Happy Traum, Bob Cohen.)

(Candyman, Fox Chase and People Who Used To See, Can't See No More appear
on a Stefan Grossman Limited Edition Cassette entitled, Babylon Is Falling)

v/g or g solo -1, bjo – 2, sp -3,
female vocalist named Suzy - 4,
with church congregation - 5,
unknown piano - 6, whistling - 7,
Annie Davis v - 8, h – 9, with Georgia Sea
Island Singers -10

New York 1962 - 1967
Stefan Grossman's Guitar Workshop
CD SGGW 130/1/2

Twelve Sticks -1, -3   "
Sally, Where'd You Get Your Liquor From   "
Babylon Is Falling -1, -3   "
What Could I Do -1, - 4   "
Children of Zion   "
Hesitation Blues   "
Candyman -2   "
Steal Away And Pray   "
Goin' To Chattanooga -1   "
Packing Up, Get Ready To Go -1,   "
Untitled - 2   "

You Cry Because I'm Leaving -1	"
Don't Let My Baby Catch You Here	"
Lord Let Me Live Longer -1, - 4	"
I Want To Be Saved - 2	Gospel Heritage LP 307/CD 07
Waltz Time Candyman -1	"
Little Boy Who Made Your Britches	"
Talks About Verses Not Sung -3	"
C Rag -1	"
Two Step Candyman -1	"
Piece Without Words -1	Gospel Heritage LP 307/CD 07
Lord Search My Heart	"
Slippin' To My Gal Comes In Partner -1	Gospel Heritage LP 307/CD 07
Sun Is Going Down	"
Raise A Ruckus Tonight	"
Save Up Your Money, John D. Rockefeller Put	"
The Panic On -1	"
Soon My Work Will All Be Done -8	"
You're Gonna Need King Jesus -2	"
I'm Going Back To Jesus-1, - 4	"
Blues In C -1	"
Saddle It Around	"
People Who Used To See	"
Italian Rag -1	Transatlantic LP 244
Candyman	"
Nobody Don't Care For Me - 7	"
Fox Chase - 9	"
Talk On Blind Boy Fuller - 3	"
Amazing Grace -5	"
Sermon -3, -5	"
I'm A Soldier In The Army Of The Lord -5	"
Sermon -3, -5	"
Lord, I Feel Just Like Goin' On -5	"
Steal Away -5	"
Can't Make This Journey By Myself -5	"
Sermon -3,-5	"
I Will Overcome Someday -3, -5,-6	"
God Be With You -5	"
	Mariposa Festival, Toronto, Canada, c. 1959. Kicking Mule LP 1
I Got Religion I'm So Glad -10	"
I'm A Soldier In The Army Of The Lord -10	"

(This album was recorded by Stefan Grossman and his voice can be heard on various titles interviewing and in conversation with Rev. Davis.)

v/g or g solo -1,
bjo solo -2.

	Various locations, c.1962/70
Dark Town Strutters' Ball -1	Kicking Mule LP 104/LP 133
Swinging Blues	TRA 244, Interstate HTCD 02
Cincinnati Flow Rag	"
West Coast Blues -2	"
Buck Rag	"
St.Louis Tickle	"
Two Step Candyman	"
Walkin' Dog Blues	"
Italien Rag	"
C – Rag	"
Waltz Time Candyman -3	"
Make Believe Stunt	"

(St. Louis Tickle and Italien Rag appear on LP TRA SAM 26)

Discography

v/g

	New York City, c.1962-63
Bill Bailey	Stefan Grossman Limited Edition Cassettes
Honey, Get Your Towel Wet	Shanachie CD 6117
You're Goin' To Quit Me, Baby	"
Don't Let My Baby Catch You Here	"
Virgin Mary	"
Babylon Is Falling	"

(Recorded at Rev. Davis's home, New York City)

g solo

	New York City, c. 1963
Sportin' Life Blues	Gospel Heritage LP 307

v/g or g solo –1. Unknown female v –2

	New York City, possibly 1963 or 68
Tired, My Soul Needs A Restin' -2	Kicking Mule LP 103
Georgia Camp Meeting –1	"
Blues in A –1	"
You're Goin' Quit Me Baby	"

(Recorded at Rev. Davis's home. Titles also appear on Stefan Grossman's Limited Edition Cassette "Let Us Get Together")

v/g

	New York City, June 1963
I Am A True Vine	Gospel Heritage LP307, Interstate HTCD 07
Lord Stand By Me	"
Won't You Hush	"
Mean Old World	"
Moon Is Going Down	"
God's Gonna Separate	"
Soon My Work Will All Be Done	"
Oh, Glory, How Happy I Am	"
Blow Gabriel	"
Candyman	"

(Titles also appear on Stefan Grossman's Limited Edition Cassette "I Am A True Vine")

v/g

	New York City, 4 Feb 1964
Keep Your Lamp Trimmed And Burning	Stefan Grossman Limited Edition Cassette
You Got To Move	"
Let Us Get Together	"
Samson And Delilah	"

(Recorded live at the Gaslight Café. Other titles on this cassette are by Bob Dylan)

g solo, bjo solo –1, h solo –2

	New York City, 2 March 1964
	New World Records LP 235
	Prestige LP 14033, 7725, OBCCD 592-2
Maple Leaf Rag	"
Slow Drag	"
The Boy Was Kissing The Girl	"
Candyman	"
United States March	"
Devil's Dream -1	"
The Coon Hunt -2	"
Mister Jim	"
Please Baby -1	"
Fast Fox Trot	"
Can't Be Satisfied	"

v/g

		New York City, c.1964
		Folkways/XTRA (E) LP 1009,
I'm On My Way To The Kingdom		
He Knows Just How Much We Can Bear		"
Lord, I'll Be With You Always		"
Yeah, (Time Is Drawing Near)		"

(Other titles on XRTA (E) LP not by Rev. Davis)

v/g, or bjo solo -1, h-2, g solo -3

		Meadville, PA., January 1964
		Document DLP 527
Cincinnati Slow Drag -3		
Harmonica Solo -2		"
Candyman		"
Banjo Instrumental -1		"
Maple Leaf Rag -3		"
I Know You'll Miss Me When I'm Gone		"
Guitar Blues -3		"
Banjo Instrumental 2-1		"

(Recorded live at Allegheny College)

v/g, h-1

		Meadville, PA., January 1964
		Wolf Records RO 915
Samson And Delilah		
Instrumental March		"
Old Time Religion		"
I Heard The Angels Singing		"
God's Unchanging Hand -1		"
Trying To Get Home		"

(Recorded live at Allegheny College, evening concert)

**v/g, h-1, g solo -2 ,
Sonny Terry h -3**

		Manchester, England (UK) 8 May 1964
		Document CD DOCD 322014
You Got To Move		"
If I Had My Way		"
The Sun Is Going Down -3		"
I'm A Soldier		"
I Got A Little Mama, Sweet As She Can Be		"
Sally, Please Come Back To Me (Worried Blues)		"
Cocaine Blues		"
Cincinnati Flow Rag-2		"
Children of Zion		"
Coon Hunt -1		"
Maple Leaf Rag -2		"

v/g, unknown bjo -1

		(Possibly) Toronto, Canada, c.1964
		Document Records DLP 521
Stovepipe Stomp (Cincinnati Flow Rag)		
She Just Put It That Way (She's Funny That Way)		"
Guitar And Banjo Duet -1		"
If I Had My Way (Samson And Delilah)		"

(Other tracks on this record
are from Folk-Lyric 125/77'LP77)

v/g

		(Possibly) Cambridge, Mass., c.63-64
		Kicking Mule LP 103
Oh Glory, How Happy I Am		
Cocaine Blues		"
Death Don't Have No Mercy		"

Let Us Get Together   "

There's Destruction In This Land   "

(Recorded at Davis's publisher's office. Titles also appear on
Stefan Grossman Limited Edition Cassette, "Let Us Get Together")

v/g, Sonny Terry h -1

                                                   Live Concert, 1964 (Possibly in UK)

Lord, Search My Heart   Groove Jams CD GJ97006

Sonny Is Going Down *(Sun Is Going Down)* -1   "

Right Now *(Great Change Since I Been Born)* -1   "

You Got To Go Down   "

Let Us Get Together *(Samson And Delilah)*   "

(These titles are incorrectly titled – the titles in italics are the correct titles where known.
There are other performers on this disc).

v/g or g solo -1, Barry Kornfeld   v/bjo -2

                                                  Newport Folk Festival, July 1965

Soldier's Drill -1   Vanguard CD 79588-2

Get Along Cindy -2   "

v/g or g solo -1. v /h -2

                                                  Newport, R.I., July 1966

                                                  Vanguard LP 3008, CD VMD 73008,

Samson And Delilah (If I Had My Way)   CD 79588-2

I Won't Be Back No More   "

Buck Dance -1   "

Twelve Sticks -1   "

Death Don't Have No Mercy   "

You Got To Move   "

Lovin' Spoonful   "

She Wouldn't Say Quit   "

I've Done All My Singing For My Lord -2   "

Twelve Gates To The City   "

I Will Do My Last Singing In This Land Somewhere   "

(Recorded live at the Newport Folk Festival)

v/g or g solo -1, h -2

                                                  Montreal, Canada, 27 January 1967

                                                  Just A Memory JAM CD 9133-2

Make Believe Stunt -1   "

Maple Leaf Rag -1   "

Coon Chase -2   "

Samson And Delilah   "

Twelve Gates To The City   "

Mind How You're Living   "

You Got To Move   "

How Much We Can Bear   "

I Will Do My Last Singing   "

Buck Dance -1   "

(Live in Concert)

v/g or g solo -1, v/bjo -2

                                                  Ann Arbor, Mi., c. 1968

She's Funny That Way -2   Kicking Mule LP 1

Baby, Let Me Lay It On You   "

Please Judy   "

The Boy Was Kissing The Girl -1   "

Hesitation Blues -2   "

(Recorded live at Michigan States University)

v/g or v/h -1. h solo -2

	Cambridge, MA., c. 1968
Twelve Gates To The City	Fontana (E) LP 914, Fontana LP 886505
Samson And Delilah (If I Had My May)	"
Keep Your Lamp Trimmed And Burning	"
The Boy Kissing The Girl (And Playing The Guitar At The Same Time)	"
Birmingham Special -2	"
Time Ain't So Long -1	"
Silvie	"
Lost John -2	"
Lo, I'll Be With You Always	"

(Recorded live at Harvard University)

v/g

	Seattle, Washington, c 1968
She Wouldn't Say Quit	Stefan Grossman Limited Edition Cassette

(Recorded live in concert. Title of cassette is "Babylon Is Falling")

v/g or v/p -1, v.h -2, v/bjo -3, h solo -4
with Larry Johnson, h -5, Sister Annie Davis, v-6,
The Apostolic Family (John Townley, Monica Bosica, Jerry Novac, Bobby Brooks), v-7.

	New York City, March 1969
	Adelphi LP 1008, Fwks LP 35
Mornin' Train	EDSEL EDCD 482
Birmingham Special (Birdshead Special) -4	"
Sun (Is) Going Down -5	"
Out On The Ocean Sailing -3	"
Soon My Work Will All Be Done – 6, 7	"
O, Glory	"
Right Now -5,6,7	"
Lo, I'll Be With You Always -5	"
God Will Take Care Of You -1,7	"
Oh, What A Beautiful City -5	Folkways LP 3542 (Not on CD)
Fast Stepping Time -5	"
Long John -4	"
We Are The Heavenly Father's Children	"
God's Unchanging Hand -2	"

(All tracks are from the original Adelphi recording session in 1969).

v/g, or g solo -1

	New Milford, CT, 12 August 1970
She's Funny That Way	American Activities UACD 103
Cincinnati Flow Rag -1	"
Sally	"
CC Rider	"
Make Believe Stunt -1	"
Delia	"
Candyman	"
Samson And Delilah	"
Let Us Get Together	"

(Recorded live at Buck's Rock Summer Camp, Conn. USA)

v/g or v/h -1, g -3 Larry Breezer g -2

	Bio CD 123	Bio LP 12030	Bio CD DK 3407	Bio CD 113
		New York City, 17 March 1971		
How Happy I Am		"		"
I Heard The Angels Singing	"	"	"	
Samson And Delilah	"	"	"	
Children Of Zion	"	"	"	
Soon My Work Will All Be Done		"		"
Talk On The Corner	"	"	"	

Sally, Where'd You Get Your Whiskey?	"	"	"	
Hesitation Blues		"		"
Whistlin' Blues		"		"
Lost John -1	"	"	"	
You Better Get Right	"	Bio BLP 12034	"	
Lord, I Wish I Could See	"	"	"	
Be Mindful Of Your Sacrament		"		
Down By The River	"	"	"	
Eagle Rocking Blues	"	"	"	
Candyman -2 -3		"		"
Crow Jane -3	"	"	"	
Cocaine Blues	"	"	"	
I'll Do My Last Singing	"	"	"	

(Biography CD 113 also has titles from Leadbelly and Rev. Dan Smith)

v/g

Cambridge Folk Festival, UK, July 1971
Catfish Records KAT CD 115

Let Us Get Together	"
There's Destruction In This Land	"
Samson And Delilah	"
You Got To Move	"
Pure Religion	"

(Recorded Live)

v/g or g solo -1

Jersey, C.I. UK, 5 August 1971
American Activities CD 103

Pure Religion	"
Mountain Jack -1	"
Cincinnati Flow Rag -1	"
Mama Let Me Lay It On You	"
I Am A True Vine	"
Candyman	"
Buck Dance -1	"
Walkin' Dog Blues (Happy Blues) -1	"
I Hear The Angels Sing	"
Whistlin' Blues	"

(Recorded live at the Royal Hotel, St Helier, Jersey, UK)

New York City, circa 1958/59, Courtesy of Stefan Grossman's Guitar Workshop, Inc.

Appendix

Albums, Cassettes & Compact Discs

Albums

(Titles are as they appear on the sleeve. The date is when released, as well as the country).

Title: "Blind Gary Davis with Sonny Terry"
Label/No: Stinson SLP 56 (USA 1954), Collectables COL-CD 5607 (USA 1995)
Death Is Riding Every Day/Jesus Met The Woman At The Well/Oh, What A Beautiful City/Say No To The Devil/Motherless Children/Bad Company Brought Me Here/I Can't Make The Journey By Myself/You Got To Move
(There are seven solo titles by Sonny Terry on the Collectables CD)

Title: "American Street Songs"
Label/No: Riverside RLP 12-611, RLP 148, (USA c. 1956) , Original Blues Classics OBC CD 524-2 (USA 1987)
Blow Gabriel/Twelve Gates To The City/Samson And Delilah/Oh, Lord, Search My Heart/Get Right Church/You Got To Go Down/Keep Your Lamps Trimmed And Burning/There Was A Time That I Went Blind
(Side One has seven tracks by Pink Anderson)

Title: "Pure Religion"
Label/No: Folk Lyric LP 125 (USA c.1957), LP'77'LA 12/14 (UK c.1965), Smithsonian/Folkways CD 40035 (USA 1991)
Pure Religion/Mountain Jack/Right Now/Buck Dance/Candyman/Devil's Dream/Moon Goes Down/Coco Blues/Runnin' To The Judgement/Hesitation Blues/Bad Company/Didn't Want To Join The Band/Evening Sun Goes Down/Seven Sisters/My Heart Is Fixed
(The CD has two extra titles: Time I Drawing Near and Crucifixion)

Title: "Harlem Street Singer"
Label/No: Prestige/Bluesville LP1015, (USA 1961), Fontana LP 688303ZL (UK c.1968), OBC CD 547 - 2 (USA 1992)
Samson And Delilah/Let Us Get Together Right Down Here/I Belong To The Band/Pure Religion/Great Change Since I Been Born/Death Don't Have No Mercy/Twelve Gates To The City/Goin' To Sit Down On The Banks Of The River/Tryin' To Get Home/Lo, I Be With You Always/I Am The Light Of This World/Lord, I Feel Just Like Goin' On

Title: "A Little More Faith"
Label/No: Prestige/Bluesville 1032, (USA 1961), Extra LP 5042 (UK c.1968), OBC CD 588-2 (USA 1999)
You Got To Move/Crucifixion/I'm Glad In That Number/There's A Table Sittin' In Heaven/Motherless Children/There's A Bright Side Somewhere/I'll Be All Right Some Day/You Better Mind/A Little More Faith/I'll Fly Away/God's Gonna Separate/When I Die I'll Live Again

Title: "Say No To The Devil"
Label/No: Bluesville (USA 1961), XTRA LP 5014 (UK c.1968), OBC CD 519-2 (USA 1991)
Say No To The Devil/Time Is Drawing Near/Hold God's Unchanging Hand/Bad Company Brought Me Here/I Decided To Go Down/Lord, I Looked Down The Road/Little Bitty Baby/No One Can Do Me Like Jesus/Lost Boy In The Wilderness/Trying To Get To Heaven In Due Time

Title: "The Guitar & Banjo Of Reverend Gary Davis"
Label/No: Prestige 7725(USA 1964), OBC CD 592-2 (USA 2001)
Maple Leaf Rag/Slow Drag/The Boy Was Kissing The Girl/Candyman/United States March/Devil's Dream/The Coon Hunt/Mister Jim/Please Baby/Fast Fox Trot/Can't Be Satisfied

Title: "Rev. Davis/Short Stuff Macon"
Label/No: Folkways (USA c.1964), XTRA 1009 (UK c.1970)
I'm On My Way To The Kingdom/He Knows Just How Much We Can Bear/Lord, I'll Be With You Always/Yeah!
(Side Two has five titles by Short Stuff Macon)

Title: "Rev. Gary Davis At Newport"
Label/No: Vanguard LP SRV-73008, (USA 1968), Vanguard CD 73008 (USA c.1993), Vanguard CD 79588-2 (USA 2001)
Samson And Delilah/I Won't Be Back No More/Buck Dance/Twelve Sticks/Death Don't Have No Mercy/You Got To Move/Lovin' Spoonful/She Wouldn't Say Quit/I've Done All My Singing For My Lord/Twelve Gates To The City/I Will Do My Last Singing In This Land Somewhere
(The 2001 Vanguard CD has two extra titles: Soldiers Drill and Get Along Cindy)

Title: "Bring Your Money, Honey"
Label/No: Fontana SFJL914 (UK 1968)
Twelve Gates To The City/Samson And Delilah (If I Had My Way)/Keep Your Lamps Trimmed And Burning/The Boy Was Kissing The Girl (And Playing Guitar At The Same Time)/Birmingham Special/Time Ain't So Long/Silvie/Lost John/Lo, I'll Be With You Always

Title: "Reverend Gary Davis 1935-1939"
Label/No: Yazoo LP L-1023 (USA c.1970), Yazoo CD 2011 (USA 1994), Document CD DOCD 5060 (UK 2003).
The Angel's Message To Me (1935)/The Great Change In Me (1935)/I'm Throwin' Up My Hand (1935)/You Got To Go Down (1935)/I Can't Bear My Burden By Myself (1949)/I Belong To The Band (1935)/I Am The True Vine (1935)/Lord, Stand By Me (1935)/Twelve Gates To The City (1935)/Have More Faith In Jesus (1935)/O Lord, Search My Heart (1935)/You Can Go Home (1935)/Meet Me At The Station (1949)/Cross And Evil Woman Blues (1935)
(The Document CD has two extra titles: Lord, I Wish I Could See and Civil War March)

Title: "Ragtime Guitar"
Label/No: Transatlantic TRA LP 244 (UK 1971)
Cincinnati Flow Rag/West Coast Blues/Buck Rag/St. Louis

Tickle/Two Step Candyman/Walkin' Dog Blues/Italien Rag/ C-Rag/Waltz Time Candyman/Make Believe Stunt

Title: "Children of Zion" (Reverend Gary Davis in concert)
Label/No: Transatlantic TRA LP 249 (UK 1971)
I'm Going To Sit Down On The Banks Of The River/Twelve Gates To The City/Angels Singing/Twelve Sticks/Long Way To Tipperary/When The Train Comes Along (Meet You At The Station)/Come Down And See Me Sometime/Buck Dance/Soldier's Drill

Title: "Blues and Gospel"
Label/No: Biograph BLP-12030 (USA 1971)
How Happy I Am/I Heard The Angels Singing/Samson and Delilah/Children of Zion/Soon My Work Will All Be Done/ Talk On The Corner/Sally Where'd You Get Your Whiskey?/ Hesitation Blues/Whistlin' Blues/Lost John

Title: "Lord I Wish I Could See"
Label/No: Biograph BLP-12034 (USA 1971)
You Better Get Right/Lord I Wish I Could See/Be Mindful Of Your Sacrament/Down By The River/Eagle Rocking Blues/Candy Man/Crow Jane/Cocaine Blues/I'll Do My Last Singing

Title: "When I Die I'll Live Again"
Label/No: Fantasy-Double LP 24704 (USA 1972)
Samson And Delilah/Let Us Get Together Right Down Here/I Belong To The Band/Pure Religion/Great Change Since I Been Born/Death Don't Have No Mercy/Twelve Gates To The City/Goin' To Sit Down On The Banks Of The River/Tryin' To Get Home/Lo, I Be With You Always/I Am The Light Of This World/Lord, I Feel Just Like Goin' On/You Got To Move/Crucifixion/I'm Glad I'm In That Number/There's A Table Sittin' In Heaven/Motherless Children/There's A Bright Side Somewhere/I'll Be All Right Some Day/You Better Mind/A Little More Faith/I'll Fly Away/God's Gonna Separate/When I Die I'll Live Again (This is Prestige 1015 and Prestige 1032)

Title: "Lo, I'll Be With You Always"
Label/No: Kicking Mule KND 1 (USA/UK 1973)
She's Funny That Way/Baby, Let Me Lay It On You/Please Judy/The Boy Was Kissing The Girl/Hesitation Blues/ Candyman/I Got Religion, I'm So Glad/I'm A Soldier In The Army Of The Lord/Children Of Zion/Whoopin' Blues/ What Could I Do/Lo' I Be With You Always

Title: "O Glory"
Label/No: Adelphi LP AD 1008 (USA 1973), Edsel EDCD 482 (USA 1996)
Right Now/Sun Goin' Down/Lo' I'll Be With You Always/ God Will Take Care Of You/Mornin' Train/Birmingham Special/Out On The Ocean Sailing/Soon My Work Will All Be Done/O' Glory

Title: "Let Us Get Together"
Label/No: Sonet/Kicking Mule, LP SNKF 103 (UK 1974)

Oh Glory, How Happy I Am/Cocaine Blues/Death Don't Have No Mercy/Let Us Get Together/There's Destruction In That Land/Tired, My Soul Needs A Restin'/Georgia Camp Meeting/Blues In A/Fox Chase/You're Goin' Quit Me Baby

Title: "Sun Is Going Down"
Label/No: Folkways LP FS3542 (USA 1976)
Sun Is Going Down/Oh, What A Beautiful City/Morning Train/Fast Stepping Time/Long John (Lost John)/God's Unchanging Hand/We Are The Heavenly Father's Children

Title: "I Am A True Vine"
Label/No: Heritage LP HT 307 (UK 1985), Heritage HT CD07 (UK 1991)
I Am A True Vine/Lord Stand By Me/Won't You Hush/Mean Old World/Moon Is Going Down/Sportin' Life Blues/Get Right Church/Blow Gabriel/Slippin' Til My Gal Comes In Partner/Wall Hollow Blues/Blues In E/Piece Without Words/ Whoopin' Blues/I Want To Be Saved

Title: "Blind Gary Davis"
Label/No: Document DLP 521 (Austria 1988)
Slow Blues/Right Now/Instrumental Guitar Rag/Candy Man No.1/Instrumental Rag/Fast Blues/Candy Man No. 2/Maple Leaf Rag/Christ Is A Friend (O My Lord)/ Instrumental (Untitled)/Untitled Rag/When The Evening Sun Goes Down/Stovepipe Stomp/She Just Put It That Way/ Guitar & Banjo Duet/If I Had My Way

Title: "At Allegheny College, Meadville, PA., 1964. Afternoon Workshop"
Label/No: Document DLP 527 (Austria 1988)
Cincinnati Slow Drag/Harmonica Solo/Candy Man/Banjo Instrumental 1/Maple Leaf Rag/I Know You'll Miss Me When I'm Gone/Guitar Blues/Banjo Instrumental 2

Title: "Live 1962-1964"
Label/No: Wolf Records 120.915 (Austria c.1988)
Death Don't Have No Mercy/Soon My Work Will Be Done/ You Got To Move/If I Had My Way/Just A Closer Walk With Thee/He Knows How Much We Can Bear/Samson And Delilah/Instrumental March/Old Time Religion/I Heard The Angels Singing/God's Unchanging Hand/Trying To Get Home

Compact Discs

Title: "Reverend Gary Davis"
Label/No: Heritage HTCD 02 (UK 1989)
(Compilation from TRA LP 249 and TRA LP 244)
I'm Going To Sit Down On The Banks Of The River/Twelve Gates To The City/(I Heard The) Angels Singing/Twelve Sticks/It's A Long Way To Tipperary/I'll Meet You At Station When The Train Comes Along/Come Down And Meet Me Sometime/Buck Dance/Soldier's Drill/Cincinnati Flow Rag/ West Coast Rag/Buck Rag/St. Louis Tickle/Two Step Candy Man/Walkin' Dog Blues/Italien Rag/C-Rag/Waltz Time Candy Man/Make Believe Stunt

Title: "Good Morning Blues"
Label/No: Biograph Records BCD 113 (USA 1990)
Candy Man/Hesitation Blues/Whistling Blues/How Happy I Am/Soon My Work Will All Be Done
(There are also titles by Leadbelly and Rev. Dan Smith on this disc)

Title: "At The Sign Of The Sun"
Label/No: Heritage HTCD 03 (UK 1990)
Sun Is Going Down/I'm Gonna Meet You At The Station/If I Had My Way/Twelve Gates To The City/God's Gonna Separate The Wheat From The Tares/Get Right Church/When The Saints Go Marching In/God Don't Work Like A Natural Man/Soon My Work Will Be Done/I'll Be Alright/Old Drunken Sally/Kitty Went A-Courtin'/Keep Your Lamp Trimmed And Burning/There's Destruction In This Land/Death Don't Have No Mercy/Near The Cross

Title: "Delia - Late Concert Recordings 1970-1971"
Label/No: American Activities CD 103 (UK 1990)
She's Funny That Way/Cincinnati Flow Rag/Sally/CC Rider/Make Believe Stunt/Delia/Candy Man/Samson And Delilah/Let Us Get Together/Pure Religion/Mountain Jack/Cincinnati Flow Rag/Mama Let Me Lay It On You/I Am A True Vine/Candy Man (version 2)/Buck Dance/Walkin' Dog Blues (Happy Blues)/I Hear The Angels Sing/Whistlin' Blues

'*Title:* "I Am A True Vine"
Label/No: Heritage HTCD 07 (UK 1991)
(This is HTLP 307 plus five unissued tracks)
I Am A True Vine/Lord, Stand By Me/Won't You Hush/Mean Old World/Moon Is Goin' Down/Sportin' Life Blues/God's Gonna Separate/Soon My Work Will Be Done/Oh Glory, How Happy I Am/Blow Gabriel/Slippin' Til My Gal Comes In Partner/Cocaine Blues/Candy Man/Wall Hollow Blues/Blues In E/Piece Without Words/Whoopin' Blues/Get Right Church/I Want To Be Saved

'*Title:* "Pure Religion And Bad Company"
Label/No: Smithsonian/Folkways, CD SF 40035 (USA 1991)
Pure Religion/Mountain Jack/Right Now/Buck Dance/Candy Man/Devil's Dream/Moon Goes Down/Cocaine Blues/Runnin' To The Judgement/Hesitation Blues/Bad Company/I Didn't Want To Join The Band/Evening Sun Goes Down/Seven Sisters/My Heart Is Fixed/Time Is Drawing Near/Crucifixion

Title: "Rev. Blind Gary Davis Complete Recorded Works 1935-49"
Label/No: Document DOCD 5060 (Austria 1991/2003)
Catfish CD 146 (UK 2000)
I'm Throwin' Up My Hands (Ain't Gonna Work No More)/Cross And Evil Woman Blues/I Am A True Vine/I Am The Light Of The World/O Lord, Search My Heart/I Saw The Light/You Can Go Home/Twelve Gates To The City/Have More Faith In Jesus/You Got To Go Down/I Belong To The Band - Hallelujah!/The Great Change In Me/Lord, I Wish I Could See/The Angel's Message To Me/Civil War March/I

Cannot Bear My Burden By Myself/I'm Gonna Meet You At The Station

Title: "From Blues To Gospel"
Label/No: Biograph BCD 123 (USA 1992)
Talk On The Corner/Sally, Where'd You Get Your Whiskey From?/Crow Jane/Eagle Rocking Blues/Cocaine Blues/Lost John/Samson And Delilah/I Heard The Angels Singing/Children of Zion/Lord I Wish I Could See/Down By The River/You Better Get Right/I'll Do My Last Singing

Title: "Blues and Ragtime"
Label/No: Shanachie LC 5762 (USA 1993)
Walkin' Dog Blues/Cincinnati Flow Rag/She's Funny That Way/ Whoopin' Blues/Twelve Sticks/Children of Zion/Buck Rag/Hesitation Blues/C-Rag/ Baby, Let Me Lay It On You/Cocaine Blues/Buck Dance/Candyman/Wall Hollow Blues/Little Boy, Little Boy Who Made Your Britches/Whistlin' Blues

Title: "Live And Kickin'"
Label/No: Just A Memory JAM 9122-2 (USA 1997)
Make Believe Stunt/Maple Leaf Rag/Coon Chase/Samson Delilah/Twelve Gates To The City/Mind How You're Living/You Got To Move/How Much We Can Bear/I Will Do My Last Singing/Buck Dance

Title: "Blues Jams"
Label/No: Groove Jams GJ 97006 (USA 1998)
Lord (Search My Heart)/Sonny Go Down/Right Now/You Got To Go Down/Let Us Get Together
(There are titles by others on this disc. All songs are incorrectly titled — see discography)

Title: "Live At Cambridge 1971"
Label/No: Catfish Records KATCD 115 (UK 1999)
Let Us Get Together/There's Destruction In This Land/Samson And Delilah/You Got Move/Pure Religion

Title: "Live At Newport"
Label/No: Vanguard CD 79588-2 (USA 2001)
Samson And Delilah (If I Had My Way)/I Won't Be Back No More/Buck Dance/Twelve Sticks/Death Don't Have No Mercy/You Got To Move/Lovin' Spoonful/She Wouldn't Say Quit/I've Done All My Singing For My Lord/Twelve Gates To The City/I Will Do My Last Singing In This Land Somewhere/Soldier's Drill/Get Along Cindy
(This supersedes Vanguard CD VMD 73008, which does not include the last two titles)

Title: "Demons And Angels: The Ultimate Collection"
Label/No: Shanachie Box Set CD 6117 (USA 2001)
Disc One: Buck Dance/ Soldier's March/ Baby, What You Going To Do/ Twelve Sticks (The Dozens)/ Save Up Your Money, John D. Rockerfeller Put The Panoc On/I Am The Light Of This World/Nobody Cares For Me/Slippin' 'til My Gal Comes In Partner/Blues/Crucifixion/Rag Blues In C/Blues In E/Square Dance Verses/Don't Know Where To Go/

He's My King/I'm Throwin' Up My Hands (Ain't Gonna Work No More) also known as Mountain Jack Blues/Cross And Evil Woman Blues/Keep Your Lamp Trimmed and Burning/I'm So Tired Of Being All Alone
Disc Two: I Am The True Vine/Lord, Stand By Me/Won't You Hush/Mean Old World/Moon Is Going Down/Sportin' Life Blues/God's Gonna Separate/Soon My Work Will All Be Done/Blow Gabriel/Get Right Church/I Want To Be Saved/Oh Glory, How Happy I Am/There's Destruction In That Land (Message From Heaven)/Tired, My Soul Needs Resting/Georgia Camp Meeting/Bill Bailey/Honey Get Your Towel Wet/She Wouldn't Say Quit/You're Going To Quit Me Baby
Disc Three: I'm Going To Sit Down On The Banks Of The River/Twelve Gates To The City/I Heard The Angels Sing/Twelve Sticks/It's A Long Way To Tipperary/When The Train Comes Along/Little Boy, Little Boy Who Made Your Britches/All Night Long/Who Shall Deliver Poor Me/Jesus Met The Woman At The Well/Lord, Search My Heart/Lord, On Your Word/Let Us Get Together/Cocaine Blues/Devil's Dream/Blow Gabriel/Sun Is Going Down/Spoonful/Whistlin' Blues/Virgin Mary

Title: "The Sun Of Our Life"
Label/No: World Arbiter (USA 2002)
Improvisation: Fast Blues In A/Improvisation: Slow Blues In E/West Coast Blues (Blind Blake)/Improvisation: Rag In A Minor/Two- Step/Horse Thief's Blues/Candy Man/Cigarette Break/Improvisation: Hills and Valleys/Seven Sisters/Crucifixion/I Decided To Go Down/Sun Is Going Down/My Heart Is Fixed/Hymn, Prayer, Song, Sermon (Church Service)/Improvisation: Coco Blues

Title: "Heroes Of The Blues: The Very Best Of Rev. Gary Davis"
Label/No: Shout Factory DK 30257 (USA 2003)
Samson And Delilah/Death Don't Have No Mercy/Cross And Evil Woman Blues/Can't Be Satisfied/Lord I Wish I Could See/Twelve Gates To The City/Out On The Ocean Sailing/Whistlin' Blues/Candy Man/How Happy I Am/I Belong To The Band - Hallelujah!/ Bad Company (Brought Me Here)/ Crucifixion/You Got To Move/Cocaine Blues/Soon My Work Will All Be Done
(This is a selection from recordings made between 1935 and 1971)

Title: "If I Had My Way"
Label/No: Smithsonian Folkways Recordings SFW 40123 (USA 2003)
If I had My Way/If The Lord Be For You/Twelve Gates To The City/You Got To Move/We Are The Heavenly Father's Children/A Friend Like Lonely Jesus/Get Right Church/Marine Band/Shine On Me/There's Destruction In This Land/He Stole Away/The Unclouded Day/Say No To The Devil/I Belong To The Band/Give Me A Heart To Love/He Never has Left Me Alone/Got On My Travelling Shoes/Civil War Parade

Title: "From Blues To Gospel"
Label/No: Biograph Records DK 34007 (USA 2004)
Talk On The Corner/Sally, Where'd You Get Your Whiskey/

Crow Jane/Eagle Rocking Blues/Cocaine Blues/Lost John/Samson And Delilah/I Heard The Angels Singing/Children of Zion/Lord I Wish I Could See/Down By The River/You Better Get Right/I'll Do My Last Singin'

Title: "Reverend Gary Davis, Manchester Free Trade Hall 1964"
Label/No: Document Records DOCD -32-20-14 (UK 2007)
You Got To Move/ If I Had My Way/ The Sun Is Going Down/ I'm A Soldier/ I Got A Little Mama, Sweet As She Can Be/ Sally, Please Come Back To Me (Worried Blues)/ Cocaine Blues/ Cincinnati Flow Rag/ Children Of Zion/ Coon Hunt / Maple Leaf Rag

Title: "Lifting The Veil: The First Bluesmen: Rev. Gary Davis & Peers"
Label/No: World Arbiter (USA 2008)
Come Down To See Me Sometime/ Lost John/ Soldier's Drill/ Slow Blues In E
(There are other performers on this disc.)

Title: "Rev. Gary - Davis Live at Gerde's Folk City, February 1962"
Label/No: Stefan Grossman's Guitar Workshop SGGW114/5/6 (USA 2009)
You Got To Move/ Intro To Come Down And See Me Sometime/ Come Down And See Me Sometime/ Wouldn't Say Quit/ Oh Lord/ Announcing Guitar Lessons/ People That Used To See, Can't See No More/ There's Destruction In This Land/ Intro To Soon My Work Will All Be Done/ Soon My Work Will All Be Done/ Intro To Oh Glory, How Happy I Am/ Oh Glory, How Happy I Am/ I Want To Be Saved/ Just A Closer Walk With Thee/ Death Don't Have No Mercy/ Lord I Won't Go Back In Sin/ Candyman/ Buck Dance/ Samson And Delilah/ Working On The Building/ I'll Fly Away/ Sun Goin' Down/ Fox Chase/ God's Gonna Separate/ Lord Search My Heart/ Jesus Met The Woman At The Well/ Say No To The Devil/ I Am A Pilgrim/ All Night Long/ Trying To Get To Heaven/ Thank You Jesus/ Twelve Sticks/ Intro. To Tesse/ Tesse/ Lord They Tell Me/ Right Or Wrong.

Title: "Rev. Gary Davis. At Home And Church. 1962-1967"
Label/No: Stefan Grossman's Guitar Workshop SGGW 103/1/2 (USA 2010)
Twelve Sticks/ Sally, Where'd You Get Your Liquor From/ Babylon Is Falling/ What Could I Do/ Children Of Zion/ Hesitation Blues/ Candyman/ Steal Away And Pray/ Goin' To Chattanooga/ Packing Up, Get Ready To Go/ Untitled/ You Cry Because I'm Leaving/ Don't Let My Baby Catch You Here/ Lord Let Me Live Longer/ I Want To Be Saved/ Waltz Time Candyman/ Little Boy Who Made Your Britches/ Talks About Verses Not Sung/ C Rag/ Two Step Candyman/ Piece Without Words/ Lord Search My Heart/ Slippin' To My Gal Comes In Partner/ Sun Is Going Down/ Raise A Ruckus Tonight/ Save Up Your Money, John D. Rockefeller Put The Panic On/ Soon My Work Will All Be Done/ You're Gonna Need King Jesus/ I'm Going Back To Jesus/ Blues In C/ Saddle It Around/ People Who Used To See/ Italian Rag/ Candyman/ Nobody Don't Care For Me/ Fox Chase/ Talk On Blind Boy Fuller/Amazing Grace/ Sermon/ I'm

A Soldier In The Army Of The Lord/ Sermon/ Lord, I Feel Just Like Goin' On/ Steal Away/ Can't Make This Journey By Myself/ Sermon/ I Will Overcome Someday/ God Be With You/ I Got Religion I'm So Glad/ I'm A Soldier In The Army of The Lord

Cassettes

Title: "I Am A True Vine"
Label/No: Stefan Grossman Limited Edition Cassette (USA 1984)
I Am A True Vine/Lord, Stand By Me/Won't You Hush/Mean Old World/Moon Is Goin' Down/Sportin' Life Blues/Tesse/ God's Gonna Separate/Soon My Work Will All De Done/Oh, Glory, How Happy I Am/Blow Gabriel/Slippin' 'Til My Gal Comes In, Partner/Cocaine Blues/Candy Man/Wall Hollow Blues/Blues In E/Piece Without Words/Talk On The Death Of Blind Boy Fuller/Whoopin' Blues/Get Right Church/I Want To Be Saved

Title: "Babylon Is Falling"
Label/No: Stefan Grossman Limited Edition Cassette (USA 1984)
Little Boy, Little Boy, Who Made Your Britches?/All Night Long/Paul and Silas/Jesus Met The Woman At The Well/Lord, Search My Heart/Lord, Oh Your Word/Let us Get Together/ Cocaine Blues/Devil's Dream/Blow Gabriel/Sun Is Goin' Down/When The Train Comes Along/Spoonful/Whistlin' Blues/Bill Bailey/Honey, Get Your Towel Wet/She Wouldn't Say Quit/You're Goin' To Quit Me, Baby/Don't Let My Baby Catch You Here/Virgin Mary/People Who Used To See, Can't See No More/Babylon Is Falling

Title: "Lo, I Be With You Always"
Label No: Stefan Grossman Limited Edition Cassettes (USA c.1984)
She's Funny That Way/Baby Let Me Follow You Down/Please Judy/The Boy Was Kissing The Girl.../Hesitation Blues/I Got Religion I'm So Glad/I'm A Soldier In The Army Of The Lord/Children of Zion/Lo' I Be With You Always/What Could I Do

Title: "Rev. Gary Davis/Bob Dylan"
Label/No: Stefan Grossman Limited Edition Cassette (USA c.1984)
Keep Your Lamps Trimmed And Burning/You Got To Move/ Let Us Get Together/Samson And Delilah
(Other tracks by Bob Dylan)

(A number of titles appear on various teaching tapes published by Stefan Grossman but these have not been included).

Selected Anthologies

(There are numerous anthologies with material from Rev. Davis - just a selection has been chosen. Only titles by Rev. Davis are listed.)

Title: "Philadelphia Folk Festival, Vol. 2"

Prestige International 13072 (USA c.1963)
If I Had My Way/Sally, Where You Get Your Liquor From?/ You Got To Move

Title: "Blues At Newport, 1963" Fontana TFLP 6037/ Vanguard (USA/UK 1964), Vanguard CD 6622 (USA 1993)
Samson And Delilah/You Got To Move

Title: "Blues Rediscoveries" RBF 11. (USA 1966)
Oh Lord, Search My Heart (1935)/You Got To Go Down (1935)

Title: "ASCH Recordings - 1939-1945 Vol. 2" ASCH AA4 (USA 1967)
Civil War Parade

Title: "Folk Blues" Continental Records Jazz Collector Series 16003 (USA c.1967)
I Cannot Bear My Burden/I'm Gonna Meet you At The Station

Title: "Blind Boy Fuller On Down Vol. 2" Matchbox Saydisc SDR 168 (UK c.1970)
Cross And Evil Woman Blues (1935)/I'm Throwing Up My Hand (1935)

Title: "Black Diamond Express To Hell" (Rev. Davis's second guitar to Bull City Red) Matchbox SCX 207/8 (UK c.1970)
I Saw The Light

Title: "Picture Rags" Transatlantic TRA SAM 26 (UK 1972)
Italien Rag/St. Louis Tickle

Title: "Some People Who Play Guitar Like A Lot of People Don't", Kicking Mule LP104 (USA 1974)
Swinging Blues/ Darktown Strutters Ball
(There are titles from other musicians on this album including Stefan Grossman, Roy Book Binder and Woody Mann)

Title: "Guitar Evangelists Vol. 2" Truth records TLP 1003 (Austria c.1975)
I Am The Light Of The World

Title: "Maple Leaf Rag" New World records NW 235 (USA 1976)
Maple Leaf Rag

Title: "The Guitar Bluesman Vol. 2" Golden Hour LP GH 879 Vanguard Records (USA/UK 1978)
Death Don't Have No Mercy

Title: "Bluesville Vol. 1- Folk Blues" ACE CH 247 (UK 1988)
You Got To Move

Title: "Good Morning Blues" Biograph CD 113 (USA 1990)
Candy Man/Hesitation Blues/Whistlin' Blues/How Happy I Am/Soon My Work Will All Be Done

Title: "Blind Boy Fuller, East Coast Piedmont Style" Columbia CD 467923 (USA 1991)
Rag, Mama, Rag/Baby You Gotta Change Your Mind

(Rev. Davis on second guitar)

Title: "Preachin' The Gospel, Holy Blues" Columbia CD 467890 (USA 1991)
Lord, I Wish I Could See (1935)
(Rag, Mama, Rag, and Baby You Gotta Change Your Mind appear on various Blind Boy Fuller releases).

Title: "Preachin' The Gospel: Holy Blues" Columbia/Sony CD 467890 (USA 1991)
Lord, I wish I could See

Title: "Blues At Newport" Vanguard Records CD 662248 (USA 1993)
Samson And Delilah/ You Got To Move

Title: "Gospel At Newport" Vanguard Records VCD 77014-2 (USA 1995)
Samson and Delilah

Title: "Blues Sweet Carolina Blues" Prestige Records CD PRCD 9914-2 (USA 1996)
The Boy Was Kissing The Girl (And Playing The Guitar At The Same Time)/Candy Man

Title: "Rare And Hot Gospel" Catfish KAT CD 171 (UK 2000)
I Belong To The Band

Title: "Blind Boy Fuller 1935 - 1938" JSP Records JSP CD JSP 7735 (UK 2004)
I'm Climbin' To The Top Of The Hill/Ain't It A Cryin' Shame/Rag, Mama, Rag: Take 1/Rag, Mama, Rag: Take 2/ Baby You Gotta Change Your Mind

Title: "Reverend Gary Davis and the Guitar Evangelists Volume Two" JSP Records 7759 (UK 2006)
All the pre - 1944 solo material.

A "bootleg" LP was published c.1970 on "Red and Green Records 1". One side was a selection of Riverside LP 12-611 and the other from Folk Lyric/77.
Records LP 12/14.

(One of Rev. Davis's most popular songs "Candyman" is often titled "Candy Man".)

Video/DVD/Teaching Aids

Rev. Gary Davis/Sonny Terry
Introduced by Taj Mahal
Masters of the Country Blues, Yazoo 501.
(USA 1991) Yazoo DVD 501
This was originally released as a twenty-six minute black and white film by the Seattle Folklore Society, directed by John Ullman (c.1965). Songs and instrumentals included:
If I Had My Way /Cincinnati Flow Rag/Candyman/ Sally, Where'd You Get Your Liquor From?/Buck Dance/ She Wouldn't Say Quit/ Oh Glory How Happy I Am/ I Heard The Angels Singing. (There is also a part of "Oh, What A

Beautiful City" over the titles. The second half of the tape has the harmonica player Sonny Terry).

There is footage of Rev. Davis playing on a series of teaching videos produced by Stefan Grossman entitled `Country Blues Guitar' (Stefan Grossman's Guitar Workshop, GW 904,905,906, USA) and on `How To Play Blues Guitar', (GW 903).

Legends of the Country Blues Guitar
Vestapol DVD 13003 (1994)
Children of Zion/Death Don't Have No Mercy
(There are also titles by other performers)

Legends of The Country Blues Guitar Volume Two
Vestapol DVD 13016 (1994)
Buck Dance/Hard Walking Blues/Make Believe Stunt/Keep Your Lamp Trimmed And Burning
(There are also titles by other performers)

Up The Country: The Country Blues Guitar Legacy
Vestapol DVD 13037 (1995)
Oh Glory How Happy I Am
(There are also titles by other performers)

The Legends of Traditional Fingerstyle Guitar
Vestapol DVD 13004 (c 1995)
I Belong To The Band
(There are also titles by other performers)

Ragtime Blues Guitar of Rev. Gary Davis: Taught by Stefan Grossman.
Stefan Grossman's Guitar Workshop GW CD 99464

Holy Blues of Rev. Gary Davis: Taught by Stefan Grossman.
Stefan Grossman's Guitar Workshop GW CD 99463
(Two audio teaching sets with a book and compact disc)

The Gospel Guitar of Rev. Gary Davis: Taught by Ernie Hawkins
Stefan Grossman's Guitar Workshop DVD 813/16 (2002)
(A four disc DVD teaching set by a student of Rev. Davis)

The Art Of Acoustic Blues Guitar: Ragtime and Gospel, With Woody Mann
Acoustic Sessions ASV/DVD 103 (2002)
(Five titles by Rev. Davis)

Roy Book Binder in Concert at the National Storytelling Festival: Roy, the Reverend and the Devil's Music.
Homespun Video/DVD (2002)
(Roy plays a number of Rev. Davis titles as well as anecdotes about his times with him.)

The Blues Guitar of Rev. Gary Davis: Taught by Ernie Hawkins
Stefan Grossman's Guitar Workshop DVD GW 97879 (2008)
(A two DVD set)

The Ragtime Guitar of Rev. Gary Davis: Taught by Ernie Hawkins
Stefan Grossman's Guitar Workshop DVD GW 98081 (2008)

Rev. Gary Davis:
The Video Collection
Stefan Grossman's Guitar Workshop/ Vestapol Productions/ Rounder DVD 13111 (2008)
(A collection of films from circa 1962 – 1972)
Sun Is Goin' Down/ Lord, I Feel Like Goin'/Children of Zion/ Oh Glory How Happy I Am / Sally Where'd You Get Your Liquor From/ Calling For Irene/ Buck Dance/ Hard Walkin' Blues/ Keep Your Lamp Trimmed And Burning/ Make Believe Stunt/ Guitar Lesson (Twelve Gates To The City)/ Twelve Gates To The City (Instrumental)/ Advice On Guitar Playing/ Twelve Sticks/ Twelve Gates To The City/ Samson And Delilah/ Cincinnati Flow Rag (Slow Drag)/ Candyman/ Sally, Where'd You Get Your Liquor From/ Buck Dance/ Wouldn't Say Quit/ Oh Glory How Happy I Am / (I Heard) The Angels Singing/ I Belong To The Band/ Talk On Death/ Death Don't Have No Mercy/ She's Funny That Way/ Samson And Delilah/ Cincinnati Flow Rag (Slow Drag)/ Spoonful/ Buck Dance.

Novelty Instrumentals of Rev. Gary Davis. Taught by Ernie Hawkins
Stefan Grossman's Guitar Workshop DVD GW 984 (USA 2009)

Rags and Minstrel Songs of Rev. Gary Davis. Taught by Ernie Hawkins
Stefan Grossman's Guitar Workshop DVD GW 98283 (USA 2009)

A Selection of Rev. Davis Titles Recorded by Other Musicians:

Peter, Paul and Mary:
If I Had My Way, Warner Bros. WS 1449 (1962)

Dave Van Ronk:
Samson And Delilah/Cocaine Blues, Prestige 13056/Fantasy 24710 (1962).
Cocaine Blues/Candyman, Sonet 885 (1982)

Dick Farina and Eric Von Schmidt:
Cocaine, Folklore Records/77 Records Fl 7 (1963)

Bob Dylan:
Baby Let Me Follow You Down, Columbia (1963)

Donovan:
Candyman, Hallmark Records HMA 200 (1965)

Hot Tuna:
Let Us Get Together, Grunt records FTR 1004 (1972).
Hesitation Blues, Death Don't Have No Mercy, Search My Heart, Victor/RCA 740.061(c.1971)

Rolling Stones:
You Gotta Move, COC 59100 (1971)

Roy Book Binder:
Delia, Cincinnati Flow Rag, Adelphi Records AD 1017 (1972)
Hesitation Blues, Blue Goose Records 2023 (1977).
Oh Glory, How Happy I Am, Flying Fish Records FF 098 (1979)

Stefan Grossman:
Soldier's March/Cincinnati Flow Rag/Candyman/Whistlin' Blues/Make Believe Stunt, Transatlantic 89501(c.1975)

George Gritzbach:
She Ain't Crazy, Kicking Mule 126 (1976)

Tom Winslow:
Tryin' To Get Home, Truth Records 13712 (1978)

Larry Johnson:
Sally, Where'd You Get Your Liquor From? /Baby Let Me Lay It On You, Spivey records LP 1034 (c.1983)

John Cephas and Phil Wiggins:
I Saw The Light, Flying Fish LP 394 (1986)

Taj Mahal:
Candyman, The Collectors Series CCSLP 180 (1987)

Catfish Keith:
You Got To Move, Fishtail Records CD 001 (1991)

Cephas and Wiggins:
Banks Of The River
Flying Fish CD FF 70580 (1992)

Roy Book Binder:
Candy Man/Hesitation Blues
Rounder Records CD 3130 (1994)

Eric Von Schmidt:
Baby, Let Me Lay It On You
Gazell GPCD 2013 (1995)

Woody Mann:
Buggy Wagon, I Will Do My Last Singing In This Land Somewhere /There Is No Sorrow/O Glory How Happy I Am
Acoustic Music Records 319 (1995)

Michael Hakanson - Stacy:
I Am The Light Of This World/I Saw The Light
Time And Strike Inc. CDTS 7778 (1995)

Ernie Hawkins:
Will There Be A Star In My Crown/Samson and Delilah/Cocaine
Say Mo' Music CD SM002 (1996)

Andy Cohen:
Oh Glory, How Happy I Am /Twelve Gates To The City/ Samson And Delilah/I Am The Light Of This World/I'll Be

Alright Someday/Pure Religion/Goin' To Sit Down On The Banks Of The River/I'm Glad I'm In That Number/God's Gonna Separate/Children Of Zion/Crucifixion/You Got To Move/Get Right Church/I Belong To The Band/Tryin' To Get To Heaven In Due Time/A Little More Faith/I Will Do My Last Singing In This Land/Oh Glory, How Happy I Am
(with Larkin Cohen)
Riverlark Music RLCD 102 (1997)

Roy Book Binder:
Let Us Get Together/Rag, Mama (Rag)
Rounder Records CD 3153 (1998)

Eric Noden:
I Heard The Angels Singing
Diving Duck Records CDDD01 (1998)

John Jackson:
Death Don't Have No Mercy
Alligator Records ALCD 4867 (1999)

Larry Johnson:
Banks Of The River/Sally Where You Get Your Liquor From/Death Don't Have No Mercy
Armadillo Music CD ARMD 00005 (1999)

Happy Traum:
Twelve Gates To The City
Lark's Nest Records CDLN01 (2000)

Ernie Hawkins:
Slow Drag/Crucifixion/Jesus Gonna Make Up My Dying Bed/I Belong To The Band
Say Mo' Music CDSM007 (2000)
Deliah (Delia)/Fast Fox Trot/Buck Dance
Say Mo' Music CDSM009 (2002)

Ralph McTell:
I Will Do My Last Singing
Leola Music TPGCD 21 (2002)

Various including:
Ari Eisinger: I'm Throwin' Up My Hand / **Ken Whiteley and Friends:** Let Us Get Together/ **Maria Muldaur:** I Am The Light Of This World/ **Ernie Hawkins:** Will There Be Stars In My Crown/ **Eric Noden:** Pure Religion/ **Pat Conte:** Devil's Dream/ **William Lee Ellis:** I Heard The Angels Singing/ **Ellen Britton:** United States March/ **Mary Flower:** Sit Down On The Banks/ **John Cephas and Phil Wiggins:** Twelve Gates To The City/ **Ian Buchanin with The Otis Brothers:** Hesitation Blues/ **Peter, Paul and Mary:** Samson And Delilah / **Mitch Greenhill and Mayne Smith:** Samson And Delilah / **Penny Lang And Friends:** God Knows How Much We Can Bear/**Jerry Ricks:** Where'd You Get Your Liquor From – Hesitation Blues/ **Dave Van Ronk And Friends:** Soon My Work Will All Be Done/ **Rick Ruskin**: I Will Do My Last Singing In This Land
Inside Sounds CD ISC 0508 (2002)

John Cephas, Woody Mann and Orville Johnson
Death Don't Have No Mercy/I Will Do My Last Singing
Acoustic Sessions CD (2004)

Eric Noden:
Cincinnati Flow Rag
Diving Duck Records CD DD 0022 (2004)

Mike Dowling:
Tryin' To Get To Heaven
Wind River Guitar CD WRG 05 (2005)

Woody Mann:
Have Mercy (Death Don't Have No Mercy In This Land) The Rev's Music (an instrumental medley of various Davis titles)
Acoustic Sessions ASR 215 (2005)

Roy Book Binder:
Baby Let Me Lay It On You/Delia/Cocaine Blues
Peg Leg Records 7005 (2005)

Ernie Hawkins:
Make Believe Stunt/The Boy Was Kissing The Girl (And Playing The Guitar At The Same Time)/I Am The Light Of This World
Say Mo' Music CD SMO22 (2006)

William Lee Ellis:
Search My Heart
Yellow Dog Records CD YDR 1343 (2006)

Grant Dermody, John Miller and Orville Johnson:
I Will Do My Last Singing
Orb Discs CD ORB 1007 (2006)

Jorma Kaukonen
There's A Table Sitting In Heaven/Will There Be Any Stars In My Crown?
Red House Records CD 202 (2007)

Willie Salomon
Mountain Jack Blues/I Heard The Angels Singing
Acoustic Music 1386.2 (2007)

Marie Knight with Larry Campbell
Lord I Feel Like Going On/Let Us Get Together/I Belong To The Band/Samson and Delilah/I Am The Light Of This World/12 Gates/I'll Fly Away/Lord I'll Be With You/ When I Die/Death Don't Have No Mercy/A Little More Faith/You Got To Move
M.C. Records MC 0058 (2007)

Jorma Kaukonen
There's A Bright Side Somewhere
Red House Records RHD CD 217 (USA 2009)

Ramblin' Jack Elliot
Death Don't Have No Mercy
Anti - Epitaph CD 4577870052 (USA 2009)

London, 1971, Georges Chatelain

Publicity Photograph, c. 1965, Lenny Schechter

Part Seven

Selected Bibliography

Major Sources:

Rev Gary Davis/The Holy Blues
Compiled by Stefan Grossman
Robbins Music Corporation, New York (1970)
(This is a collection of eighty songs with music, guitar chords and many interesting photographs.)

Nothing But The Blues
Hanover Books, London (1971)
(Includes an essay entitled "The Reverend Gary Davis" by Richard Noblett, Stephen Rye and John Offord.)

Crying For The Carolines
Bruce Bastin
Studio Vista, London (1972)
(A survey of musicians from the East Coast States including a great deal of information about Rev. Davis. A pioneering book.)

Rev. Gary Davis/Blues Guitar
Stefan Grossman
Oak Publications, New York/Music Sales Limited, London (1974)
(This is an excellent tablature guitar teaching book which includes twenty titles. Also included is a long interview with Rev. Davis, an essay by Steve Calt and many photographs.)

A Rare Interview With Rev. Gary Davis
Stefan Grossman, Sing Out! Magazine, USA March (1974)

Sweet Showers of Rain
(The Bluesmen, Vol. Two)
Samuel Charters
Oak Publications, New York (1977)
(A survey of individual blues musicians with a chapter dealing with Rev. Davis and Sonny Terry.)
.

Red River Blues
Bruce Bastin
Macmillan Press, London (1986)
(An essential award winning book with a chapter dealing with Rev. Davis's time living in Durham, North Carolina. A very important book.)

A selection of books, album notes, and magazines which contain major essays:

The Record Changer, (USA) Vol. 14 No. 8 circa 1956
(Includes essay by Kenneth S. Goldstein and two photographs by Lawrence Shustak, one is on the cover.)

Rolling Stone Magazine (USA) December 23rd 1971
(Includes a long excellent essay by Alex Shoumatoff, with photographs by David Gahr.)

Sing Out! Magazine. (USA) Vol. 23 No.1 1974
(Includes an informative interview with Rev. Davis by Stefan Grossman during 1962-1968.)

Southern Exposure Magazine (USA) Vol. 2 No. 1 1974
(Contains an essay by Bill Phillips, 'Piedmont Country Blues', which has much information about Rev. Davis's days in North Carolina during the 1930's and the early 1940's.)

Blues Guitarists
Essays collected from Guitar Player Magazine (UK) 1975
(Includes an interview with Rev. Davis by Stefan Grossman.)

The Folk Music Sourcebook (USA) 1976
Larry Sandberg and Dick Weissman
Alfred A. Knopf, New York.

Blues Magazine (Canada) Vol. 2 No. 2 No. 3, 1976
(Both volumes are dedicated to his music and contain essays and tablature to a number of songs.)

The Folk Music Encyclopedia (UK) 1977
Kristin Baggelaar and Donald Milton
Omnibus Press.

Blues Who's Who (USA) 1979
Sheldon Harris
Arlington House, New York.

Hoot! : A Twenty Five Year History of the Greenwich Village Music Scene, Robbie Woliver, (USA) 1986
St. Martin's Press.

Living Blues magazine, (USA) May/June 1989
(Contains an essay by Mary Katherine Aldin entitled "The Living Country Blues: Rev. Gary Davis".)

Guitar Extra! Magazine (USA) Vol 1 No. 2 1990,
(Contains an essay entitled "Sons of the Pioneer" with contributions by a number of musicians who have been influenced by his music.)

Acoustic Guitar (USA) November/December 1994
(Contains an essay by Robert Tilling entitled "Divine Inspiration".)

Blues & Rhythm magazine, (UK) April 1996
(Contains an essay by Robert Tilling entitled "Eagle Rocking Blues".)

Blues & Rhythm magazine, (UK) October 1997
(Contains an essay by Robert Tilling entitled "Reverend Gary Davis On Compact Disc".)

Booklet in Shanachie compact disc box set (CD 6117), "Demons and Angels: Rev. Gary Davis: The Ultimate

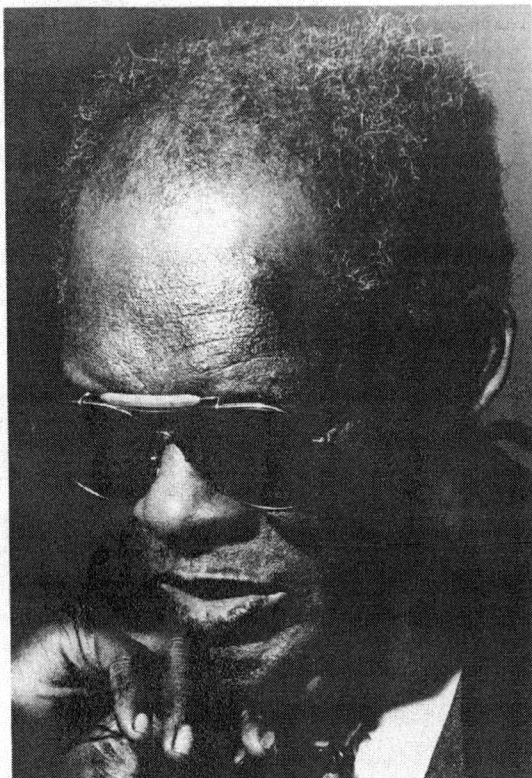

Record Changer magazine, 1956, Lawrence Shustak

Collection" (USA) 2001
(Compiled by Stefan Grossman including excellent biographical notes by Bruce Bastin)

Blues & Rhythm magazine, (UK) May 2002
(Contains an essay by Robert Tilling entitled "I was never shy around none of those guitar players".)

Booklet in World Arbiter compact disc (CD 200) "The Sun of Our Life; Solos, Songs, A Sermon 1955-1957." (USA) 2002.
(Contains essay by Allan Evans. This is the first time a live sermon by Rev. Davis has been released on disc.)

Between Midnight And Day: The Last Unpublished Blues Archive, Dick Waterman. (USA) 2003
Thunder's Mouth Press.

Booklet in Smithsonian/Folkways compact disc (CD SFW 40123) "If I Had My Way: Early Home Recordings" (USA) 2003.
(Contains essay and notes by John Cohen and Horace Clarence Boyer.)

The Mayor of MacDougal Street: A Memoir, Dave Van Ronk with Elijah Wald, (USA) 2005 Da Capo Press.

The Fretboard Journal, Number 1, Winter, (USA 2005)
(Contains essay by Allan Evans entitled "Learning from the

Reverend: Guitar lessons with Gary Davis.")

Booklet in World Arbiter compact disc (CD 2008) "Lifting The Veil: The First Bluesmen: Rev. Gary Davis And Peers." (USA) 2008.
(Contains notes by Allan Evans, and extracts from an interview made by Elizabeth Lyttleton Harold with Rev. Davis during 1951.)

Sing Out! magazine, Vol. 51 No. 4   (USA) Winter 2008
(Contains an essay by Eric von Schmidt with John Kruth.)

No Depression, Volume 78, University of Texas Press (USA 2009)
(Contains essay by John Milward entitled "Sons Of The Preacher Man. Legendary guitarist Gary Davis had no children, but his prodigies became his artistic progeny.")

Selected Magazines
(including reviews and articles)

Record Changer (USA): Vol. 14 No. 8 1956/ Jazz Journal (UK): March 1959, June 1962, June 1964, December 1970, July 1972/ Sing Out! (USA): No. 4 1960, Nov. 1965, Vol. 21 No. 5 1972, Vol. 23 No.1 1974, Vol. 23 No. 3 1974, Vol.51 No.4 2008 / The New York Times: 30 Jan. 1950, 19 July 1959, Sept. 1960, 19 March 1961, 31 July 1961/Saturday Review (USA): Feb 25th 1961/ Music Memories (USA): May 1962/ Oberlin Review (USA): Nov. 1963/ Jazz Monthly (UK): July 1964/ Coda (USA): Oct. 1964, Feb. 1970/ Blues Unlimited (UK): No. 20 March 1965, No. 22 May 1965, September 1965, No. 38 and 39 1966, No. 84 1971, No. 85 1971, July 1972, April 1973, No.104 November 1973, No. 108 June 1974/ Blues World (UK): No. 3 1965, No. 37 1970, No. 41 1971, No. 42 1972, No. 43 1972, No. 45 1973/ Jazzbeat (USA): Aug. 1965/ Melody Maker (UK): July 30th 1966/ Boston After Dark (USA): October 12th 1966/ Billboard (USA): August 1968/ Tennessee Folk (USA): Vol. 61 No. 2 1969/ Sounds (UK): Nov. 1970/ The Times (UK): Nov. 29th 1970/ B.M.G. Magazine (UK): December 1971/ Blues (Japan): No. 8, 1972/ Rolling Stone (USA): December 1971/ Melody Maker(UK): May 1972/ Guitar Magazine (UK): December 1972, January 1973, September 1973, October 1975, January 1978, June 1980/ Living Blues (USA): Nos. 5, 8, 9,11,12,13,14,15,16,17,18,19, 20, 24, Spring 1972, Summer 1973, Winter 2007, Spring 2008 / Spring 2009/ Summer 2009/ Blues Link (UK): No. 2 January 1974, No. 5 1974/ Folk Scene (USA): February 1975/ Blues Magazine (Canada): Vol. 2 No. 4 1976/ Talking Blues (UK): No.1 1976, No. 6 and No. 7 1977, September 1977, December 1977/ Guitar Player (UK): December 1977, June 1978, April 1981, May 1981/ Blues (Canada): No.10 1987/ Juke Blues (UK): No. 10 1987/ Frets (USA): December 1988/ Record Collector (UK): No.142 1991/ Blues and Rhythm (UK): No. 38 1988, No. 69 1992, July 1993, April 1995, April 1996, April 1997, May 1997, October 1997, March 1998, September 2000, February 2003, April 2003 / April 2004, August 2006, April 2008 / Folk Roots (UK): October 1991; July 1993; October 1993 /

Blueprint (UK): January 1992, February 1992, / Acoustic Guitar (USA): January 1992/ Blues Review Quarterly (USA): No. 4 1992/Acoustic Guitar (UK): December 1993/ Acoustic Guitar (USA): December 1994 /Jefferson (Sweden): August 1995/ Blues Review (USA) September 2003 / Acoustic Guitar (USA): October 2003.

Acoustic Guitar Magazine, September 1996, included the compact disc *Pure Religion and Bad Company*, Smithsonian/Folkways 40009 (1989) in their *100 Essential CD's* supplement.

Selected General Sources:

Blues Fell This Morning (The Meaning of the Blues), Paul Oliver, Collier Books (1960/63); The Story of the Blues, Paul Oliver, Barrie and Jenkins (1969); Nothing But The Blues, Mike Leadbitter, Hanover Books (1971); The Blues Revival, Bob Groom, Studio Vista (1971); The Devil's Music/A History of the Blues, Giles Oakley, British Broadcasting Corporation (1976); Blues Who's Who, Sheldon Harris, Da Capo Paperback, (1979); The Blackwell Guide to Blues Records, edited by Paul Oliver, Blackwell (1989); Blues and Gospel Records 1902-1943, R.M.W. Dixon and J. Godrich, Storyville (1982); Blues Records 1943-1970 Vol. One, Mike Leadbitter and Neil Slaven, Record Information Services (1987); The Penguin Encyclopedia of Popular Music, Edited by Donald Clarke, Penguin Books (1989); No Direction Home, The Life and Music of Bob Dylan, Robert Shelton, New English Library 1986); Baby Let Me Follow You Down, Eric Von Schmidt and Jim Rooney, Anchor Books (1979); The Blues Line, Eric Sackheim, Mushinsha Books (1969); The

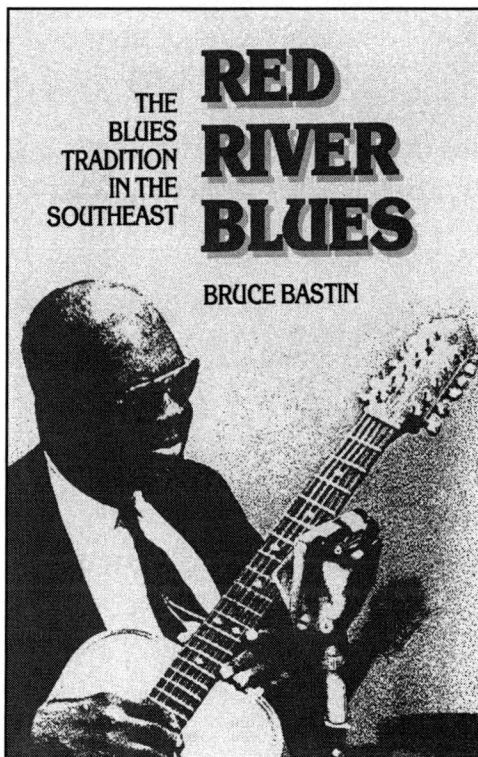

Book Cover, 1986, Photograph Robert Tilling

New Grove/Gospel, Blues and Jazz, Paul Oliver, Max Harrison and William Bolcom, MacMillan (1986); Guitars, Tom and Mary Anne Evans, Paddington Press, London (1977); The Guitar, Allan Kozinn, Quarto Books, 1984; The Jazz Scene, Charles Fox/Val Wilmer, Hamlyn Books (1972); Yazoo 21-83 (Lyrics from songs on Yazoo Albums), R.R. Macleod, PAT Publications (1992); The Big Book of Blues, Robert Santelli, Penguin Books, 1993 (USA); Nothing But the Blues: The Music And Musicians, Lawrence Cohn, Abbeville Press 1993 (USA); All Music Guide To The Blues, Various Contributors, Miller Freeman Books 1996 (USA); The New Blackwell Guide to Recorded Blues, Edited by John Cowley and Paul Oliver, Blackwell 1996 (UK); The Virgin Encyclopedia of the Blues, Colin Larkin, Virgin Books 1998 (UK); There Is No Eye, John Cohen Photographs, Powerhouse Books 2000(USA); Bill Wyman's Blues Odyssey, Dorling Kindersley Books 2001 (UK); Can't Be Satisfied: The Life And Times of Muddy Waters, Robert Gordon, Pimlico 2003 (UK); The American Blues Guitar, Rick Batey, Hal Leonard 2003 (UK); Chronicles, Volume One, Bob Dylan, Simon and Schuster, 2004 (USA/UK); Encyclopedia of American Gospel Music, W.K. McNeil, Routledge 2005 (UK); The Penguin Guide to Blues Recordings, Tony Russell and Chris Smith, Penguin Books 2006 (USA/UK); The Bob Dylan Encyclopedia, Michael Gray, Continuum Books 2006 (UK); White Bicycles: Making Music in the 1960's, Joe Boyd, Serpent's Tail 2006 (UK); Folklore Productions, The First Fifty Years, Folklore Productions (2007 USA).

The following selection of guitar tuition books contain songs and instrumentals by Rev. Davis: Instrumental Techniques of American Folk Guitar, Harry Taussig, Oak Publications (1965); Masters of Instrumental Blues Guitar, Donald Garwood, Oak Publications (1968); Something to Sing About, Milton Okun, Collier Books (1968); Ragtime Blues Guitarists, Stefan Grossman, Oak Publications (1970); Six Early Blues Guitarists, Woody Mann, Oak Publications (1973); Rev. Gary Davis/ Blues Guitar, Stefan Grossman, Oak Publications (1974); Masters of Country Blues Guitar: Rev. Gary Davis, Stefan Grossman, Belwin Inc., (1991); Masters of Country Blues Guitar: The Anthology of Country Blues Guitar, Stefan Grossman, Belwin Inc., (1992); Early Masters of American Blues Guitar: Rev. Gary Davis, Stefan Grossman, Alfred Publishing Co., Inc (2007).

Club 47, Cambridge, Mass., 1963, Dick Waterman

Rev. Davis is also mentioned in the novels: "Deliverance" by James Dickey (1970) and "The Steel Guitar" by Linda Barnes (1992).

Reading the Bible with Roy Book Binder, New York, April 1972, Robert Tilling

One Little Rose

I would rather have one little rose
From the garden of a friend
Than to have the choicest flowers
When my stay on earth must end.
I would rather have one pleasant word
In kindness said to me
Than flattery when my heart is still
And life has ceased to be.
I would rather have a loving smile
From friends I know are true
Than tears shed round my casket
When this world I've bid adieu.
Bring me all your flowers today
Whether pink or white or red;
I'd rather have one blossom now
Than a truckload when I'm dead.

A poem chosen by Mother Annie Davis
New York, August 1992

Peter Mourant

Robert Tilling was born 1944, in Bristol, England and first became interested in blues and jazz as a teenager and his enthusiasm for Reverend Davis started during the early sixties. For the past thirty nine years he has regularly contributed to various blues and folk magazines in both Britain and the United States. He has lectured at universities, colleges, guitar teaching camps, and at blues festivals on both sides of the Atlantic. Since 1968 he has been living in Jersey, Channel Islands, and is married with two daughters. Robert Tilling is also a member of The Royal Institute of Painters in Water Colours, London, and has held over thirty five solo exhibitions of his paintings, prints and drawings. He was appointed M.B.E. during 2006.

"Well thought-out and beautifully illustrated with dozens of rare photographs, *Oh, What A Beautiful City* is a welcome addition to the library of any true blues lover"

BRETT BONNER
LIVING BLUES (USA) OCTOBER 1993.

"Reading this book makes you want to hear the man's music and if that is Tilling's objective then he has done Rev. Davis proud."

DAVID LANDS
JAZZ JOURNAL (UK) MARCH 1994

"Tilling is not trying to be comprehensive, but rather produce a tribute and memorial to a wonderful man. He has succeeded beautifully."

E.W.
SING OUT! (USA) 1993

"Recommended to all blues lovers and guitarists of every stripe"

LARRY HOLLIS
CADENCE (USA) DECEMBER 1995

Selected reviews of the first edition (Paul Mill Press 1992)